Coming Soon

Principles of
SAN Design

by **Josh Judd**

**Watch for news about this and other
forthcoming titles on the**
SAN Administrator's Bookshelf **website**

http://www.brocade.com/bookshelf

**Membership on this <u>FREE</u> website
also provides a discount on this and
other titles in the series**

<u>NOTICE</u>

This is the **first edition** of *Multiprotocol Routing for SANs*, the first in a series of real-world-focused books designed to aid SAN professionals in the performance of their jobs.

Since multiprotocol SAN routers are a relatively new technology, **changes will be made** to this content as the technology continues to evolve. Change is always probable with high technology, but in this case it is particularly likely since much of the material in this book is related to untried and still emerging IP SAN technologies like iSCSI.

To receive **FREE** updates discussing such changes, log on to the *SAN Administrator's Bookshelf*[TM] website:

http://www.brocade.com/bookshelf

Brocade and the author actively solicit **your feedback** on this book in order to improve the next edition. Please send **comments, corrections,** or ideas for **enhancements** to the *SAN Administrator's Bookshelf* team:

bookshelf@brocade.com

First Edition

Multiprotocol
Routing
for SANs

by **Josh Judd**

ISBN: 0-7414-2306-5

SAN Administrator's Bookshelf™
  Series designed by Josh Judd

Multiprotocol Routing for SANs
  Written by Josh Judd
  Graphics, diagrams, and layouts by Josh Judd
  Edited by Kent Hanson and Josh Judd
  Reviewed by the Brocade Marketing and Engineering teams
  Cover designed by Josh Judd, Jed Bleess, and Brocade Marketing

Printing History
  "Advance Edition" printed from June to August 2004
  "First Edition" initially printed October 2004

Published by:

1094 New Dehaven St.
West Conshohocken, PA 19428
info@InfinityPublishing.com
www.InfinityPublishing.com
www.BuyBooksOnTheWeb.com
Toll-free: (877) BUY-BOOK
Local Phone: (610) 941-9999
Fax: (610) 941-9959

Printed on Recycled Paper in the United States of America

Legal Information

Brocade Corporate Headquarters
San Jose, CA USA
T: (408) 333-8000
info@brocade.com

Brocade European Headquarters
Geneva, Switzerland
T: +41 22 799 56 40
europe-info@brocade.com

Brocade Asia Pacific Headquarters
Tokyo, Japan
T: +81 3 5402 5300
apac-info@brocade.com

Acknowledgements

Special thanks are due to Greg Reyes and Tom Buiocchi for executive-level support.

Nick Moezidis, Mark Sausville, and Ron Totah should be acknowledged for their early efforts to champion the FC-FC Router product concept within Brocade.

Material was adapted from the *FCR, iSCSI,* and *FCIP Functional* and *Design Specifications* by Brocade Engineering. (Dennis Makishima; Suresh Vobbilisetty; et al.) Other concepts were adapted from Brocade Education Services and/or Marketing material. (Eric Wolff; Lisa Guess; et al.) Ezio Valdevit provided FSPF information. Joey Yep and Forrest Farman provided information on the serial port. Robert Snively and Steve Wilson provided information on standards.

Information about third-party products was provided by Jane Circle of CNT, Gregg Pugmire of LightSand, and Dave Stoner of SANRAD.

Finally, this book would not have been possible without review cycles from the following people: Mario Blandini, Jed Bleess, Daniel Chung, Todd Einck, Derek Granath, Lisa Guess, Kent Hanson, Jim Heuser, Justin Jones, Jay Kidd, Dennis Makishima, Charles Milhans, Michael O'Connor, Martin Skagen, Robert Snively, Suresh Vobbilisetty, Doug Wesolek, Steve Wilson, Eric Wolff, and Joey Yep.

Special thanks to Martin Skagen for insisting that the diagrams needed to be more readable. Keep picking those nits.

About the Author

Josh Judd is a Principal Engineer at Brocade Communications Systems, Inc. reporting to Technical Marketing. In addition to writing technical literature, he provides support for roadmap activities, writes new product requirements, and works directly with systems engineers, OEMs and end-users worldwide.

When he first went to work for Brocade, Josh was the company's senior IT technical contributor, responsible for the network, server, and desktop infrastructure.[1] His career in IT has given him a diverse skill set, including senior-level expertise in both UNIX and Windows administration, RAID configuration and optimization, storage virtualization and volume management, clustering, and network engineering. Before joining Brocade in early 1997, Josh worked in Silicon Valley at IBM Global Services, LSI Logic, and Taos Mountain Consulting, as well as at various smaller companies.

In addition to relevant work experience, he has a long list of vendor-specific technical certifications and a degree with highest honors in Computer and Information Science.

To name just a few of his outside interests: he is an avid reader, travels extensively, climbs very, *very* large rocks, fences, plays chess, races cars occasionally, goes SCUBA diving, and dabbles in music and the theater arts.

Josh currently lives in San Jose, California.

---

[1] Actually, when he *first* started, he was the company's *only* IT technical contributor. That's a startup for you.

About the Book

What does this book contain?

This book provides general information about multiprotocol routing for Storage Area Networks (SANs) as well as guidance and reference material specific to the Brocade® SilkWorm® Multiprotocol Router platform and software. It can therefore be considered a reference work on the subject as a whole as well as being useful for customers deploying Brocade products.

The subjects covered for each router protocol and service include theory of operations, usage cases, and advice on designing, implementing, and managing routed SANs. All of the capabilities of the Brocade router are discussed as they stand at the time of this writing, as well as the hardware platforms that the software currently runs on. Planned near-future capabilities are discussed where they are expected to be available at or near the publication date of this book.

The material in each chapter is intended to be useful both for tutorial and reference. However, the four sections into which the book is divided each have a different focus.

The first section focuses on the theory behind each platform and service: why it is needed and how the Brocade implementation works at a high level. These chapters are for readers who want an overview of the routing services and the platforms that they run on.

The second section discusses practical usage cases. It provides high-level SAN designs that show how the router can solve real-world business problems. It gives the business case for why multiprotocol SAN routers are needed, and how the Brocade product addresses real business needs.

The third section gives more specific deployment guidance, discussing design, installation, configuration, troubleshooting, and management. Most of this material is likely to apply to current and future router implementations.

The last section contains reference material. First, it has a basic reference covering things like media types and cabling. Next, it has an advanced chapter that goes into more detail on the routing services. Finally, it has a glossary and index.

. While some material might seem repetitious when reading the book from cover to cover, each section deals with overlapping topics in different ways. This is intended to explain complex concepts thoroughly, reinforce key points, and provide a larger number of examples than would be possible if each topic were dealt with only once.

What is a multiprotocol router?

Routers are used to connect different networks together, as opposed to bridging segments of the same network. In this context, "multiprotocol" means connecting networks using different protocols, generally at the lower levels of the stack.

For example, one network could use SCSI over Fibre Channel (FC) and another could use SCSI over IP. In general usage, a router that can merely handle multiple Upper Layer Protocols (ULPs) but *not* different lower layer protocols is *not* considered multiprotocol.[2] For example, the ability to handle both SCSI/FC and FICON/FC would not qualify a product as a multiprotocol router, whereas handling both SCSI/FC and SCSI/IP does qualify for the term.

---

[2] For differing ULPs, a router may not need any special capabilities. For example, an IP/Ethernet router can handle both HTTP/IP/Ethernet and Telnet/IP/Ethernet without being "multiprotocol" per se: the ULP is transparent to the router.

In the context of SANs, a multiprotocol router must connect Fibre Channel (FC) fabrics to each other and/or to some other networking protocol. Fibre Channel is mandatory since it is by far the leading protocol for use in SANs. Other protocols that a router may connect to include IP storage protocols such as FCIP and the emerging iSCSI standard.

There are a number of SAN devices sometimes incorrectly called storage routers. Some companies have built protocol bridges that they called routers for marketing reasons. For example, a device that converts SCSI-3 to Fibre Channel is not a router per se, since SCSI-3 is not a network protocol, and to be a true router a device must connect different networks together.

The Brocade router provides three functions critical to modern enterprise SAN deployments, and is designed to provide more in the future. At the time of this writing, the router software provides:

- FC-FC Routing Service for enabling greater connectivity than traditional Fibre Channel SANs provide
- FCIP Tunneling Service for extending Fibre Channel fabrics over distance using IP wide area networks
- iSCSI Gateway Service for sharing Fibre Channel storage resources with iSCSI initiators

In addition to running these services, the Brocade router is a high-performance Fibre Channel fabric switch.

What is new in this edition?

This is the first generally available (GA) version of *Multiprotocol Routing for SANs*, and therefore the entire work could be considered "new in this edition." However, there was a limited "advance edition" released for attendees of the 2004 Brocade Conference Road Show and selected other events, and there have been a number of changes since that version.

For example, this edition represents a complete rewrite of the advance edition for enhanced readability. Every word and diagram on every page was reconsidered to determine if it could be clarified. Some sections were improved substantially, and bear only structural resemblance to the original.

In addition to improved readability, a number of changes to technical content were made. For example, this edition:

- Added the "wire once" business driver for FC-FC Routing Service to chapters 1 and 7.
- Added additional details on selected third-party multiprotocol routing products to chapter 2.
- Added material in chapter 14 discussing how to integrate the router into fabrics that do not currently use zoning.
- Expanded the glossary, adding more terms and definitions.
- Added to the content on troubleshooting.
- Added to the FAQs at the end of each section.

How should this book be used?

For readers completely unfamiliar with multiprotocol SAN routing, it would be best to start at the beginning and read to the end of at least the first section. This section is written as a set of tutorials.

Readers familiar with SAN routing who want to learn how it can solve a specific business problems should browse the second section to locate a similar design. The examples in section two coupled with the guidance in section three should be sufficient to lead to a candidate network design.

For readers familiar with the technology and its business applications who are interested in routed SAN design theory, or readers actively engaged in deploying the router, starting with section three could be appropriate.

In all cases, if a section fails clarify a point, try reading the section FAQ first. All of the major router concepts are discussed differently in each section, so also try looking for similar material in other parts of the book. The appendices may also help to clarify more advanced concepts.

Who should read this book?

There are many groups for whom this book is appropriate. For example, it is appropriate for:

- Administrators currently responsible for SANs
- Administrators intending to deploy SANs in the future
- Third parties implementing router management software
- Systems Engineers who design and deploy SANs
- OEM personnel who sell and support the router
- Industry analysts who need an in-depth understanding of the direction in which storage networks are evolving
- Technology evangelists helping to direct that evolution
- Network Engineers wishing to expand their skill sets

Where can more information be found?

The Basic Reference appendix is useful for those familiar with SANs but unclear on specific technologies such as media and cable types, or external networking equipment that may be connected to the Multiprotocol Router such as IP network switches and routers. The glossary is a good starting place if a particular term is unfamiliar. Each section ends with a FAQ that may shed light on more difficult subjects.

This is not a data or storage networking primer. It is assumed that the reader is at least passingly familiar with concepts related to SANs and Fibre Channel and with general network concepts like switches and IP routers. For readers less familiar with IP concepts, Section 4 (Reference Material) has some relevant information, but it is not a comprehensive tutorial on data networking. There are already many books available on that subject. For readers less familiar with basic Fibre Channel and SAN concepts, there are a number of books available with introductory-level material on SANs. For example, both Dan Pollack's *Practical Storage Area Networking*, and *Building SANs with Brocade Fabric Switch* by Josh Judd have good introductory material. Perhaps the most effective resource would be *Principles of SAN Design*. This is another *SAN Administrator's Bookshelf* title by Josh Judd, and has an entire section devoted to basic SAN tutorials.

To learn more about operation of the Brocade Multiprotocol Router platform and XPath OS, refer to the product manuals, including but not limited to:

- Brocade SilkWorm Fabric AP7420 Hardware Reference Manual
- Brocade XPath OS Advanced Web Tools – AP Edition
- Brocade XPath OS Command Reference Manual
- Brocade XPath OS Procedures Guide
- Brocade XPath OS System Error Message Reference Manual

Information about this and other books can be found at **http://www.brocade.com/bookshelf**. Users of Brocade products should consider joining Brocade Connect at **http://www.brocade.com/connect.** This provides access to forums, documentation, and scripts. There is a similar online community designed for Brocade partners and OEMs: **http://partner.brocade.com..** Brocade Education Services offers relevant classes, and can be reached on the web at **http://www.brocade.com/education_services**.

How can errors or omissions be reported?

Feedback may be sent to **bookshelf@brocade.com**. Please include the name of the book, the edition, and the publication date, and if applicable the page number and paragraph to which each comment applies. Using figure and/or table numbers is also acceptable.

It will not always be possible to reply to such e-mails, but they will be reviewed prior to publication of the next edition. In addition, updated material often will be posted as it becomes available to the *SAN Administrator's Bookshelf* website. This site will carry major updates to existing content. Modifications such as minor readability enhancements, spelling and grammar changes, or large sections of new content will be made available in the next printed edition.

Contents

Table of Contents

Table of Figures

Table of Tables

Figure Legend

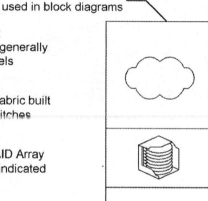

Generic Network
May be FC or IP; generally
indicated with labels

Brocade Fabric
A Fibre Channel fabric built
using Brocade switches

Storage Array
Fibre Channel RAID Array
unless otherwise indicated

Enterprise Host
High-end server using FC HBAs
unless otherwise indicated

Low-End Host
Low-end iSCSI host or desktop
client unless otherwise indicated

Multiprotocol Router
SilkWorm AP7420 platform
unless otherwise indicated

FC Switch
Brocade pizzabox switch, such
as SilkWorm 2x00 or 3x00

FC Director
Brocade modular chassis, such
as SilkWorm 12000 or 24000

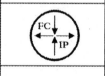

Generic Link
May be FC or IP connection;
generally indicated with labels

Section One

Technology Overview

Section Topics

- Need for Storage Routers
- Descriptions of Router Platforms
- Overview of FC-FC Router
- Overview of iSCSI Gateway
- Overview of FCIP Tunneling
- Frequently Asked Questions

1: Storage Network Evolution

The driving force behind the rapid adoption of multiprotocol Storage Area Network (SAN) routers has been the rapid growth and increasing complexity of production SANs. As organizations continue to expand, they require more comprehensive solutions than traditional Fibre Channel (FC) fabrics can provide. To address these needs, Brocade® has developed routing services that increase SAN functionality, scalability, and versatility. These services are a natural evolution for storage networks, and track the evolution that data networks went through.

For example, consider the non–hierarchical nature of Fibre Channel fabrics. Early efforts to create flat segments (e.g. Ethernet or ThickNet) hit a ceiling beyond which they could not grow or be managed. Today, FC fabrics are hitting a similar limit. An FC router solves this problem, but unlike IP routers, it is optimized for the more stringent performance and reliability needs of the SAN market. An FC router is to an FC fabric as an IP router is to an Ethernet segment, so the FC-FC Routing Service allows the same kind of hierarchical network design for Fibre Channel that was required to make technologies like Ethernet work. However, it uses the more reliable underlying FC protocol to do so, instead of IP. Fibre Channel routers are expected to be critical to the future of SANs. As Thomas Weisel Partners recently stated, the next phase of SAN evolution "...is likely to rely heavily on storage routers [to interconnect SAN islands]."

In addition to scalability enhancements, FC routers can also be used to enable a "wire once" environment for SANs.

It is possible for a SAN to start with a high degree of order: the SAN designer may know exactly which nodes need to communicate with each other, and be able to arrange matters such that most traffic is localized at the switch or at the even port-group level. The "wiring" of the SAN may be set up in a manner optimal for the initial traffic patterns. This is a very good way to tune a SAN for best performance.

However, ever changing business and technical requirements inevitably create *operational entropy*.[3] Well-ordered connectivity patterns change as equipment is added, removed, or relocated, and applications are upgraded or migrate between hosts. If the SAN is physically wired to optimize for a particular traffic pattern, it will need to be re-wired as the traffic patterns change.

It is possible to prevent the need to re-wire by using a network design that allows connectivity outside the originally anticipated traffic patterns. This is referred to as a "wire once" design method. Solving SAN design problems in such as way as to account for operational entropy in the past meant creating large flat fabrics: there simply was no alternative that provided the needed data-plane connectivity. However, very large fabrics also came with administrative and technical challenges that might not be desired. Using FC routers between smaller fabrics solves the connectivity problem without the manageability and scalability headaches.[4]

In addition to enhancing Fibre Channel solutions for existing SAN markets, the Brocade router also brings SAN connectivity to totally new markets.

---

[3] "Entropy" in this context is a measure of the disorder in a system. Specifically, the tendency for IO patterns to change to disorder as business needs change. There are other kinds of operational entropy as well: indeed, any change from the initial plan could be considered entropic.

[4] To fully understand this, it is useful to consider both the rate and scope of change. Large fabrics minimize the effects of IO pattern entropy because they allow IO patterns to change without requiring the SAN to be rewired. However, when large fabrics *do* require changes, the impact is higher, because it is operationally difficult to restructure any large, flat network.

With the explosive growth of storage networking, a new market segment has opened up on the far low-end. Fibre Channel is ideally suited for all levels of enterprise use. However, at the very lowest end of the SAN market, for small businesses just getting started with SAN deployments and for some low-end applications in small enterprises, Fibre Channel may simply be too expensive. The iSCSI Gateway Service expands the total available market for FC storage, and indeed for SANs in general, by allowing connectivity between low-end hosts and enterprise-class fabrics.

The iSCSI service also has an analogy to the data networking world. Data networks usually consist of enterprise-class switches, routers, and protocols, which are typically deployed in mission-critical datacenter environments. These tend to form the core or *backbone* of the network. But data networks also include entry-level technologies deployed around the farthest edges, where cost would otherwise preclude networking altogether.

For example, in a traditional data network, a datacenter core might use modular layer 3 (L3) switching chassis with Gigabit Ethernet interfaces and potentially 10Gbit backbone links. Servers generally attach to this class of network product. On the other hand, very low end servers on the edges of the network might attach to commodity L2 Ethernet switches running 10/100baseT. These tend to be much less reliable, and so the servers will have lower performance and availability, but the network attachment is also lower cost. Similarly, in the datacenter SAN of the future, the bulk of deployments will consist of Fibre Channel backbones that attach all storage and most servers, but some lowest-tier applications may benefit from iSCSI attachment, even at the expense of most of their performance and reliability metrics.

Low-end technologies have never gained wide acceptance at the core of the enterprise datacenter due to their inherent performance and reliability limitations: a 10baseT hub is no substitute for a modular chassis. For similar reasons, it is not expected that iSCSI will displace or even substantially disturb Fibre Channel as the datacenter SAN protocol of choice. Thomas Weisel Partners also recently stated that end-to-end iSCSI would remain a relatively small part of the SAN market going forward, with the majority of the market being pure FC fabrics, or FC SANs using routers for limited "edge" iSCSI connectivity. iSCSI will remain at the fringes of the network – like the commodity L2 Ethernet switches – and Fibre Channel will continue to form the center of the SAN and much of the edge – like enterprise-class L3 switches at the heart of the datacenter. The iSCSI gateway service was designed to facilitate this usage case.

Finally, SANs have been increasingly used in long-distance applications for resource consolidation and disaster recovery. The FCIP service addresses this need. In data networks, it is often the case that the technology used within a site (e.g. Ethernet) will not be the same as is used between sites (e.g. frame relay), which is why data networks have used multiprotocol WAN routers for years. Similarly, in long distance SAN solutions, it may be desirable to use other protocols in the WAN. The geographical expansion of SANs is enabled by multiprotocol routers for this reason.

In fact, the Brocade Multiprotocol Router can enhance distance solutions in several ways: it has a fully-integrated FCIP service, it can support native FC links over long distances due to its large per-port buffering, and it can be combined with external extension products like xWDMs and SONET/SDH gateways. It can even combine with and augment FCIP and/or iSCSI products from best-in-class providers like CNT.

At each level, the Brocade Multiprotocol Router tracks the data network evolution: it meets deep, real-world customer needs by solving the same basic problems for SANs that were solved by analogous data networking technologies. However, unlike IP routers, the Brocade solution does so in ways specifically optimized for the demands of mission-critical storage traffic.

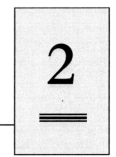

2: Router Hardware Platforms

This chapter discusses the capabilities of the different platforms that the Multiprotocol Router software can run on.[5] In addition, it provides examples of several best-in-class products from Brocade partners. This is by no means a complete list of Brocade partners; it is simply intended to illustrate a few of the *kinds* of third-party products which might complement the Brocade router.

Licensing Model

The Brocade SilkWorm® Multiprotocol Router software is activated using license keys on platforms with appropriate hardware support. In addition to many of the options available for other Brocade platforms, separate keys are available for router-specific features such as:

- Ports on Demand
- FC-FC Routing Service
- FCIP Tunneling Service

iSCSI is an emerging protocol, without any production track record, so at the time of this writing the iSCSI Gateway Service is included in the base platform price without additional licensing cost.[6]

---

[5] Some platform *hardware* capabilities may not be enabled in *software* immediately, and different channels may have varying release schedules.

[6] Since iSCSI is the least mature protocol in the SAN market, it is critically important to check for *end to end* support before deploying any iSCSI solution from any

Licensed features may be purchased separately, but in many cases they can be purchased in bundles, which can be more cost effective. Either way, be sure to obtain the correct licenses when making a router platform purchase.

SilkWorm AP7420

The first platform that the multiprotocol routing services will be delivered on is the Brocade SilkWorm Fabric Application Platform (AP7420), which is shown in Figure 1. Support is planned for additional platforms over time.

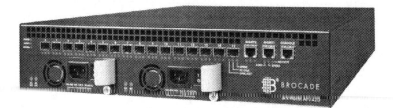

Figure 1 – SilkWorm AP7420

Multiprotocol routing is a subset of the capabilities of the AP7420: as well as performing its roles as a multiprotocol router and an FC fabric switch, it was designed to handle storage application processing requirements (a.k.a. "virtualization") for environments ranging all the way from small business to large-scale enterprises.

At only two RETMA units (2U) in height, the AP7420 allows deployment of fabric-based applications and multiprotocol routing using very little space. With "ports on demand" licensing, a single platform can be purchased with as few as eight ports and is scalable to sixteen ports with the addition of a license key. Its advanced networking capabilities allow scalability far beyond that level.

---

vendor. This must include all applications, IP infrastructure, iSCSI drivers and HBAs, storage devices, the iSCSI gateways and FC infrastructure.

The platform operating system is based on the Brocade XPath™ Architecture, which is compatible with switches running Brocade Fabric OS. This allows users to enhance their existing SANs without costly "forklift" upgrades.

The AP7420 can make switching decisions using any protocol layers up to the very top of the protocol stack. This means that the platform hardware is able to function as a standard Fibre Channel fabric switch, an FC-FC router, a virtualization switch, or all three in combination. Similarly, it could function as any level of Ethernet or IP switch from layer 2 to layer 4.[7] The platform has considerable flexibility, since every port has its own ASIC with multiple embedded CPUs and both Ethernet and FC protocol support.

Side Note

Each port of the SilkWorm AP7420 has its own dedicated ASIC (codenamed FiGeRo), each of which has dedicated RAM and three CPUs. Imagine the performance and flexibility of a network switch with the power of three RISC processors embedded at every single port: when new applications are invented that have not even been conceived of yet, the existing platform hardware should often be able to accommodate them. For more information about the FiGeRo ASIC and the XPath virtualization architecture, download the whitepaper "Optimizing Fabric Applications With Brocade XPath Technology" from the Brocade web site.[8]

The SilkWorm AP7420 Fabric Application Platform provides the following features:[9]

---

[7] As a practical matter, not all combinations of features will be available in software from all support channels just because the platform *hardware* is capable of delivering them.

[8] http://www.brocade.com/san/pdf/whitepapers/XPath_Tech_WP_00.pdf

[9] This section refers briefly to features – such as EX_Ports – that are covered in much greater detail in later chapters.

- 16 ports with software selectable modes, including auto-sensing 1Gbit/2Gbit FC, and 1Gbit Ethernet

- 2U rack-mountable enclosure about 25 inches deep

- High–availability features including redundant hot-swappable power supplies and fan Field-Replaceable Units (FRUs)

- Forward and backward compatibility within fabrics with Brocade 2000-series and later SilkWorm switches

- Management access via dual 10/100Base-T RJ45 Ethernet ports and one RJ45 serial port

- When in Fibre Channel mode:
  - o Auto-sensing ports negotiate to the highest speed supported by attached devices
  - o FC ports auto-negotiate as E_ or F_Ports. Any port may be manually configured as an FL_Port to permit an NL_Port device to be attached, or configured as an EX_Port for FC-FC routing.
  - o Exchange-based Inter-Switch Link (ISL) and Inter-Fabric Link (IFL) routing[10]

- When in Gigabit Ethernet mode:
  - o Ports support hardware acceleration by offloading TCP to the port ASICs' three ARM[11] processors.
  - o FCIP is available under license to deliver TCP/IP distance extension of FC virtual E_Port traffic
  - o iSCSI initiator to FC target protocol mediation

- Per-port XPath ASICs for rapid data manipulation

- The XPath Fabric ASIC provides non-blocking connectivity between Port ASICs

---

[10] Exchange-based routing is much like frame-level trunking, in that it uses hardware to balance IO across multiple switch-to-switch links better than FSPF would on its own. The differences are that exchange routing balances whenever the exchange ID changes (usually every SCSI command) rather than every frame, and does not need to be implemented only between ASIC port groups. This is also discussed in the FSPF subsection of Appendix B.

[11] Advanced RISC Multiprocessor

- Small Form-Factor Pluggable (SFP) optical transceivers allow any combination of supported Short and Long Wavelength Laser (SWL, LWL, and ELWL) media.[12]
- Latency is minimized through the use of storage application service processors inside each port ASIC.[13]
- Each port has three LEDs to indicate behavior and status
- Air is pulled into the non-cable-side of the chassis, and exits cable-side above the SFPs

Physical Interfaces

The router uses optical interfaces for data ports and copper for management ports. When deploying connections from an IP network to the router for an iSCSI or FCIP solution, use *optical* Gigabit Ethernet such as 1000baseSX.[14]

Note that the SFPs which ship with the router support 1000baseSX in addition to Fibre Channel, but other SFPs may not. (See Figure 117 p282 and the surrounding text for a more detailed discussion of SFPs.) If only 1000baseT *copper* is available, use a media converter. (See "Copper to Fiber Gigabit Ethernet Converter" p296.) When connecting to an IP management network, use 10/100baseT copper Ethernet.

The router includes a standard DB9 adapter for the RJ45 serial management port, but may require special handling in some cases. (See Figure 121 p287, Figure 122 p288, and

---

[12] See Table 2 p101 for more information on supported media.

[13] Latency refers to the amount of time that elapses between when a frame enters a network and when it leaves the network, if the network is uncongested. Delay is a more general term that also covers congestion. To avoid performance degradation, storage applications tend to require latency in the microsecond range, *not* in the millisecond range as this is the order of magnitude in which disk seek delay occurs. (IP networks tend to have latency measured in milliseconds if not seconds, which is one of the reasons why IP SANs have historically failed to function properly.) By implementing application processors in ASIC hardware, latencies are not only kept to the right order of magnitude, but are in fact on the low-end of that range.

[14] Of course, external Ethernet fan-in switches may use copper 1000baseT to connect to hosts, as in Figure 21 p56.

Table 30 p289.) In general, see Appendix A for more details
about physical interfaces and cabling.

The SilkWorm 24000 Director

The SilkWorm 24000 Fibre Channel Director (Figure 2)
is an evolution of the highly successful SilkWorm 12000 design, which has been used in thousands of mission-critical
production deployments for years. Because they use a common design, the two directors are blade-compatible with
each other, meaning that blades from a SilkWorm 24000 can
be used to populate a SilkWorm 12000 chassis and vice versa.
Both directors use the same operating system, and all of the
FRUs are identical except for the port and CP blades.

Figure 2 - SilkWorm 24000 Director

In addition to the AP7420, at the time of this writing
Brocade is in the process of designing an router blade for the
SilkWorm 24000. The intention is to be able to populate the
chassis with any combination of standard Fibre Channel or
router blades. The system should be able to support full performance router configurations of at least 128 ports. Contact

your sales representative to inquire about timing and availability of this and other future Brocade products.

The director platform in which the router blade will reside has industry-leading performance and HA characteristics. Each blade is hot-pluggable, as are the fans and power supplies. The chassis has redundant control processors (CPs) with redundant active-active non-blocking[15] backplane switching elements, which of course support hot (i.e. non-disruptive) code load and activation (HCL/A).

The bulk of the information in this book is expected to apply to the router software whether running on the AP7420 or the future director blade. However, since the application blade has not yet been released, all specific examples outside of this subsection use the AP7420. When the blade is generally available, updated information will be released. Register online to receive free updates on current content in this book, and brief discussions of net-new features for planned future editions. (Use the *SAN Administrator's Bookshelf* series URL: http://www.brocade.com/bookshelf.)

The SilkWorm 24000 Director has the following features:

- 128 ports per chassis configured in 16-port increments
- Current port blades are 1Gbit/2Gbit Fibre Channel
- Planned 16-port application blade will have software selectable modes similar to the AP7420
- Planned 4Gbit and 10Gbit port blades provide platform longevity. (Next generation Brocade ASIC technology.)

---

[15] There has been debate in the industry about the definition of the term "blocking." When Brocade uses the word, it refers to Head of Line Blocking (HoLB). The SilkWorm 24000 is not subject to HoLB because it uses virtual channels internally as well as externally, and can guarantee that any given port combination will not overlap on a VC queue. In addition, its backplane supports more *bandwidth* than current Fibre Channel blades are capable of, so it will support future higher speed blades. All ports can run full-speed full-duplex at the same time. This means that the SilkWorm 24000 is both *non-blocking* and capable of *uncongested operation*.

- Management access via 10/100Base-T RJ45 Ethernet ports and DB9 serial ports
- 14U rack mountable enclosure less than 30 inches deep
- High-availability features include hot-swappable FRUs for port blades, redundant power supplies and fans, and redundant control processor (CP) blades
- Diagnostics and monitoring capabilities deliver unprecedented Reliability, Availability, and Serviceability (RAS)
- Non-disruptive software upgrades (HCL/A)
- Non-blocking multi-terabit passive backplane architecture enables all 128 ports to operate at line rate in full-duplex mode simultaneously
- Forward and backward compatibility within fabrics with all Brocade 2000-series and later SilkWorm switches
- SilkWorm 12000s are upgradeable to SilkWorm 24000s
- Brocade director roadmap is based on the SilkWorm 24000 "CE" architecture for design longevity.
- Small Form-Factor Pluggable (SFP) optical transceivers allow any combination of supported Short and Long Wavelength Laser (SWL, LWL, and ELWL) media
- Blade assemblies and power supplies are serviced from the cable-side and fans from the non-cable-side
- Air is pulled into the non-cable-side of the chassis and exits cable-side both above the port and CP blades and through the power supplies to the right of the blade cage

Software Layering

From a software layering standpoint, the components of the SAN Routing Services package sit below storage services and above lower level protocols such as Ethernet and Fibre Channel, as shown in Figure 3.

This applies to all planned Brocade Multiprotocol Router platforms. Moving forward, this layered approach will allow the router to support additional routing methods independent of mid-level services, and additional services independent of protocols, both without requiring changes to the application layers. It may be possible in the future to combine virtualization applications with routing within a network and even in many cases within a single platform.

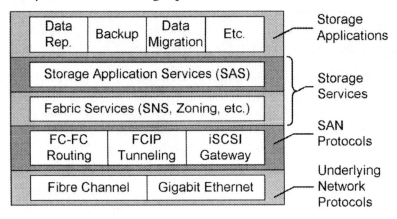

Figure 3 - Multiprotocol Router Layers

The end-user benefits of this layered approach are numerous, including but not limited to:

- **Manageability**: Router features are configured and managed with familiar existing tools
- **Reliability**: Already tested fabric services continue to work as before when upper layers are changed
- **Extensibility**: Platforms can deliver future services in addition to current capabilities without re-architecture

Other Multiprotocol Platforms

The Brocade Multiprotocol Router is a world-class product overall, and is by far the best-in-class FC-FC routing solution on the market today. However, no single product can be perfectly optimized for every possible usage case. In some environments, it will be desirable to use a product from another vendor in conjunction with Brocade switches and routers. This subsection discusses a subset of the third-party multiprotocol platforms that work in conjunction with Bro-

15

cade platforms. Most of these and many other options have been tested in the Brocade Fabric Aware labs.

CNT Ultra Edge 3000

The integration of the FCIP service with FC switching and routing into a single platform makes the Brocade router a cost-effective FCIP distance extension solution. This integration also simplifies installation and ongoing management.

In addition to offering FCIP on the AP7420, Brocade has a long history of partnering with CNT to deliver best-in-class distance extension solutions. This strategy is continued with the Multiprotocol Router. Users may wish to deploy the CNT solution because the Brocade platform does not yet implement some of the more advanced FCIP features like tape pipelining and data compression.

The CNT UltraNet 3000 gateway (Figure 4) can be purchased with a selection of distance extension interfaces, including FCIP via Fast Ethernet or Gigabit Ethernet interfaces, ATM, and packet over SONET/SDH.

Figure 4 – CNT FCIP; ATM; SONET/SDH Gateway

It is possible to combine the Brocade Multiprotocol Router running the FC-FC Routing Service with the CNT Ultra Edge 3000 to get best-in-class solutions for both tunneling and inter-fabric routing. Combining these products is appropriate for users who need the CNT advanced FCIP features more than they the need lower cost and complexity of an integrated gateway. Figure 43 (p128) illustrates one way to combine the Brocade router with third-party distance extension platforms such as the CNT gateway.

SANRAD and Stringbean Software

The Brocade router can be purchased through some channels without the optional "ports on demand" license. In this case, it is a cost-effective 8-port multiprotocol routing platform. For FC-FC routing and FCIP, this can be ideal.

However, given that iSCSI is inherently a cost- rather than feature- or performance-driven market, some users may need an even cheaper alternative for iSCSI translation. The SANRAD (www.sanrad.com) iSCSI gateway, shown in Figure 5, is one example. It has two iSCSI portals, and two Fibre Channel ports. While it is missing some of the advanced features of the Brocade router, it may have a lower entry-level cost point in some configurations.

Figure 5 - SANRAD iSCSI Gateway

The iSCSI gateway offered on the SANRAD platform is similar in principal to the Brocade iSCSI Gateway Service offered on the AP7420. Because the SANRAD platform is smaller and offers far fewer features, it can be less expensive, and may be adequate for users who desire the lowest entry point into the iSCSI bridging market. However, there are a number of differences between the platforms besides cost and port count which must be considered when making a product selection.

The SANRAD product is not capable of providing FC fabric switching, FCIP distance extension, or FC-FC routing. The products use different methods of projecting iSCSI hosts into the FC fabrics: while the Brocade product uses zoning and standard E_Port methods to control and represent iSCSI hosts, a SANRAD gateway will present either N_Port or NL_Port interfaces. The Gigabit Ethernet interfaces on the SANRAD product are low-end copper, whereas the Brocade product uses more reliable optical ports capable of spanning greater distances and of running protocols other than Gigabit Ethernet. Perhaps most importantly, this third-party solution

17

is not integrated into most SAN management software, whereas Brocade products tend to be more widely supported.

Stringbean Software (www.stringbeansoftware.com) offers an even lower-end solution. Their WinTarget package allows a standard Microsoft Windows 2000/XP/2003 host to become a software-only iSCSI gateway. While this and similar software solutions may have lower performance and reliability in some cases, they also use commodity hardware, and are usually the most cost effective from a hardware standpoint. However, software solutions require additional integration and testing to install, which may be expensive.

One of these solutions should be considered under the following conditions:

- Need lowest possible cost entry point into the iSCSI bridging market above all else[16]

- Need a higher per-port session count than the Brocade platform can support in the current release[17]

- Requires RJ45 copper GE interfaces on the gateway itself, rather than just on the iSCSI hosts[18]

- Solution is needed before the Brocade iSCSI gateway is generally available from the relevant support provider[19]

---

[16] *Total* cost is important. For example, be sure to calculate the cost of increased downtime before deploying iSCSI...

[17] High per-portal over-subscription has an impact on both performance and availability on all iSCSI gateway products. Evaluate these impacts carefully before deploying iSCSI.

[18] In data networking, it is normal to use optical ports for backbone platforms like routers, and copper for edge switches. To connect them, it is possible to use a device such as the one discussed under "Copper to Fiber Gigabit Ethernet Converter" (p296), but the more common approach is to use edge switches with both optical and copper ports as in Figure 21 (p56) and Figure 123 (p291).

[19] Note that this assumes that the Brocade solution is not supported *and* that the alternative *is* supported. At the time of this writing, all major OEMs are at some stage of the release process. Most have completed qualification of the AP7420 hardware, FC-FC routing, and/or FCIP. Due to limited demand for iSCSI in general, some vendors have not prioritized testing that feature, though all have expressed interest.

LightSand S-2500-B

The LightSand S-2500-B (Figure 6) is able to interconnect Fibre Channel across a SONET/SDH MAN or WAN. The Fibre Channel input ports on the platform can carry native SCSI traffic (FCP) or mainframe traffic (FICON).

Figure 6 - LightSand SONET/SDH Gateway

SONET/SDH provides an ideal infrastructure for extending SANs over distance. It is usually more reliable and faster than FCIP, since the SONET/SDH transport eliminates the overhead and latency that comes from encapsulation. Perhaps more importantly, the packet loss typical on IP networks may force protocols such as FCIP, TCP, or even SCSI to retransmit, which reduces throughput considerably. SONET/SDH has a much more reliable process than is typically used for IP networks. Fully-coupled flow control across the MAN/WAN ensures that the data is never lost, providing the guaranteed delivery that SANs expect and require.

The major trade-offs between FCIP and FC over SONET/SDH are that using an FCIP transport is usually less expensive while SONET/SDH is more reliable and performs better. Also, the Brocade FCIP solution has greater integration, resulting in simpler installation and management. Users who require best-in-class performance and reliability should consider using the Brocade router for inter-fabric routing in combination with a SONET/SDH product such as the LightSand gateway.

3: FC-FC Routing Service

FCR and LSANs

The Brocade FC–FC Routing Service provides connectivity between two or more fabrics without merging them.[20] It can potentially run on a number of different platforms. Any platform it is running on can be referred to as an *FC router*, or *FCR* for short. The service allows the creation of Logical Storage Area Networks, or *LSANs*, which provide connectivity that can span fabrics. The fact that an FCR can connect autonomous fabrics without merging them has advantages in terms of change management, network management, scalability, reliability, availability, and serviceability to name just a few areas.

An FC router is to an FC fabric as an IP router is to an Ethernet subnet.[21] An LSAN is also somewhat analogous to a Virtual Private Network: it creates connectivity between different networks, but only allows designated devices on those networks to communicate rather than opening the floodgates

---

[20] Merging fabrics causes, for example, their name servers to become a single distributed name server, their FSPF databases to become one, and their zoning configurations to join. There are also fabric-wide events that increase in scope and effect, such as certain RSCN types and fabric reconfigurations. Merging fabrics combines configurations and faults that would otherwise be isolated and managed separately. Large-scale merges may provide the desired connectivity, but also may have undesired consequences. The router provides the connectivity without the consequences.

[21] An FC router is actually more analogous to a Layer 3 switch in that each frame is routed by ASICs rather than software.

between them as a pure router would.[22] Following that analogy, an FC router is like a switching firewall, or a router with
hardware–enforced access control lists. As a result, LSANs
may occasionally be called Logical *Private* SANs. However, it
is most useful to think of an LSAN in terms of Brocade Advanced Zoning: an LSAN is a zone that spans fabrics.

The customer needs for this product are similar to those
that brought first routers and then Layer 3 switches to the
data networking world. Early efforts were made to create
large, flat Ethernet LANs without routers. These efforts hit a
ceiling beyond which they could not grow effectively. In
many cases, Ethernet broadcast storms would create reliability
issues, or it would become impossible to resolve dependencies for change control. Perhaps merging Ethernet networks
that grew independently would involve too much effort and
risk. An analogous situation exists today with flat Fibre
Channel fabrics.

For example, a customer with many Fibre Channel SAN
islands might not be willing to merge them because it would
involve resolving domain ID and zoning conflicts, fabric-
wide parameter mismatches, and overcoming other challenges. It might take too much effort and risk to justify the
added benefit of connectivity. With the FC router, users can
interconnect fabrics, gaining the desired device connectivity
without the challenges a fabric merge would pose. Each
SAN island remains an independent Fibre Channel fabric, in
this context referred to as an *edge fabric*.

It is important to understand that edge fabrics retain their
own separate fabric services: name servers, zoning databases,
routing tables, domain ID spaces, etc., are all unique within
an edge fabric. Without an FC router, fabrics could not be
merged until such conflicts were resolved, which can be time
consuming and can introduce risk to a production environment. With a router, such conflicts are simply irrelevant.

---

[22] That is, unless the router *also* had firewall software and/or used access control
lists (ACLs).

To name just a few areas where an FCR provides advantages vs. merging fabrics: the scalability of one edge fabric does not affect another, fabric reconfigurations do not propagate between edge fabrics, and faults in fabric services are contained. Furthermore, if Meta SANs are constructed with legacy switches, the overall network size can vastly exceed the hardware and software capabilities of those switches. None of these things are true with large merged fabrics.

 Side Note

When evaluating multiprotocol routing products, be sure that all candidate solutions truly isolate separate fabrics. Some implementations only appear to be routers, but retain major inter-fabric dependencies. They may require all router ports to attach to fabrics at the same software versions, or run their "routing" code for all fabrics on common CPs, or – worst of all – require fabric-wide parameters and domain IDs to be synchronized. (All of these are characteristics of VSAN switches.) These products may appear superficially to be routers in marketing slides, but they miss the technical business cases for FC-FC routing.

Meta SANs

The resulting routed storage network is a level above the common definition of SAN, in which a "SAN" = "a fabric" and a "Dual Redundant SAN" = "an unconnected pair of parallel redundant fabrics." This new kind of storage network is therefore called a *Meta SAN*.[23] The equivalent object in data networks is sometimes called an *internetwork*, though this term is now confusing to many readers because of it's implied connection to the Internet.

---

23 "Meta," from the Greek, meaning: (1) Beyond; transcending; more comprehensive. (2) At a higher state of development. This does not imply a reference to e.g. Meta Data. It is acceptable simply to refer to a Meta SAN as "the SAN," but only if context makes the meaning clear.

Figure 7 illustrates a generic Meta SAN comprised of two Fibre Channel routers and two edge fabrics. Note that the number of edge fabrics can be (and generally is) much greater than two.

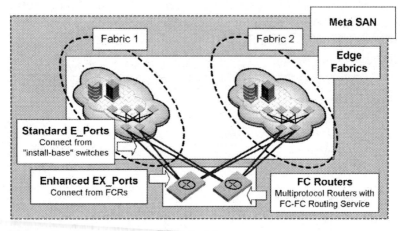

Figure 7 – Generic Meta SAN

EX_Ports, FC-NAT, and IFLs

FC routers connect to edge fabrics and export devices between them using *EX_Ports*. These are like normal E_Ports from the perspective of the edge fabrics, and the protocols that run across them are E_Port standards–compliant. The distinction is that EX_Ports limit what each edge fabric sees by using Fibre Channel Network Address Translation, or *FC-NAT*. This is similar to the "hide behind" NAT used by IP firewalls. An FCR can "hide" an entire *n*-domain edge fabric behind one phantom domain (explained later). This is analogous to the translation performed by fabric switches when connecting to private loop devices.

An EX_Port can be thought of as being an "E_Port lite." It is fully compatible with standard Brocade fabric switches, since to the edge fabric it behaves like a regular E_Port. An E_Port-to-EX_Port connection is called an "Inter-Fabric

Link" or *IFL*,[24] similar to the Inter-Switch Links (ISLs) used within fabrics. Unlike a traditional E_Port, an EX_Port terminates at the router, and does not propagate fabric services or FSPF routing information to other edge fabrics.

☑ Side Note

EX_Ports are in many ways an advancement over traditional E_Ports, but they still follow E_Port standards. This is why EX_Ports can seamlessly connect to installed base FC switches. The EX_Port enhancements (e.g. FCRP) are higher up the protocol stack than the E_Port standards. This is in stark contrast to proprietary tagged VSAN ports, which violate standards at every level down to the frame format itself, and are guaranteed to be incompatible with all installed base FC devices in the world.

Exporting Devices with LSANs

The act of projecting a node into another fabric is called *exporting*. When a host is *exported* from Fabric 1 into Fabric 2, it also must be *imported* into Fabric 2 from Fabric 1. To create an LSAN, both exporting and importing must occur, so these statements are functionally equivalent in normal cases. This book uses the term 'export' for consistency. Figure 8 shows a pair of devices that have been exported between two edge fabrics.

Each EX_Port has a user-configured Fabric Identifier, or *FID*, that specifies to which fabric it is attached. Any number of EX_Ports can (and must) have the same FID if they attach to the same edge fabric. In the Figure 8 example, all EX_Ports on all routers connected to Fabric 1 would have FID=1 set.

---

[24] An EX_Port to E_Port IFL is also called an EX-IFL to distinguish it from a hypothetical future EX_Port to EX_Port link called an EX^2-IFL. (Pronounced Ee Ex Two Eye Ef El.)

In a Meta SAN, a fabric reconfiguration in one edge fabric is not propagated to the others. Fabric convergence time scalability issues simply do not exist between edge fabrics in a Meta SAN. Similarly, zoning database and fabric topology data is not propagated between edge fabrics, so scalability is not limited by the sum of all fabrics' zoning, routing, or convergence timing.[25] Even Storage Name Server (SNS) entries only cross fabrics for those devices that have been explicitly added to LSANs for sharing. This means that certain scalability effects *can* cross fabric boundaries even with the router, but only to the extent that devices are actually exported between fabrics.

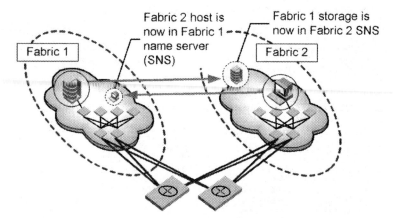

Figure 8 - Exporting Devices Between Edge Fabrics

For example, if Fabric 1 has a scalability limit of 1024 name server entries and currently has 768 devices, and so does Fabric 2, an administrator could not merge the fabrics without going beyond each fabric's name server capabilities. However, if two fabrics were connected via FC routers, then

---

[25] When building a large, flat fabric, all fabric services on all switches relate directly to the services on all other switches in that fabric. This is known as an n^2 problem, and in order to make it work, it is necessary not only to make the protocols work, but also to make the timing work. For example, if a switch does not respond to a name server request in a certain time, it can cause other switches or hosts to give up on it. Similarly, if FSPF updates are delayed, the fabric can segment. By using routers, the n^2 nature of scalability problems is eliminated because switches on different fabrics do *not* talk directly to each other.

up to a third of the devices could be shared between them without hitting SNS scalability limits.

It would therefore be appropriate to refer to the router as being an "any subset to any subset" connectivity solution. While the router *can* provide all-to-all connectivity across fabrics, doing so is not desirable because it does not improve Meta SAN scalability or reliability to any great extent vs. what could be achieved by merging fabrics. However, since storage networks rarely require all-to-all connectivity, this is not a real-world issue.

For example, it is not expected that *all hosts* in one edge fabric will need to communicate with *all hosts* in *all other* edge fabrics, or, for that matter, with *any* hosts in *any* edge fabrics in most SANs: Hosts tend to talk to a *subset* of *storage* ports. Correct Meta SAN configuration tends to involve exporting only some devices to only some other fabrics, rather than taking a blanket approach.

When a set of devices on different edge fabrics are allowed to communicate through an FC router, the resulting connectivity group is known as an LSAN. This is illustrated in Figure 9.

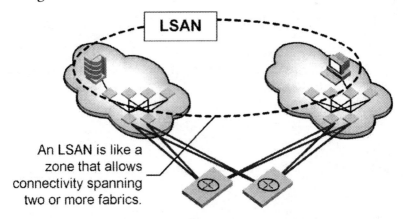

Figure 9 – LSAN Spanning Two Fabrics

Many different LSANs can exist in a Meta SAN. Indeed many different LSANs can exist between any given pair of edge fabrics. Devices can be members of multiple LSANs, and LSANs can overlap with traditional zoning mechanisms on local fabrics as well.

Installation and Management [26]

Installing an FC router is a simple and non-disruptive process.[27] The initial steps are the same as those performed to install any other Brocade switch, such as configuring an IP address for management and rack mounting the platform.

Next, the appropriate ports must be configured as EX_Ports, and set to appropriate FIDs. This is accomplished by using the same familiar tools used for traditional switch administrative tasks: WEB TOOLS, Fabric Manager, the Fabric OS CLI, etc.. Finally, cables are connected between the EX_Ports on the router and E_Ports on the existing fabrics.[28] The process is simple enough that less experienced SAN administrators should be able to install an FC router platform.[29]

Once the routers are installed, day-to-day administration is performed using zoning within each edge fabric. This allows existing tools from both Brocade and many third parties to work as usual, and minimizes the need to retrain SAN administrators. If a specially named zone called an "LSAN zone" is created on each of two edge fabrics that an FC router has access to, the router will automatically create the LSAN (including any needed FC-NAT entries) between those fabrics. If an LSAN spans two fabrics, there are two LSAN zones that define it – one on each fabric. An LSAN that spans three fabrics would have three LSAN zones, and so

---

[26] This is covered in more detail in Section Three.

[27] This is true of the Brocade router, but not generally of other vendors.

[28] Before doing this, make sure that the EX_Ports really *are* configured as EX_Ports. If they are still in U_Port mode, they will come up as E_Ports and merge fabrics instead of creating a Meta SAN.

[29] This cannot be said of similar platforms from other vendors, and is a unique advantage of the Brocade approach.

on. Figure 10 illustrates the LSAN zones used to create the LSAN shown previously in Figure 9.

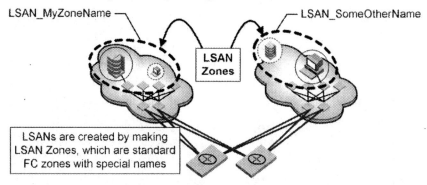

Figure 10 – Creating an LSAN Using LSAN Zones

FC routers automatically obtain the zoning database from each edge fabric and parse the database for zones with "LSAN_" as the prefix of the zone name.[30] The router compares the port WWNs from LSAN zones from each fabric with entries from each of the other fabrics. Matching entries define which devices can communicate across fabrics. These devices are considered to be in the same LSAN. The user-defined portion of the LSAN zone name from one fabric does *not* have to match the user defined portion of the LSAN zone name from another fabric for devices to be included in the same LSAN. Also, node membership does not need to be identical. It is only required that the port WWNs that need to communicate across fabrics be in both zones. In Figure 10, the host and storage port WWNs need to be in the LSAN zones on both fabrics, but those zones may also contain non-matching entries.[31]

It is important to note that these are real zones in the edge fabrics and the devices that exist in these zones are sub-

---

[30] The prefix is not case sensitive to the router, so "LSAN_" and "lsan_" are equivalent. Case may, however, matter to the switches in the edge fabrics. Remember: an LSAN zone is a real zone within an edge fabric, and all of the normal zoning access control rules and methods apply.

[31] Note that this is *possible*, but not *recommended* for manageability reasons. Section Three has a discussion of this.

29

ject to normal zoning enforcement by the switches in each edge fabric. Even if the router somehow malfunctioned and exported a device erroneously, zoning on each edge fabric would still provide access control. If the administrator of Fabric 1 does not zone his host together with the storage array from Fabric 2, it does not matter if the Fabric 2 administrator did so. The devices will only be able to communicate when the zoning policy on *both* fabrics allows it.

There are two major administration models for SAN environments, and LSANs support both. There is the case where one admin owns the routers and all edge fabrics involved, and the case where different admins own each fabric.

An administrator who wants to allow connectivity between two fabrics and has administrative access to both can accomplish this using either traditional zoning tools or the Brocade Fabric Manager (FM).[32] Because FM can access both fabrics, it can create both LSAN zones at once. When instructed to create an LSAN, FM determines which fabrics the devices are in and creates the appropriate LSAN zones in each fabric. This is known as the "Super Admin" model.

If different administrators have access to each fabric, each must create matching LSAN zones containing the devices they want to share. This is the "Multi Admin" model.

Look again at Figure 8. Let's say that two different administrative organizations exist. An administrator of Fabric 1 could ask the admin of Fabric 2 that one of his FID 1 hosts be allowed to communicate with an FID 2 storage port. He could email the other admin the WWN of his host. The other admin could create an LSAN zone called "LSAN_xyz" that contained his storage port's WWN and the WWN of the FID 1 host. He would then reply to the first admin with this data. The FID 1 admin would create a matching zone in his fabric. The FC routers would receive this and automatically create FC-NAT entries, and the devices would then be able

---

[32] Certain minimum firmware and FM versions are required.

to communicate. This prevents unintended or unauthorized access between fabrics in a multiple–administrator model: one administrator creating an LSAN zone in one fabric does *not* result in connectivity between the two fabrics. Only after *both* admins have agreed on what devices should be allowed to communicate and have created correct LSAN zones will the FC–NAT entries be created by the routers and the zoning policies on each fabric allow connectivity.

LSAN zones are indistinguishable to an edge fabric from any other kind of zone, which is why they are compatible with previous Brocade Fabric Operating System (Fabric OS) versions. There are just two distinguishing features of an LSAN zone. First, they must begin with the prefix "LSAN_"[33] so that routers will recognize them. Second, they must contain only port WWNs or aliases of devices intended for inter-fabric sharing. This is because Fibre Channel Port IDs (PIDs) are not unique identifiers in a Meta SAN. The same PID can exist in multiple edge fabrics, so a router would not know what the administrator wanted to do if PIDs were used to create LSAN zones. This constraint, however, does not in any way preclude the use of PID-based zoning in edge fabrics for other zones. Those zones continue to work as usual.

In addition to supporting day-to-day administration of LSANs through familiar zoning mechanisms, the FC–FC Routing Service provides for element management of the routers themselves. For example, an administrator might be troubleshooting an LSAN connectivity problem and want to know if a port is online and in EX_Port mode, and if so to which edge fabric it is attached. On a standard switch an admin familiar with Brocade's CLI would expect to use the "switchShow" command, so that command has been en-hanced to provide the intuitive output, including the EX_Port designation and FID as shown below:

---

[33] The prefix is not case sensitive.

```
router:admin> switchShow

Switch Name  :  router
    [...]
Port Media Speed State      Info
=====================================
  0  id  AN  No_Light
  1  id  AN  No_Light
  2  id  AN  Online
  3  id  N2  Online EX_PORT 10:00:00:60:69:c0:20:ed "sw1" (fabric id = 2)
  4  id  N2  Online  E_PORT 10:00:00:60:69:90:10:dc "bb1" (upstream)
  5  id  AN  No_Light  Disabled
  6  id  AN  Online
  7  --  AN  No_Module
  8  id  AN  No_Light
  9  id  AN  No_Light  Disabled
 10  id  AN  No_Light
 11  id  N2  Online  F_PORT 10:00:00:00:c9:33:3e:3f
 12  id  AN  No_Light
 13  id  2G  No_Light
 14  id  AN  No_Light
 15  id  N1  Online  F_PORT 10:00:00:00:c9:30:11:0e
```

Similarly intuitive extensions are provided throughout a router's element management interfaces. This allows an already trained SAN administrator to have a rapid learning curve. There are a small number of new commands to perform functions that have no prior analogue, such as *portCfgEXport* which can put a port into EX_Port mode and set its fabric ID, and *fcrProxyDevShow* which displays proxy devices presented by EX_Ports and information about them.

Here is an example showing how the multi-administrator model can be useful. Figure 11 illustrates two router-connected fabrics running different Fabric OS versions during an upgrade test period.

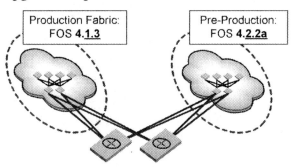

Figure 11 - Upgrading One Fabric at a Time

This example has a pre-production fabric that needs to be managed by developers, and a production fabric managed by the IT department. The fabrics need to be fault-isolated so that a problem in pre-production does not cause downtime for production. Connectivity is desired so that a production database can be copied to pre-production systems, allowing developers to work with up-to-date data.

The pre-production fabric is also used to test changes: a Fabric OS upgrade can be executed on the pre-production fabric, and only after it is successful will it be applied to production fabrics. This only works because the two fabrics are completely separate: if they shared hardware or software, then they would have dependencies. As it is, the only interdependencies between the fabrics are devices that are members of LSANs spanning between them.

A similar technique can be used in data and server migrations. Many large enterprises have hosts and storage arrays constantly coming off leases, or fabrics being re-architected and/or upgraded, or hosts being moved to new locations. The router facilitates all of these operations.

Backbone Fabrics

If a large number of fabrics need to be combined into a Meta SAN, routers can be networked over a centralized *Backbone Fabric* (BB fabric) as in Figure 12.

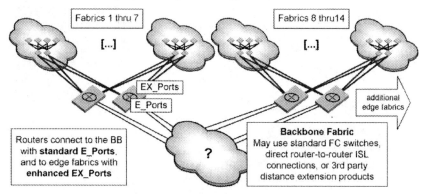

Figure 12 – Elements of a Backbone Fabric

Look at the overall structure of the network: edge fabrics on the upper tier, routers in the middle, and a standard fabric

33

to interconnect the routers. The backbone allows a host in Fabric 1 to be exported to Fabric 14 even though those fabrics are not attached to any common FC routers.

To allow the routers to coordinate this activity, Brocade has authored the Fibre Channel Router Protocol. FCRP operates on backbone-attached E_Ports.[34] Routers do not use EX_Ports for router-to-backbone connections: they use standard E_Ports. Each router on the backbone uses standard Fibre Channel protocols to determine that other routers have entered the fabric, and then sends them FCRP messages. FCRP also operates between EX_Ports on edge fabrics. In addition to routing per se, FCRP coordinates Translation Phantom Domains (discussed later), LSAN zones, and device and fabric states.

It is possible to build redundant *parallel* backbone[35] fabrics. Each router can only have one backbone attachment, so redundant backbones requires redundant routers as well.[36]

Each router also projects special virtual N_Ports onto the backbone fabric. These are known as an *NR_Ports*, which denotes "Fibre Channel standard <u>N</u>ode ports for <u>R</u>outer use." NR_Ports serve as sources and destinations for data frames sent across the backbone. They are analogous to router ports in IP networks.[37] NR_Ports can be thought of as being "the reverse side of an EX_Port." They are discovered via FCRP and do not exist in the name sever of the backbone fabric. (Since nothing but another router port ever needs to send data to an NR_Port it would be superfluous to do this, and could have adverse scalability effects.) Each

---

[34] And/or VE_Ports, which are discussed in the FCIP chapter.

[35] Edge – Routers 1 & 2 – BB 1 & 2 – Routers 3 & 4 – Edge. Section Three has details on redundant topologies.

[36] If you tried to connect one router to two different backbone switches, the two would merge into a single backbone fabric through the router itself. Remember, backbone connections are E_Ports, not EX_Ports.

[37] The reference section at the end contains some background information on basic IP concepts. Briefly, a router port is used as a target by devices that want to get off segment. NR_Ports use each other as targets to get off the backbone.

NR_Port has a valid PID on the backbone fabric so that standard switches can route frames between them. The PID of an NR_Port has a domain matching the backbone domain of the router, an area matching the external port of the associated EX_Port, and an AL_PA of zero.

Data frames sent between NR_Ports use an encapsulated "global header" which contains the source and destination fabric IDs so that a receiving router knows where the frame really came from and to which edge fabric it is supposed to go. Unlike proprietary tagging mechanisms used by other vendors, this is transparent to standard switches in the backbone fabric because the FCR-specific data is encapsulated. This means that it is placed in the data portion of a frame with a standard Fibre Channel header in front of it, and "looks" just like any other data frame to existing non-FCR switches.[38]

The number of edge fabrics that can be practically joined into a Meta SAN by using backbone fabrics is quite large. Since each edge fabric can also be large, the overall scalability of routed SANs is one or more *orders of magnitude* ahead of non-routed fabric scalability. As always, it is necessary to refer to documentation from the appropriate support vendor for site-specific limitations.

In order to allow this degree of scalability, edge fabric devices are not projected into the name server of the backbone fabric. Otherwise BB fabric scalability limitations would become Meta SAN scalability limits: the entire network would be limited by the capabilities of one section of the network. A side effect of this is that currently the FCR does not support routing between an edge fabric and a node attached to the BB fabric. This means that a node attached directly to a router or to a switch in the backbone fabric will not be able to communicate with a node attached to a switch in any edge fabric, because the edge fabric SNS entries are not present in

---

[38] Figure 137 (p310) and the surrounding text in Appendix B has more detail on frame formats.

the backbone fabric[39]. Brocade has devised a strategy for addressing this limitation in a forthcoming release, but for now backbone fabrics should be used only for interconnecting routers.

Redundant Deployments

It is possible to deploy multiple backbone fabrics, and even multiple independent Meta SANs. For customers who implement dual redundant fabrics today, there is usually little or no benefit to connecting the A/B SAN pairs together and there *is* an availability and reliability benefit to *not* doing so. In most cases, a customer who has many A/B fabric pairs today would implement A/B Meta SANs.

For example, a customer might have 16 SAN islands, each of which consists of two separate fabrics in redundant (A/B) configurations. The customer could create a single 32-fabric Meta SAN, or two 16-fabric Meta SANs – a dual redundant Meta SAN. Unless connectivity is actually needed between the A/B pairs, the latter option is preferable. This is discussed further in Section Three.

Phantom Topologies and Proxy Devices

As mentioned earlier, FC-NAT uses a mechanism known as *Phantom Domain Addressing*. This is related to topology.

Fibre Channel fabrics traditionally have a *physical* topology where physical ports of physical devices connect via physical cables to physical ports of other physical devices. Fibre Channel protocols such as FSPF discover the *logical* topology of switch and device connectivity. The logical topology is used for routing calculations. Historically, physical and logical topologies were identical.

---

[39] Note that devices in the BB fabric *can* communicate with each other. This is useful for some iSCSI deployments.

The router introduces a new model where a *phantom topology* is presented which consists of phantom domains and phantom devices. It does not necessarily correlate to physical entities. The phantom topology is presented via protocols such as Fabric Shortest Path First, Storage Name Server, Management Server, etc..

An EX_Port connected to Fabric 1 projects a *Front Phantom Domain* for itself, and projects a route to a set of *Translation Phantom Domains*: up to one for each other fabric in the Meta SAN. Front Phantom Domains may be called *front domains* for short, and Translation Phantom Domains are abbreviated as *xlate domains*. (Abbreviating "translation" as "xlate" is common usage in many IP firewall NAT solutions.) Even if a remote edge fabric has ten, twenty, thirty, or more Fibre Channel switches in it, just one xlate domain is projected into any other edge fabric to represent the entire fabric. Figure 13 shows how the device export example from Figure 8 would create a phantom topology in Fabric 1.

In this example, Fabric 1 consists of six domains in a core/edge topology: domains 11 through 16 in the upper left corner of Figure 13. The core domains (11 and 12) are connected to two FC routers, each with two EX_Ports. (Four EX_Ports total.) Each EX_Port receives one front domain: domains 1 through 4 in this example were assigned by the Fabric 1 principal switch. The routers coordinate with each other using FCRP to decide how to consistently present devices from remote edge fabrics that they have access to. In this case, since they both have access to Fabric 2, one of the routers presents that domain to the principal switch for assignment, and receives domain 5. *All of Fabric 2 is represented by this one domain.* There is one host physically located in Fabric 2 that has been configured in an LSAN with a storage port in Fabric 1. This host shows up in Fabric 1 looking as if it were physically attached to domain 5. None of the other hosts in Fabric 2 are projected into Fabric 1 unless additional LSANs are created.

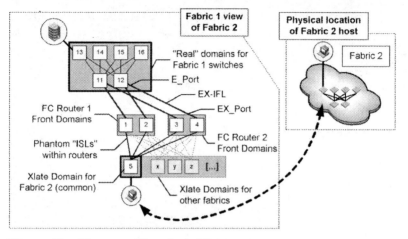

Figure 13 - Phantom Topology View

All devices that are translated between fabrics are "hung off of" xlate domains. To maximize usable NAT address space, translated devices are given Fibre Channel PIDs using both the area and port bytes, so to the human eye xlate addresses may look like NL_Port devices in destination fabrics even if they are really N_Ports in their source fabrics.

Note that this is how the router can represent more than 256 nodes from a given source fabric. One byte of the PID represents the xlate domain (i.e. remote fabric) while the other two bytes represent the particular node. Two bytes can represent many tens of thousands of nodes. If only the middle byte were used for remote nodes, then only 256 nodes could be represented as coming from a given fabric.

While these PIDs are "made up" by the router, whatever PID is used for any given device exported into any given edge fabric is persistent. Even simultaneously rebooting every host, storage, and network device in the Meta SAN - including all routers - will not cause any xlate PIDs to change. Furthermore, the translation table can be saved and loaded using the *configUpload* / *configDownload* commands, so even in the case of catastrophic failure of all routers in a Meta SAN the mappings can be restored.

A device's PID will usually be different in the source fabric vs. the destination fabric, but its WWN is always the same. Therefore a WWN is a unique identifier in a Meta SAN, whereas a PID is not. This is why LSAN zones must use port WWNs or aliases.

Look again at Figure 13. The disk on Fabric 1 might have a PID of 13,01,00 if it were attached to domain 13 port 1. The host on Fabric 2 could potentially *also* have a PID of 13,01,00 since the same [domain,port] can exist in both fabrics. When the host is projected into Fabric 1, it is translated to a domain 5 PID, e.g. 05,00,01. A Fibre Channel analyzer on Fabric 1 would view the conversation as being between 13,01,00 and 05,00,01, regardless of the real PID the host had in Fabric 2. To know what devices were really involved would require looking at the WWNs, or using element management on the routers.

A device that has been exported into another fabric is called a "proxy device" by the destination fabric. Proxy devices are brought online by routers when LSAN zones dictate their creation *and* the devices specified by the zones are online. (There is no need to bring a proxy device online if the real devices are offline.) Devices are notified that proxy devices are brought on- or offline through normal fabric mechanisms such as RSCNs and name server registrations.

Scalability

Translation domains are created *up to* one per remote fabric. No xlate domain is created unless a relevant device is actually exported. For example, if fabrics 1 and 2 had an FC router between them, but no devices were exported between those fabrics via LSANs, then no xlate domains would be created for Fabric 1 on Fabric 2 or vice versa. This is a substantial advantage for Meta SANs consisting of a large number of fabrics in which only a subset of fabrics need to export devices to each other.

The router itself does not limit the number of name server entries or domains in edge fabrics: those are limited by the support characteristics of the switches in the fabrics. The router does limit the number of devices that can be exported, but these limits are high relative to fabric scalability limits. At the time of this writing, more devices can be exported using a given xlate phantom domain than can be supported by the scalability limit of any fabric from any vendor, so the router is not expected to be a limiting factor.[40]

Side Note

Early in the evolution of Fibre Channel, some vendors did not believe that three-byte fabric addressing was needed. They built nodes that could understand just one byte. This was a standard known as FC-AL private loop. As it turned out, customers needed more connectivity than one byte could provide. Unfortunately, many customers still had legacy devices with only private loop support. To connect these devices to fabrics, Brocade built a NAT mechanism known as phantom logic *into each switch port. The phantom logic in Brocade ASICs created one byte addresses for fabric devices that needed to be seen on private loops, and three byte addresses for private devices so that they could be registered in a fabric. Since many devices could not attach to a fabric at all without this feature, phantom logic turned out to be a key Brocade advantage. An analogous situation exists today with inter-fabric addressing and FC-NAT. In effect, the advent of the Fabric ID (FID) provides a fourth byte to the Fibre Channel address space.*

---

[40] Not all Brocade partners support the scalability levels that Brocade has designed for and tested to, and there may be other limitations besides the router. This is true of SANs in general, not just Meta SANs. It is always important to check with the vendor support organization before deploying a large solution.

Fabric Multi-Pathing

From the perspective of FSPF, EX_Ports create a phantom topology such as the one depicted in Figure 13 (p38). Figure 14 shows how FSPF uses the phantom topology to multi-path to the exported host.

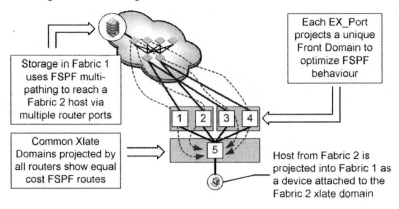

Figure 14 – Phantom Topology Multi-Pathing

This figure shows that Fabric 1 receives one front domain for each EX_Port (1-4), plus up to one xlate domain for each remote fabric (domain 5 represents Fabric 2). All routers project equal cost paths to the xlate domain(s) which are *common* to all routers. Therefore FSPF will make use of all EX_Ports when allocating routes to the Fabric 2 host.

This ensures "sane" behavior on hosts and storage devices by presenting an exported device *once* in the edge fabric name server, even when it is presented by *n* different routers. If the FCR used F_ or FL_Ports, or E_Ports with just one level of domain hierarchy, then one exported host could appear as *n* different SNS entries, and it would be left to other nodes to understand that these were really the same host. The Phantom Topology approach achieves active-active load sharing in the same way that standard Fibre Channel fabrics achieve it, rather than relying on host intelligence to work with a non-standard presentation of devices. Whatever multi-pathing mechanism was working in the edge fabric before the introduction of the FCR will work with the FCR the same way.

Detailed Walkthroughs

This subsection goes through some of the more complex FCR concepts step-by-step. It is targeted at readers interested in a deep understanding of the product. Most readers can skip to the chapter summary. In addition expanding on points already made, this subsection introduces the flow and timing between certain operations which has not previously been discussed.

Figure 15 through Figure 17 are used for reference throughout this subsection.[41] Text that appears in **bold** correlates to diagram labels.

Walkthrough of Steady State

In Figure 15, two fabrics are connected via routers in a redundant manner. Each fabric has two core switches, each core is connected to two different routers, each router connected with two ISLs to its own backbone fabric.

During normal operation, any device on **Fabric 2** can be exported to **Fabric 1**. It will appear to **Fabric 1** as being attached to **Xlate Phantom Domain Q**, which was assigned ID 5 by the **Fabric 1** Principal Switch. Both routers **E** and **F** will show routes to this domain. The FSPF processes running on the **Fabric 1** edge switches (domains 13 to 16) will show equal-cost routes to domain 5 via the two **Fabric 1** core switches (11 and 12) and the routers' **Front Phantom Domains** (1 to 4). Similarly, any **Fabric 1** device can be exported to **Fabric 2** by routers **K** and **L**.

Routers **E** and **F** use different backbones to get to **Fabric 2**. Router **E** uses **Backbone 1 (I)** whereas router **F** uses **Backbone 2 (J)**. Should the BB1 fabric fail completely, F1 can still reach F2.

---

[41] Note that the examples use the same domain IDs for each fabric. This is allowed but not required by the router. Overlapping domain IDs are used in the example because this is likely to be the rule rather than the exception. (This is one reason to be very sure that any FC-FC routing solution supports FC-NAT.)

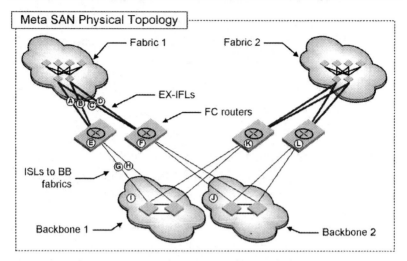

Figure 15 – FCR Walkthrough Physical Topology

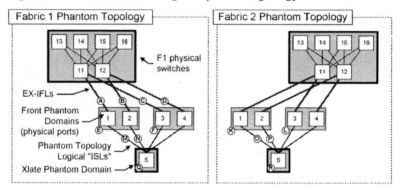

Figure 16 - FCR Walkthrough Edge Fabric Topologies

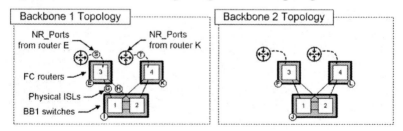

Figure 17 - FCR Walkthrough BB Fabric Topologies[42]

---

[42] In this configuration the BB fabrics must *not* have duplicate FIDs. In *redundant* Meta SANs, BB and even edge fabric FIDs can be duplicated, but this is a *resilient* Meta SAN…

43

The two BB1 routers "see" each other through their mutual connections to that fabric. FCRP on each router detects the other router, and automatically synchronizes xlate behaviors and LSAN data. The same is true of the two BB2 routers. Routers **E** and **K** talk via **Backbone 1**, while routers **F** and **L** see each other across **Backbone 2**.

There is no BB connection between **E** and **L** or **F** and **K** since the two backbone fabrics have no connectivity between them. The xlate and LSAN synchronization between these routers occurs over each of the two *edge* fabrics: routers **E** and **F** can see each other across **Fabric 1**, and routers **K** and **L** communicate via **Fabric 2**. FCRP operates between the front domains of each router. The routers therefore form a ring of synchronization: **E** is in sync with **K** via BB1, **K** is in sync with **L** vi F2, **L** is in sync with **F** via BB2, and **F** is in sync with **E** via F1.

When there are redundant connections into an edge fabric there must be a single primary owner for that fabric's xlate tables. The owner is one of the routers' front domains, and owner selection occurs as the routers first come up.

Suppose that everything is up and running except IFLs **C** and **D**. That is, router **F** is not connected to **Fabric 1** yet. When IFL **C** is attached, it gets assigned a front phantom domain – domain 3 in this example – by the **Fabric 1** principal switch. It then looks for other routers in the fabric. Since IFL **A** is already there (domain 1), the **C** front domain "talks" to it using FCRP. They discover that they both have access to **Fabric 2**, albeit via different BBs. Since **A** was there first, it "owns" the xlate map. It had already been assigned domain 5 for use as the xlate domain to represent **Fabric 2**. The newly added front domain **C** from router **F** accepts this, and tells **Fabric 1** that it has a route to that domain using FSPF. Similarly, if any LSANs are configured between the two fabrics, router **F** will use the same xlate PIDs that router **E** already used for **Fabric 2** devices when "hanging them off of" the common xlate domain.

Frame headers are rewritten as frames pass between F1 and F2. The device *sending* the frame will use its *real* Source ID (SID) and the Destination ID (DID) of the *xlate PID* of the destination. While crossing a backbone, the frame gets wrapped in a global header which is wrapped in a Fibre Channel standard encapsulation header. The encapsulation header has a SID of the NR_Port that represents the far side of the EX_Port that the frame came in from. If it came in on IFL **A**, it would have a SID of NR_Port **S** while crossing **BB1**. The DID would be NR_Port **T**: the back-side of the IFL going to the destination fabric. When the frame gets onto the destination fabric, the global and encapsulation headers are removed. The SID is that of the *xlate PID* for the *sender*, and the DID is the *real PID* of the *destination*.

Walkthrough of Failure Modes

An IFL is an ISL from the point of view of the edge fab ric to which it is attached. This is why the router can attach to a standard Fibre Channel fabric without special hardware or software running in that fabric. This also means that a failure on an IFL will act just like an ISL failure in that fabric: it will cause a fabric reconfiguration.

If IFL **A** were to fail, the **Fabric 1** switches would reallocate relevant routes onto IFLs **B**, **C** and **D**. This does not cause an IO interruption within the edge fabric, or for devices using IFLs **B**, **C** or **D**. Any traffic that had been using IFL **A** would be disturbed in that frames in flight on the IFL would be dropped: just like an ISL failure in a standard fabric. If IFL **A** were added back to the fabric, this would again be like an ISL being added within a standard fabric: it will not cause a fabric reconfiguration. The specific behavior would depend on the DLS setting for that fabric. If DLS is on (generally the default) then adding the IFL back into the fabric would cause switches to reallocate routes back onto it. (Although this is really up to the switches themselves. With Brocade switches, this depends on the settings for the DLS and IOD parameters.) There would be no impact to anything other than traffic associated with IFL **A**.

If an E_Port on a BB fabric fails, it has the same impact as any E_Port failure in a fabric: the BB fabric might reconfigure, depending on whether or not the ISL was an upstream link.   In any case, this will *not* translate into reconfigurations on any edge fabric.

Suppose that backbone ISL **G** goes down. Router **E** still has a path to router **K**, so neither router needs to make any change to its phantom topology presentation. The BB1 fabric might reconfigure, but this would not impact IO. If ISL **H** were to fail also, then **E** and **K** would have no routes to each other. In this case, they would delete phantom ISLs **M**, **N** and **O**, **P** respectively. Since a phantom domain cannot be a principal switch, it is not possible for these phantom links to be downstream links. No fabric reconfiguration will occur, but switches in each edge fabric will be notified, and will shift routes away from IFLs **A** and **B** in F1, and the equivalent links in F2.

If the ISLs to BB2 from router **F** were to fail *at the same time*, there would be no path from F1 to F2. All of the routers would respond by removing relevant xlate PIDs from the name servers of their fabrics and sending an RSCN to devices in that fabric in relevant LSANs. It would look to F1 switches as though all of the F2 exported devices had been unplugged. The xlate phantom domain (**Q**) would not be removed, however, so no fabric reconfiguration would occur. This prevents "flapping" links in one fabric from causing a flapping reconfiguration in another.

(Note that this is only true because the Brocade router completely separates fabrics. Other vendors do not do so − particularly in the case of VSANs − and these "routers" are vulnerable to propagation of this and many similar errors.)

The same occurs if both BB1 (**I**) and BB2 (**J**) fabrics fail, e.g. if a user powers off all four switches.

If a BB switch were to fail or to be rebooted, its fabric would reconfigure but no edge fabric impact would occur.

Frames in flight across it would be dropped, and edge devices would need to retry, as in any other switch failure.

If a router fails or is rebooted, it causes a reconfiguration in its edge fabric(s) and its BB fabric. It also may cause phantom topology changes on routers that were using it to access its edge fabrics.

For example, if router **E** were to fail, router **K** would have no path to F1. It would be as if both ISLs **G** and **H** both failed (above). **K** would delete its phantom ISLs to its F1 xlate domain (**R**), but F2 would not reconfigure. If router **F** also failed, router **L** would remove the xlate PIDs but not the last phantom ISL, so F2 would still not reconfigure.

Even if an entire edge fabric is removed, no other fabrics will reconfigure. E.g. if F2 is shut down, routers **E** and **F** will remove their xlate PIDs, but not the xlate domain. Remote edge fabrics accessing F2 will have FSPF updates, but only hosts actually accessing devices on F2 would receive RSCNs. And since they really do need to know that their remote devices went away, this is a desirable behavior.

(Again, this is a key feature of the Brocade router. Because it uses a light-weight E_Port (i.e. EX_Port) to connect to fabrics and uses FC-NAT between them, the Brocade router can do a much better job of fault isolation than others are architecturally capable of doing. With Brocade, only devices that really need to know about remote fabric events are notified.)

✓ Side Note

Logical links internal to routers in the phantom topology do not count as hops. Only physical links count, including E_Port to E_Port and E_Port to EX_Port links. To determine end-to-end hops in a Meta SAN, count all physical ISLs and IFLs traversed in the edge and backbone fabrics.

FC-FC Routing Service Summary

By adding hierarchical networking to Fibre Channel, Brocade has combined the flexibility and scalability of data networks with the performance and reliability of FC fabrics. The FCR brings unprecedented reliability, manageability, security, flexibility, and scalability to SANs, and makes deployments practical that were not even theoretically possible before its introduction.

4: iSCSI Gateway Service

SCSI over TCP/IP

iSCSI is an emerging protocol for transporting SCSI across IP networks. This is similar in concept to the mapping already provided by FCP for Fibre Channel. In addition to defining the transport, iSCSI defines naming, discovery, access control, and security. Again, this is similar to the already existing Fibre Channel standards. In theory at least, iSCSI should save on equipment costs in certain areas, with the major trade-offs being in the areas of maturity, performance, and reliability. For this reason, many in the industry view iSCSI as being a "poor man's Fibre Channel."

iSCSI is a newcomer to the SAN arena: it was not ratified until 2003, almost a decade behind Fibre Channel in development and adoption. iSCSI adoption has been so slow that some have concluded that – vendor hype aside – it is a dead-end protocol. There is merit to this position, but most observers believe that there are cases where iSCSI can play a role. This is mainly by providing connectivity into FC fabrics for low-end hosts. This quote from IDC illustrates why:

At first glance, it would appear that iSCSI should have a negative effect on FC switch sales into [the low-end volume server and blade server] markets. The promise of lower cost hardware and reuse of existing infrastructure would appear to make iSCSI far more attractive than FC in this sector. ... In reality, expanded use of volume servers is an important trend in large organizations (especially blade server variants) that already have significant FC infrastructure in place.

49

In other words, the customers most likely to buy iSCSI solutions are the same customers who already have substantial investments in Fibre Channel. These customers are unlikely to throw out those investments. Doing so would cost rather than save money, and would involve massive risk to production environments. At best, the "rip and replace" approach would cost more money while providing lower performance and reliability. Any practical iSCSI product must therefore work within the existing Fibre Channel SAN framework, and acknowledge the lead that FC has in market penetration.

This chapter discusses what iSCSI is appropriate for in that context, how Brocade has addressed the need to connect iSCSI hosts into FC fabrics, and some of the tradeoffs associated with its use. Details are provided for iSCSI networking concepts such as naming and name services, redundancy, and security. Comparisons are made with technologies like Fibre Channel and network filesystems (as in NAS). Finally, a subsection is provided that illustrates some of the possible high-level iSCSI networking models and discusses which are more appropriate and why, separating the reality of iSCSI from vendor marketing hype.

iSCSI Killer App

There is one class of applications that is – at least in the near term – addressed well by iSCSI: non-critical low-tier connectivity, such as departmental web servers or low-end Windows clusters. These applications do not require high performance or reliability, but are extremely cost sensitive. Yet they can benefit from the SAN model in much the same way as enterprise-class applications, provided that this can be done cost effectively.

Certain pieces of the Fibre Channel network are traditionally more expensive than their iSCSI counterparts. The primary example is 2Gbit Fibre Channel HBAs vs. *non-accelerated* 1Gbit Ethernet NICs that use *software-only* iSCSI stacks. Fibre Channel HBAs are cost-competitive with accelerated iSCSI cards that have TCP Offload Engines (TOEs) on them, and outperform these by at least 2:1. (Usually much more.) However, lowest-tier severs may not require performance either in the network or for their processor and memory resources, and so the use of software iSCSI stacks may be acceptable.[43]

For a host to be a good candidate for iSCSI SAN attachment, at least four things need to be true. If a host meets these requirements, then it might be a candidate for iSCSI.

- The host requires <u>block-level access</u> to networked storage. If block-level access is *not* required, then network filesystem solutions with FC SAN back-ends will be a better option. If networked storage is not a requirement, then direct attached storage might even work just as well.

- The host already has an <u>extra Gigabit Ethernet NIC</u>. As demonstrated later, it is rarely desirable to use a single network for both iSCSI and data networks, and if an additional NIC needs to be installed anyway the host may be a better candidate for a low cost Fibre Channel HBA.

- The host does <u>not require fast access</u> to storage.[44] If, for example, the host is a standby cluster server, then downtime may not be an issue, and disk access may be rare.

- The host does <u>not require its CPU for other operations</u>. A software iSCSI stack relies on the main CPU for all operations, whereas hardware in an FC HBA offloads such tasks. If the host needs CPU cycles to run its applications, Fibre Channel would be a better approach.[45]

---

[43] At this time, 2Gbit FC HBA prices are dropping fast, and 4Gbit is on the immediate horizon. As a result, the long-term viability of the this business case is uncertain.

[44] Even an entry level Fibre Channel switch from Brocade can route a frame between ports in a matter of nanoseconds. Even a high-end Ethernet switch typically is quite a few orders of magnitude slower. Just look at the output of the data network "ping" command: it cannot even resolve round trip times on the scale at which SANs operate.

[45] The same thing could be done with an iSCSI TOE card, but the cost would be equivalent and the performance would be at best half of the FC solution: not a compelling use case…

Connecting iSCSI to Fibre Channel

There are quite a few ways to construct the top-level network architecture for an iSCSI SAN. This subsection discusses some of the options, and gives general recommendations.

While it is theoretically possible to deploy end-to-end iSCSI solutions, most organizations have a Fibre Channel installed base that they want to maintain. There is no reason to assume that there will be cost advantages associated with iSCSI-native storage arrays, so there is no incentive to throw out the capital investment in Fibre Channel storage and replace it with slower and less reliable iSCSI.

A more attractive solution that does not require forklift upgrades is to keep the primary storage network running Fibre Channel and use a tiered approach to attaching hosts.

First tier business-critical hosts would be dual-attached to a pair of Fibre Channel fabrics. This approach has been the industry best-practice for years. Multipathing software on hosts and/or storage devices allows application uptime even in the event of catastrophic failure of an entire fabric.

Middle tier hosts – important but not critical – might have single connections into a Fibre Channel fabric. One approach is to divide the middle tier hosts into two groups and connect half to each of the A/B fabrics. If a host is part of a cluster, split the hosts in that group between fabrics.

Lower tier hosts would either use low cost Fibre Channel HBAs or access the SAN through iSCSI. In this case, a dedicated IP SAN would be connected to a gateway to convert from iSCSI to Fibre Channel. Figure 18 illustrates tiered SAN attachment.

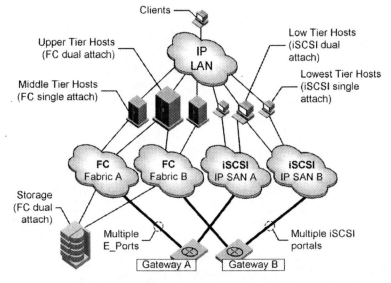

Figure 18 - iSCSI/FC Integration with Tiered Approach

When studying new networking technologies, it often helps to visualize the relationships of the various protocols. Figure 19 illustrates the block-level gateway architecture.

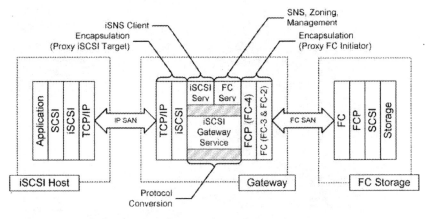

Figure 19 - iSCSI to FC Protocol Stack Map

The effect is that an iSCSI host appears to Fibre Channel storage devices as if it were a locally attached FC host, and an FC storage port appears to iSCSI hosts as if it were a locally attached iSCSI target.

Stranded Servers

In addition to scenarios in which cost vs. performance tradeoffs may make iSCSI attractive, there are cases in which it may be useful for distance extension. For stranded locations with more than a few hosts, FCIP is a better solution. However, if a company has just a few hosts at each of many locations, then FCIP may be unattractive since it requires a gateway at each end. Figure 20 illustrates such a case.

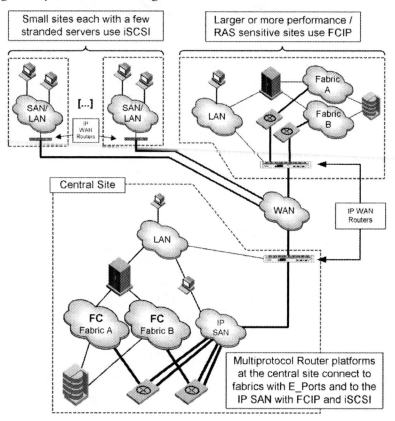

Figure 20 - iSCSI Stranded Servers

There are many factors that must align to make iSCSI the correct solution. For example:

- There are a large number of small sites
    - o   If the sites were large, FCIP would be better

o If there were too few sites, the cost of providing the
   iSCSI gateways might be prohibitive

- Hosts at the remote sites are not business critical or running performance intensive applications
  o If the hosts were important, they would use FC
  o Performance in this example will be at best half of
     that provided by even low cost FC HBAs
- Storage cannot be co-located with the remote servers.
  o In general, localization of primary storage is desired
     for performance and reliability reasons.

Remote storage is needed for applications like backups –
which would not require iSCSI since there are already several
backup-over-LAN protocols – and disaster tolerance solutions
– which are not generally appropriate for iSCSI due to its inherent performance and reliability issues, and are not usually
needed for non-critical hosts in any case.

The only reason to use iSCSI this way is to connect many
small sites running non-business critical applications where it
is not practical to co-locate the storage with the server.

IP SAN Subnet Configuration

As mentioned earlier, it may sometimes be desired to
configure two IP SANs for redundancy. However, it may
even be desirable to configure many separate IP SANs simply
because connectivity between them is not required, and
eliminating it may both save cost and improve reliability.
Traffic will always flow between iSCSI hosts and the gateway
ports, so as long as each host has *that* connectivity, making
the subnet any larger would not be helpful.

Figure 21 illustrates a "right sized" IP SAN subnet approach. Each Ethernet switch in the diagram is an isolated IP
subnet. None of the Ethernet switches can reach each other,
but all iSCSI hosts can reach all *disks* in a fully redundant
manner. Also note that the IP *LAN* connections from the
iSCSI hosts may well all go to a single fully-connected network even if the IP *SAN* segments are unconnected.

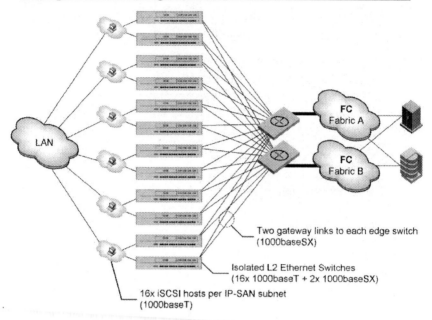

Two gateway links to each edge switch (1000baseSX)

Isolated L2 Ethernet Switches (16x 1000baseT + 2x 1000baseSX)

16x iSCSI hosts per IP-SAN subnet (1000baseT)

Figure 21 - iSCSI Subnet Sizing

iSCSI vs. FC SAN Models

This subsection discusses some perceived vs. actual differences between iSCSI and FC, and specifically focuses on top-level network architecture.

At the most abstract level, the iSCSI network model does not look much different from the Fibre Channel model. Hosts attach to a network using HBAs (FC) or NICs (iSCSI), traverse the network which is built from switches and/or routers, and arrive at storage, which can be shared between many hosts. The business needs that iSCSI could architecturally address are the same as those already provided for by Fibre Channel, though FC solutions are faster and have been in production for years while iSCSI is new.

At this point it is worth saying a few words about that performance difference. Aside from the fact that 2Gbit FC is inherently twice as fast as 1Gbit iSCSI – and 4Gbit FC doubles the gap again – it is also the case that iSCSI software solutions do not even come close to 1Gbit in the real world.

Look at Figure 22. This shows two performance metrics taken from a single host running different block sizes. One set of tests was run using an iSCSI software driver.[46] The other test used an FC HBA.[47] In both cases, they accessed the same FC storage.[48]

On the left, the overall throughput is compared. The FC throughput was five times that of iSCSI, running on the same host, with the same application,[49] to the same disk. On the right, the difference in CPU utilization is shown: iSCSI predictably taking far more CPU resources than FC.

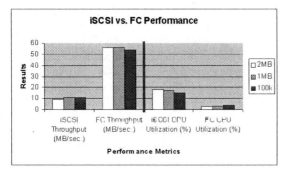

Figure 22 – iSCSI vs. FC Performance

It is possible to get an iSCSI software solution to run at 1Gbit full-duplex, but this requires a host to dedicate a *massive* amount of CPU cycles to protocol processing. Testing in Brocade labs has shown that it requires about 1Ghz of CPU speed just to handle half-duplex 1Gbit iSCSI protocol overhead. Assuming that applications also require equivalent CPU cycles (typical) this means that it would take 4Ghz of CPU on a host to run an application over a single full-duplex

---

[46] The Cisco iSCSI driver on a Windows host. The iSCSI <> FC gateway used was the Cisco SN5420/8.

[47] An Emulex 1Gbit PCI adapter. Other HBAs show even better results. In fact, using an obsolete FC card to make the test "fair" to iSCSI substantially reduced FC performance, yet even this old HBA outperformed iSCSI handily.

[48] A JBOD in this test. Other devices show similar results.

[49] The test used IOmeter. The gap is greater when running a real application that competes with iSCSI for CPU cycles.

software iSCSI link, achieving equivalent performance to a 2Ghz system with a 1Gbit Fibre Channel HBA.

Some commentators state that increasing CPU speeds will obviate the performance advantages of Fibre Channel. This is only true if users accept that most of their new, greater CPU performance will be spent on iSCSI framing, rather than – for example – on running their business applications faster. In effect, the cost of iSCSI performance is either a new, fast, dedicated CPU (not free) or an iSCSI HBA that costs as much as a Fibre Channel HBA.

Given all that, the difference between FC and iSCSI might seem to be Fibre Channel's greater performance, reliability, and maturity vs. iSCSI's ability to use existing network infrastructure. Figure 23 and Figure 24 illustrate how the two architectures would look if iSCSI used a common network for data and storage.

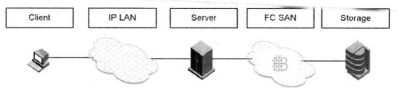

Figure 23 – Generic Fibre Channel SAN Architecture

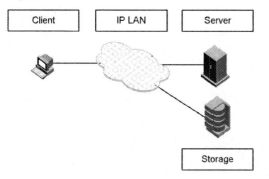

Figure 24 – Generic iSCSI Single Network Architecture

While this might make a nice marketing diagram for iSCSI, it does not reflect what users are likely to deploy. It turns out that a physically separate network for storage is required or at least strongly desired regardless of protocol.

Consider security. Attaching storage directly to a production IP network exposes it to denial of service attacks, network-aware viruses, network unreliability, and hackers, both internal and external. That is, if there is a physical connection between the IP SAN and a network known to be exposed to this category of problem as in Figure 24, then the IP SAN is also exposed. If there is *no* physical connection as in the Figure 23 model, it is impossible for e.g. hackers on the data network to attack the SAN directly.

✓ Side Note

One frequently expressed concern with iSCSI is, "Spanning Tree problems," or words to that effect. Some users find that troubleshooting IP networks is difficult enough, and are wary of throwing storage into the mix. It may take a customer longer to isolate an IP problem than the maximum time their SAN is allowed to be down.

This is not an irresolvable problem with iSCSI: it is just another reason to keep iSCSI subnets isolated and small. The deployment in Figure 21 (p56) will never have an STP issue, and indeed is not subject to most of the complex failure scenarios of IP networks. Not only is the likelihood of a failure sharply reduced, so too is the scope of a failure should one occur since errors cannot propagate from one of the Ethernet switches to another.

Also note that at the time of this writing there has never been a published instance of a hacker breaking into a Fibre Channel network, whereas IP networks are attacked daily. There are several reasons for this. Most Fibre Channel vendors have value-added security packages specifically designed to prevent attacks, and the hacker communities simply do not have access to the tools and knowledge necessary to attack FC SANs in even basic ways. In contrast, information on and tools for attacking IP networks are universally available. However, it is likely that the biggest factor is that Fibre

Channel networks are generally inaccessible to hackers due to their physical isolation from the data network.

Side Note

Here are three things to keep in mind when comparing iSCSI and Fibre Channel solutions:

1. The cost of building a SAN with iSCSI TOE NICs and enterprise Ethernet switches is comparable to building the same SAN with FC HBAs and switches. Similarly, iSCSI arrays are expected to be identical in cost with FC arrays, and FC HBA prices seem to be falling faster than iSCSI NICs.

2. In 2005, the dominant Fibre Channel speed will become 4Gbps[50] and this will cost about the same as a 1Gbps iSCSI TOE solution. 10Gbit technology is expected to be available equally for both Fibre Channel and Ethernet, but most servers will not be able to actually use that high of a speed for years to come. Trunked 4Gbit solutions can outperform 10Gbit by more than 2:1 for ISLs, and at a much lower price. 4Gbit Fibre Channel therefore will be the dominant player in most SAN environments since it "wins" from a price / performance standpoint.

3. FC products were in mission-critical environments years before iSCSI was conceived. iSCSI still has yet to mature, and is unlikely to ever surpass FC in maturity.

Even in environments where security is not a concern, iSCSI can place an arbitrarily high load onto a company's production LAN that can bring down applications such as email, databases, and file services. For example, most IP networks have over subscription deliberately designed into them in many places, such as edge-to-backbone uplinks. This may work well for existing data network traffic patterns which

---

[50] From Gartner/Dataquest: 4Gbps FC will grow at nearly 300 percent through 2007 compounded annually, and will become the dominant speed for new Fibre Channel products.

tend to come in small bursts, but not be sufficient for SAN traffic that may come in long, sustained sequences e.g. during a backup operation, when running a data migration, or when transferring other large data streams like videos or uncompressed graphics. Indeed, many companies implemented SANs for backup traffic specifically to get it off of LANs that were not capable of handling the sustained load.

Finally, the load on the server's single NIC in this architecture is potentially doubled, which can cause performance issues for both SAN and LAN access. This issue is straightforward, since the interface now carries both the back-end storage traffic and the front-end LAN traffic. Keep in mind that the time when performance is most critical to end users is often the time when the LAN interface is already most fully utilized: i.e. the time that the user is connecting to the server to run their application. This is also the time that the SAN load is likely to be at its highest, and when CPU and memory resources on the host are in the most demand. (Highly relevant for iSCSI software stacks.) By combining all traffic onto one interface and simultaneously increasing demand on the CPU, it is probable that iSCSI performance will be unacceptable if deployed in this way, even for lowest-tier applications.

One reason that iSCSI has been so slow to catch on is that historically IP and Ethernet equipment was not designed for the performance and reliability needs of storage. It was common for even enterprise-class IP/Ethernet switches to drop 0.1% or even 1% of packets and to rely on hosts to retransmit the lost data. Storage networks cannot withstand that kind of data loss. While IP networks now *can* be designed to meet the requirements for storage, this requires that all IP nodes and network devices be tightly controlled, up-to-date, firewalled or – better – physically isolated, and enterprise-class at all tiers. This is relatively difficult to arrange across an entire production IP network, which would be necessary if iSCSI and data network traffic were combined as in Figure 24. These problems are shown in Figure 25.

The preceding analysis is not an indictment of the iSCSI protocol. Rather, it illustrates a situation in which marketing hype must be separated from reality. There is a way to make iSCSI work. In fact, the solution to the issues above is straightforward: deploy a totally separate iSCSI network. In this case, the top-level network architecture for iSCSI looks much like the Fibre Channel diagram. There is a front-end data network and a back-end storage network. Compare the illustrations in Figure 23 (p58) vs. Figure 26.

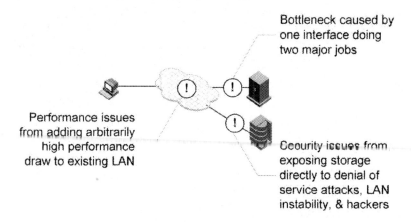

Figure 25 - Issues with the iSCSI Single Network Model

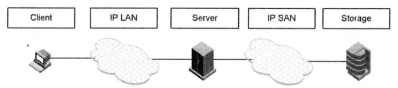

Figure 26 - Generic iSCSI SAN Architecture (Corrected)

Note that this architecture is now being recommended even by iSCSI-centric companies. It is considered a best-practice to use a physically isolated iSCSI SAN with a physically separate iSCSI interface, preferably two of them.[51]

---

[51] This is an area where SAN administrators will be surprised. Even though SAN best practices have required redundant controllers for years, many iSCSI clients do not support multipathing at the time of this writing. Many vendors make broad statements that e.g. "iSCSI should support the same multipathing options as FC" without mentioning that – "should" aside – they don't. Shop carefully...

✅ Side Note

*For Figure 26 to resolve some of the security and perform-
ance problems with iSCSI, one of two things must be true:*

- *There is* no *connection between the SAN and LAN*
- *The* only *connection is through a secure firewall*

*Using VLANs to separate the networks is insufficient.
VLANs appear to isolate failure modes, but in reality they
share hardware resource and software images. If a hacker,
virus, or rogue device makes an intentional or unintentional
denial of service attack against a VLAN switch, it may affect
VLANs that the attacker did not have direct access to. For
example, if a hacker discovers a denial of service attack that
can cause an IP switch to crash, all VLANs on that switch
will be equally affected, not just the VLAN that the attacker
used to reach the switch. In data networks, the risk of catastrophic failure in such cases is simply accepted. However,
the business impact of a data network failure is miniscule
compared to the impact of such a failure in a SAN...*

iSCSI vs. Network Filesystems

Both iSCSI and network filesystems such as NFS and
CIFS allow accessing storage via IP networks. Like iSCSI,
these may either use a single LAN or a separate network.
The major difference is that network filesystems use protocols
and methods that have been in production for decades, and
are present and well-understood in nearly all IT environments, while iSCSI does not yet have widespread market
acceptance and has no installed base with associated expertise.

Another difference is that iSCSI allows "raw," or block-
level access to storage, while network filesystems allow access
to "cooked" filesystems. While the average laptop or desktop
user *prefers* filesystem-level access, block-level access is required for some client-server applications such as large-scale
databases and enterprise email systems. It would seem that

iSCSI would be an acceptable choice for connecting servers, while network filesystems would be the preferred method for connecting clients.

On the other hand, most server applications that require block IO also require or at least benefit from the perform-ance, reliability, and security of Fibre Channel. If a server needs block-level access, it probably also needs Fibre Chan-nel. If it does not need block-level access, then it probably would be better to use a network filesystem.

The bottom line is that if a company is small and does not anticipate growth, network filesystems are probably the right solution, and iSCSI is not needed. If a company is larger and/or anticipates growth, then a low cost Fibre Channel SAN is a better option.

Side Note

NAS and SAN are sometimes thought of as competitors. In fact, they are complementary. NAS heads (filers) are spe-cialized pieces of hardware that project network filesystems in much the same way as general-purpose UNIX or NT serv-ers. They just do it more efficiently.

If a NAS solution is deployed, thought should be given to how it could evolve into a Fibre Channel solution down the road. Just as general-purpose servers use SANs, it is com-mon for a NAS head to use a Fibre Channel SAN as its back end, which provides both NAS front-end simplicity and SAN back-end performance. Ask your NAS provider for products with Brocade Fibre Channel fabric support.

Internet Storage Name Server

iSCSI defines a service called the Internet Storage Name Server (iSNS) which is similar to Fibre Channel's SNS. Be-fore deploying an iSCSI SAN, it is necessary to become familiar with all iSCSI services. Unlike the Fibre Channel name server which is implemented on every Fibre Channel switch, the iSNS is absent on almost all Ethernet and IP switches, which means that the SAN administrator will need to do quite a bit of manual configuration and ongoing administration. In order to build an iSCSI network it is necessary to do one of three things:

1. Deploy at least two external iSNS servers. While this adds cost and deployment complexity, it is the best option for scalability and RAS. Figure 27 (p66) shows how external iSNS servers could be added to the example from Figure 18 (p53).

2. Manually configure nodes instead of using a name server. This is not scalable or manageable. It is analogous to building an IP network with no DNS server. This should only be done if there will never be more than a dozen or so iSCSI nodes.

3. Use special-purpose iSCSI switches for attachment of hosts and storage instead of using standard IP/Ethernet equipment. This obviates the cost advantages of iSCSI, since these switches tend to be extremely expensive. In addition, these products tend to require as much administrative overhead as external name servers.

Given that most iSCSI customers will choose the first option, the Brocade gateway service implements an iSNS client so that it can integrate with external third party iSNS servers. The gateway's client presents SNS entries from the fabric to the primary external iSNS server: it acts as a bridge between an iSNS server and the gateway's native FC SNS database. If the external iSNS server supports redundant deployments, once the data is transferred to the primary it can synchronize with its subsidiaries.[52] Some iSCSI host drivers can be con-

---

[52] This is similar to the DNS server model. It would be "odd" for any DNS server not to support server-to-server redundancy, and it would be similarly "odd" for iSNS servers to lack the feature. All Fibre Channel SNS servers have database replication and redundancy, and the iSCSI standard allows redundancy as well. This is only worth mentioning because – as with any extremely new technology – some implementations may be sub-par at this time, so it is important to look very closely even for features that could are *assumed* to be provided with mature technologies like FC.

figured for redundant iSNS servers so that operations will not be interrupted when an iSNS server crashes.

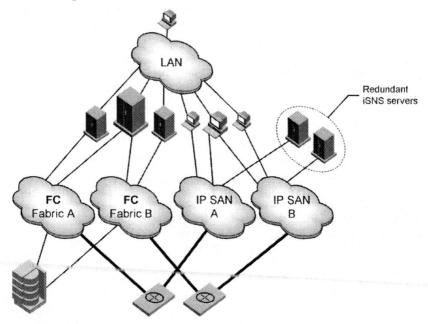

Figure 27 - External iSNS Servers

The responsibilities of the iSNS client are:

- Support the IETF standard iSNS Client Protocol
- Interface into Fibre Channel services on the router to retrieve zoning and name service information
- Convert Fibre Channel name server entries and zones into their iSCSI analogues
- Send the converted objects to the external iSNS server

This illustrates one of the fundamental differences between Fibre Channel and iSCSI. iSCSI in general assumes that there will be no intelligence in the network, since IP/Ethernet switches and routers were not designed for and indeed are almost all entirely unaware of storage, and do not, for example, implement storage name services. This means that some of the cost savings apparently associated with iSCSI is illusory: it moves some of the cost out of one component and into another. Some cost may be saved by using Ethernet instead of Fibre Channel switches, but needing to deploy multiple external name servers will use up some of this savings, not to mention adding deployment and ongoing management complexity.[53]

Sessions Limits

A session in this context is a group of TCP connections between a given iSCSI host and a given iSCSI target. Each session has a Session ID (SSID) to define it, broken up into an initiator part (ISID) and target part (Target Portal Group Tag). Each TCP connection within that session has a Connection ID (CID).

With protocols like Fibre Channel, equivalent mechanisms exist, but are designed in such a way that end users do not need to be aware of them. iSCSI sessions can be extremely resource intensive, however, so it is important to consider them carefully when designing an iSCSI solution. It is not recommended that an administrator attempt to deploy iSCSI in production without careful consideration and understanding of this issue. Each iSCSI target that a host needs to access takes processor and memory resources from the host, and each host accessing a target requires similar resources on its controller card. All iSCSI devices – including the Brocade gateway – can support a limited number of sessions per port because of this. Check session count limits on all devices and consider what else those resources could be used for before purchasing any iSCSI products.

iSCSI Naming

In order to identify an iSCSI device in a network, a unique name is required. Since any IP technology could

---

[53] At the time of this writing the iSNS client on the router accesses the external iSNS server(s) through its RJ45 Ethernet management ports. It is therefore required that the management network have connectivity to the IP SAN(s).

theoretically have worldwide scope, iSCSI name formats should be unique worldwide.

According to the standard, iSCSI names must be globally unique, permanently associated with the same device, rely on existing naming authorities, and not imply a physical location or changeable network address. Furthermore, the scheme must consist only of displayable non-whitespace characters.

It might seem intuitive to use IP addresses or DNS names. However, IP addresses may change as devices move or are given different assignments by DHCP, and similarly DNS host names cannot be assumed to be permanently associated with a node. Moreover, iSCSI names are supposed to identify an entire node, *not* one interface on that node. IP addresses vary by interface. Therefore iSCSI defines another method for identifying devices. In fact, it defines three new formats that iSCSI administrators must become knowledgeable about: IQN, EUI, and NAA.

In all three cases, the iSCSI name is associated with a *node*, and not with an *adapter*. This is intended to ensure that if, for example, a host loses its NIC, when the failed card is replaced the iSCSI name will remain the same, so configurations (such as zoning) associated with the name will not need to be modified. Also, it allows access control configuration to be more intuitive. (It is almost never intended to allow access to one interface on a node and deny it to another on the same node.)

At the time of this writing, almost all iSCSI devices use the IQN scheme. As a result, this is the only format that the iSCSI Gateway Service currently recognizes. The other two formats are described briefly since they may be supported in the future.

iSCSI Qualified Names

iSCSI Qualified Names (IQNs) are intended to be used when an end-user wishes to assign iSCSI names themselves, rather than relying on names supplied by a vendor. However, this is not a requirement for an IQN. To ensure worldwide uniqueness of an IQN it is only necessary that the organization doing the assignment own a valid Internet domain name and that they use globally unique numbers for a portion of the identifier string.

An IQN is formatted as a string starting with "iqn." to distinguish it from EUI and NAA format names. (That's lowercase "iqn" and a period.) This is followed by a date code in "yyyy-mm." format that is used to indicate a time when the naming authority had ownership of the domain. (Four-digit year, a dash, and a *two*-digit month. January must be represented as "01" for example.) Next, the domain name is added in reversed format. ("com.brocade" instead of "brocade.com".) Finally, there will be a colon followed by a site-assigned string to uniquely identify the particular node. This string can include alpha-numeric characters and many special characters such as dashes, periods, and colons, and may be up to 256 bytes long. Following the iSCSI standard, there must be no whitespace or non-printable characters. Fully formatted, an IQN for a personal web server at an individual employee's desk assigned by an administrator at Brocade might look like this:

`iqn.2002-12.com.brocade:host:http:personal.001`

Table 1 shows some more examples of valid IQNs.

Table 1 - Parts of an IQN

Type	Date	Authority	User Defined String
iqn	1996-02	com.mydomain	host:test-sys.1
iqn	2000-10	org.xyzyx	1BA0359D8
iqn	2001-05	edu.college	host:low.tier.1
iqn	2003-12	com.company	host.2k.cluster.1
iqn	2002-01	com.iownthis	Swe45_gEA1045a

The user defined string for a host can be whatever the local administrator wants it to be as long as it is unique. It is advisable to make it hierarchical and meaningful. For example, it might start with "host:" to distinguish it from storage devices on the chance that any might ever be deployed down the road. Then it might indicate the OS, or the priority level of the host, or anything else that was structured in a meaningful way to the site administrators. If organizations already have a unique identification system for hosts (asset tags for example) it would be possible to use this as well.

When the iSCSI Gateway Service exports a storage port from the Fibre Channel fabric for use by an iSCSI host, it must assign a unique IQN. This is generated automatically by the gateway according to a formula. The first part of the IQN will always be "iqn.2002-12.com.brocade:" and will be followed by the WWN of the storage port.

For example, if the Fibre Channel storage port has a port WWN of 10:00:00:60:69:51:10:42, then the IQN assigned by the gateway would be:

```
iqn.2002-12.com.brocade:1000006069511042
```

This way, all names assigned by the gateway are both unique and predictable. Only Brocade can assign IQNs with the string "com.brocade" and all WWNs are guaranteed unique. Since it is easy for a user to determine the WWN of a storage port, and the rest of the IQN is fixed, it is easy for a user to predict the IQN that will be assigned to any given storage port. This facilitates configuration of iSCSI hosts.

IEEE EUI

Extended Unique Identifiers (EUIs) are assigned by the IEEE Registration Authority. These names cannot be arbitrarily assigned by end users. The format starts with the string "eui." to distinguish it from IQN and NAA names. The rest of the string is the sixteen ASCII-encoded hexadecimal digits of the uniquely assigned EUI identifier. Fully formatted, an iSCSI EUI name might look something like this:

```
eui.1BA035891B2569D8
```

This format will only be used by manufacturers registered with the IEEE Registration Authority to configure unique iSCSI names in products at the factory, rather than on-site. At the time of this writing, EUI names are not supported by the Brocade iSCSI gateway, but support will be added in a future release if there is sufficient demand.

IEEE NAA

Network Address Authority (NAA) names are currently used by Fibre Channel. (WWNs are an examples of NAA format names.) Like EUI names, blocks of addresses are assigned by the IEEE Registration Authority for companies that assign addresses within their range at the time of device manufacture. They must start with "naa." to distinguish them from other formats, must use ASCII hexadecimal characters, and can only contain up to 32 characters. An iSCSI NAA formatted name might look something like:

```
naa.4200006178249B30
```

When printed out in documentation or human-readable interfaces, it is traditional to delimit the bytes in an NAA name with colons (e.g. 42:00:00:61:78:24:9B:30) but this is not done in NAA format iSCSI names.

At the time of this writing, the NAA name format is only a proposed extension to the iSCSI standard, and is not actually used by any vendors. As a result, NAA names are not supported by the Brocade iSCSI gateway, but support may be added if this format is adopted widely. Note that the usage case for NAA names is very similar to the way that Brocade already uses IQNs for representing Fibre Channel storage to iSCSI hosts.

Fibre Channel Identifiers

In addition to describing the three different iSCSI name formats, the previous subsection explained how the iSCSI Gateway Service automatically generates a unique IQN for a Fibre Channel storage port when presenting it to an iSCSI host. It is also necessary to generate appropriate unique Fibre Channel identifiers for iSCSI hosts when presenting them to Fibre Channel targets. There are three Fibre Channel identifiers needed for each iSCSI host: Node World Wide Name, Port World Wide Name, and Port Identifier.

The Fibre Channel identifiers are assigned dynamically the first time an iSCSI host accesses a Fibre Channel target through the gateway, or if the IQN is used to create a zone, or can be manually created by an administrator using the command line interface.

WWN Assignment

Proxy WWNs for the Fibre Channel representation of an iSCSI initiator are assigned from address blocks that Brocade has been allocated by the IEEE Naming Authority. These WWNs can be used to create Fibre Channel zones for the initiator. Brocade assigns a block of WWNs to each AP7420 platform, and the iSCSI Gateway Service allocates WWNs from this pool. It is also possible for an administrator to override this assignment from the CLI.

The association between an IQN and the allocated WWN in a given fabric is persistent: once a set of WWNs are assigned to an IQN, they will remain consistent throughout that fabric even if the initiator enters the fabric from a different port on a different gateway. If the initiator accesses a totally different fabric, its assigned WWNs will be different.

PID Assignment

Port Identifiers have three bytes, which are traditionally used for switch domain, switch port, and AL_PA address. The first two bytes of a proxy PID represent the gateway switch domain and port that it is coming into the fabric from, and the third byte differentiates between multiple iSCSI hosts using that port.

It is important to note that this means that the PID of a single initiator will be different depending on the iSCSI portal through which it entered the fabric, whereas proxy WWNs follow the device and not the port. As a result, zoning for iSCSI hosts should be WWN-based, and it may be inappropriate to use PID binding or PID-based LUN masking on some arrays.

✓ Side Note

Brocade frequently hears words to this effect from users:
iSCSI is a synonym for "the HBA is too expensive"
But Fibre Channel HBA prices are dropping fast, so this remaining iSCSI value proposition is tenuous. Check with the appropriate sales channel for availability of low cost Fibre Channel HBAs before deploying iSCSI.

Zoning and SNS Integration

Just as in existing Fibre Channel networks, access control between initiators and targets is managed by zoning. The gateway provides two important extensions to fabric services to facilitate management.

1. If zoning commands are executed on the gateway itself, it is possible to specify iSCSI hosts using their IQNs in addition to their proxy WWNs. This is more intuitive.

2. When the gateway inserts an iSCSI host into the SNS database, the IQN and IP address of the initiator are inserted into the Symbolic Port Name field. This is usually used to show SCSI Inquiry output and can be thought of as a comment field. When executing name server commands like nsShow, this clarifies the identity of the host.

The zoning extension allows ease of administration when using the gateway to control zoning. If an iSCSI host has been configured, and the administrator wants to allow it access to an FC target, they could create a zone from the gateway using the IQN of the host and the node WWN of the storage port. The gateway would then automatically create the appropriate proxy WWNs and PID for the host and allow access.

The following example shows an administrator creating and verifying a zone from the gateway.

```
gateway:admin> zoneCreate "iSCSI_001","iqn.1991-05.com.microsoft:testHost,
50:06:04:82:bf:d0:fb:92"
Zone Create Successful

gateway:admin> zoneShow -i
Defined configurations:
zone:    iSCSI_001
         iqn.1991-05.com.microsoft:testHost,50:06:04:82:bf:d0:fb:92
gateway:admin>
```

Note the use of the "–i" flag for *zoneShow*. This allows display of IQNs. Otherwise, the proxy WWN of the iSCSI host would be shown.

To allow backwards compatibility with existing Fibre Channel switches, the gateway only sends the proxy WWNs of an iSCSI host when transferring the zoning database across the fabric, and not the IQN. This is necessary because the Fibre Channel zoning standards do not define IQN objects. This also means that it is possible to administer iSCSI access control even from existing Fibre Channel switches as long as the proxies have already been created and the administrator knows the proxy WWNs of the host.

This example shows an administrator displaying the name server and finding an IQN to WWN mapping.

```
gateway:admin> nsShow
{
 Type Pid      COS     PortName                NodeName
 NL   020700;  3;      57:00:51:e1:37:00:00:02; 56:00:51:e1:37:00:00:02
                  [iqn.1991-05.com.microsoft:testHost::10.0.0.1]
     Fabric Port Name: 20:07:00:05:1e:13:70:00
The Local Name Server has 1 entries }
```

Because of the name server extension, figuring out the proxy WWNs of an iSCSI host is easy: simply search the name server for either the IQN or IP address of the host, and the database entry containing them will also have the WWNs for that initiator. In the previous example, iqn.1991-05.com.microsoft:testHost has a node WWN of 56:00:51:e1:37:00:00:02. Once the mapping is known, it would be possible to create a zone using the proxy NWWN of the initiator and real NWWN of the target(s) from any switch in the fabric.

Note that it is necessary for node name zoning to be enabled in the fabric for the gateway to work properly. Unless it has been explicitly disabled, it should already be enabled, but this can be verified using the *configureZoning* CLI command.

iSCSI CHAP Authentication

The gateway supports the Challenge Handshake Authentication Protocol (CHAP) to ensure that the iSCSI host attempting access to a given proxy target is authorized to do so. This helps prevent unauthorized access on IP networks that are not tightly controlled at all levels. In fact, it is always recommended to use CHAP authentication for iSCSI hosts even when the IP network is secure.

CHAP was originally created for PPP under RFC 1994 by the Point-to-Point Protocol Working Group of the IETF. Since then, it has been adapted by many other protocols. Under the iSCSI standard, CHAP follows roughly the following sequence:

1. The basic iSCSI link is established by the initiator.
2. The initiator sends a "challenge" message to the target
3. The target responds with a value calculated using a "one-way hash" function such as MD5.
4. The initiator checks the response.
5. If the response was correct, the authentication is acknowledged; otherwise the connection is terminated.

The challenge and response messages that are scrambled using the one-way hash are based on a username and password that must be configured the same way for both sides of the connection. That is, the entity on each side can have its own username and password, but each side needs to know the username and password of the other side as well.

To configure CHAP, first decide on a username and password for each device. Target passwords and host usernames/passwords can be selected by the administrator. However, the gateway requires that the username of targets be equal to their IQNs. These will be assigned by the gateway according to the formula:

```
iqn.2002-12.com.brocade:<PWWN>
```

...where PWWN is the Port World Wide Name of the FC target without colons.

Use the command *iscsiAuthCfg* to perform CHAP configuration on the gateway. Configure the usernames and passwords selected in the previous step for iSCSI initiators and the proxy targets to which they will connect. Follow the instructions provided with the iSCSI initiator driver to configure the CHAP username and password on each host, and those for each target it will access. With the Microsoft iSCSI driver, the initiator's CHAP settings are on the "Initiator Settings" tab. The settings for each target are on the "Advanced" dialogue that is available when adding a target under the "Add Portal" dialogue.

IP Fabric Configuration Server

The iSCSI Gateway Service uses translation mappings to present devices into networks with incompatible addressing schemes. When mapping from a Fibre Channel WWN to an iSCSI IQN, a formula is used such that all gateways on a fabric will automatically use the same IQN to represent the device. Similarly, the PID selected to represent an iSCSI device onto a Fibre Channel fabric is based on the actual port of the actual gateway the connection arrived on, so no coordination is needed.

However, iSCSI devices must also be assigned WWNs on the Fibre Channel fabric, and the method of assignment is not formulaic. Furthermore, since the WWN is used to enforce zoning it is necessary for the mapping to be consistent and persistent. Therefore Brocade has created a service for synchronizing address translation across a fabric. This is known as the IP Fabric Configuration Server, or iFCS.

The iFCS has several responsibilities. The primary two are synchronization of IQN to WWN mappings and CHAP information on a fabric-wide basis. The objective of the service is to allow an iSCSI initiator to move to different entry points in the fabric without much if any reconfiguration being required.

Like most fabric-wide services, iFCS has built-in distribution, synchronization, and redundancy mechanisms. When the service is enabled on a gateway platform, it will create a database with all of the relevant information available to that platform. It will then seek out other gateways in the fabric and automatically cause them to become iFCS secondary servers, gathering more information for its database. It will then transfer the database to each secondary, and maintain synchronization continually. If the primary server should fail, then a new primary will automatically be elected from the pool of secondaries, each of which will have a complete and up-to-date iFCS database.

There are two implementation notes at the time of this writing:

1. It is necessary to manually enable the service the first time it is used. The command *iFCSenable* must be executed on one gateway. This will automatically cause the other gateways to be enabled as secondaries. Once enabled, iFCS will stay persistently enabled across reboots.

2. All gateways must have connectivity between their RJ45 10/100baseT Ethernet management ports. That is, it must be possible for IP traffic to flow between the RJ45 Ethernet management ports on all switches being used as iSCSI gateways. Some of the synchronization tasks use those interfaces. It is also advisable that these interfaces have connectivity to the IP SAN, since they are used for internal iSNS client to external iSNS server synchronization.

Redundant Configurations

The gateway supports active/active redundant configurations in two ways: via either the gateway or the iSCSI host.

It is possible to take any given pair of gateways in the same fabric and assign them to each other as failover partners using the *iscsiFailoverAdd* CLI command. Figure 28 shows two gateways configured as a redundant pair.

The administrator would first use the CLI command to give each gateway the ID of the other for use as an HA partner. When the iSCSI host (C) then sends a SendTargets request to one iSCSI portal (A), the gateway would respond with each target as also being reachable via the second portal's iSCSI interface(s) (B). This should automatically configure failover on the host.

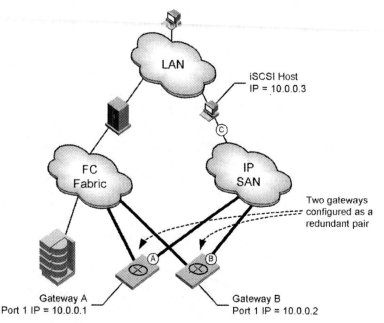

Figure 28 - iSCSI Gateway HA Configuration

The second option does not require any special configuration on the gateway, but does require configuration on each host and requires HA support in the host's iSCSI driver.

(Note that many iSCSI drivers do not support HA configurations at the time of this writing.) Since the presentation of targets is active/active even if the gateways are not configured as a pair, a user could configure the IP addresses of both portals when setting up its target(s).

Detailed Walkthrough

This subsection goes through some of the iSCSI Gateway concepts step-by-step.

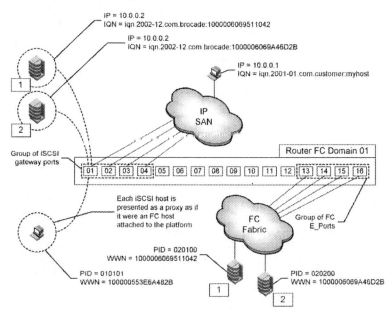

Figure 29 – Walkthrough of iSCSI to FC Mapping

Figure 29 shows an iSCSI host projected into a Fibre Channel fabric accessing two storage ports. The gateway has domain 01 in the fabric. The two storage ports are attached to the domain 02 switch. Ports 01 – 04 on the router have been set up as gateway ports on the 10.0.0.x IP subnet. (Only one is used in this example.) The administrator first configures zoning to allow the IQN of the host at 10.0.0.1 to access the WWNs of the two storage ports. This causes the gateway to create a set of proxy WWNs from its pool for that

IQN and allocate proxy IQNs for the storage ports according to a formula.

Then the administrator configures the host to access those proxy storage IQNs at the IP address of one of the gateway ports. Port #1 at address 10.0.0.2 in this case. When the host tries to access the storage, it is allocated a PID with the domain and port matching the Fibre Channel domain and port number of the router. (Domain 01 and port 01 in this case.) The AL_PA indicates the particular host on the port. In this case there is only one host, and it gets AL_PA 01.

iSCSI Gateway Summary

The iSCSI Gateway Service is intended to extend the benefits of Fibre Channel storage networks to hosts that previously could not cost-justify an HBA for SAN attachment. It is complementary to Fibre Channel in that it allows the existing investment in fabrics to be preserved, and even expands the scope of these fabrics by allowing more hosts to use Fibre Channel storage resources.

For hosts that have existing, unused Ethernet interfaces but do *not* require high performance, secure, highly reliable Fibre Channel connections, iSCSI may be a good fit. It also is possible that new low cost Fibre Channel HBAs will solve the cost-sensitive connectivity problem for hosts without the trade-offs, so check for availability of these devices before deploying iSCSI.

In general, customers should strongly consider technologies such as Fibre Channel, network filesystems with SAN back-ends, and even in some cases direct attached storage before deploying emerging technologies like iSCSI. Make sure that the business case for iSCSI cannot be equally met by more mature technologies before committing to it.

5: FCIP Tunneling Service

E_Port Over TCP/IP

FCIP is a mechanism for connecting Fibre Channel E_Ports together across medium to long distances using IP infrastructure. It is *possible* to configure FCIP links in a point-to-point manner without intermediate IP network equipment between them as if they were ISLs. However, such a design could be built more economically and with better performance using point-to-point Fibre Channel links, so real world FCIP deployments use IP switches and/or routers between FCIP gateways. See Figure 30.

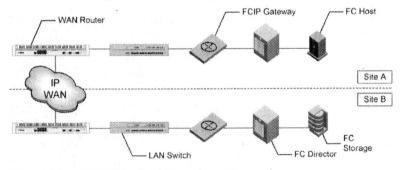
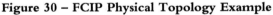

Figure 30 – FCIP Physical Topology Example

In this example, two sites are connected across an IP WAN. Each site has a Fibre Channel director (e.g. Silk-Worm 24000) and an FCIP gateway (e.g. SilkWorm AP7420 with the FCIP license). The gateway is connected to a LAN switch, which is connected to a WAN router. Once the solution is configured, a host at one site will be able to access storage at the other site as if the switches were directly connected and there were no intermediate IP network.

81

FCIP is a transparent tunneling protocol, which means that it is invisible to the Fibre Channel fabric. The only Fibre Channel devices that need to be aware of the existence of the tunnel at all are the gateways themselves. To all other devices, each tunnel appears to be an ISL. This means that the Fibre Channel devices on both sides of the link form one fabric.[54] Figure 31 shows how the fabric formed by the example in Figure 30 might appear.

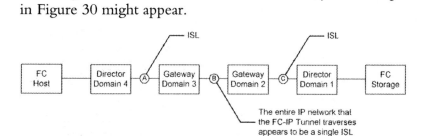

Figure 31 - FCIP Fabric Topology Example

Any port on a Multiprotocol Router platform can be configured for FCIP. An FCIP port presents itself to other switch ports and to the operating system as though it were a standard Fibre Channel E_Port, so it may also be called a VE_Port (Virtual E_Port). Once a connection is established between two gateways, the two VE_Ports form a virtual ISL. This virtual ISL is also called an FCIP tunnel. Fibre Channel frames are encapsulated with FCIP headers and forwarded to the remote switch via a TCP/IP connection.[55] Upon arrival, the FCIP frames are extracted from the TCP/IP stream, the FCIP encapsulation is removed, and the Fibre Channel frame is classified by the VE_Port and forwarded to the appropriate destination. Figure 32 shows how the protocol stacks relate to each other for the devices in the previous examples.

---

[54] There are a few exceptions, which are described in the FCR Integration subsection later in this chapter.

[55] In point of fact, it may be necessary to break up an FCIP frame into multiple IP packets since IP networks tend to use smaller packet sizes than FC uses.

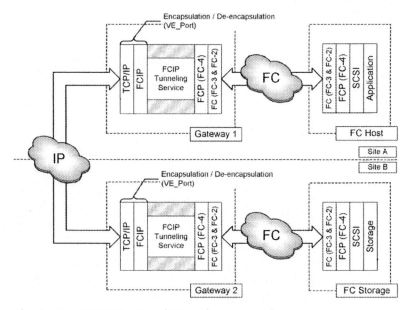

Figure 32 - FCIP Protocol Mapping Example

FCIP Applications

Like any networking technology, FCIP has many potential applications. However there are certain "killer apps" for the protocol that fall broadly into three categories: wide, metropolitan, and campus area network extension:

1. Connecting SANs over wide area distances (e.g. 200km or more) to facilitate business continuance solutions. Other technologies such as SONET/SDH gateways can do this with higher performance and reliability, but lower cost is usually in favor of FCIP.

2. Connecting SANs over medium distances (e.g. 50km or so). This could be done to facilitate backup / recovery operations within a metropolitan area, or server / data migration, or temporary provisioning of storage for applications in different buildings in a city.

3. Connecting SANs over short distances (e.g. 1km or less) to facilitate normal SAN operations within a campus in cases where dark fiber between buildings is unavailable.

The chapters in Section 2 have additional examples of usage cases for FCIP.

✅ Side Note

Encapsulation is similar to but not quite the same as protocol conversion. When a frame is encapsulated, it is "wrapped" in another protocol, which really means that the data stream simply has another set of headers tacked onto the front. This does create inefficiencies, since the extra headers consume bandwidth and add latency, but it is more efficient than conversion. Generally, none of the protocol headers already there are modified. This is a computationally inexpensive operation, as is encapsulation header removal at the other end of the connection. A protocol conversion in contrast may involve complex manipulations of existing headers, and even manipulation of the payload.

FCR Integration

One of the most appealing features of the FCIP Tunneling Service is its seamless integration with the FC-FC Routing Service. [56] When used in this way, the fabrics at each site remain separate edge fabrics and the FCIP tunnel(s) become one or more backbone fabrics. Since this is expected to be by far the most popular deployment method, most of the FCIP examples throughout this book also use the FCR integration features.

Take another look at Figure 31 (p82). If ISLs A and C were IFLs instead – in other words EX_Ports instead of E_Ports on the router – then the domain 4 director would be an edge fabric isolated by an IFL (A), the virtual ISL within the tunnel (B) would be a backbone fabric, and the director at domain 1 would be a second edge fabric isolated by an-

---

[56] This subsection assumes that the reader is familiar with FC-FC Routing. See the FCR Overview chapter if not.

other IFL (C). Of course, there would no longer be any reason to ensure unique domain IDs between the two sites, so
both directors could just as easily be domain 1. Figure 33
shows a similar case with redundancy and domain ID overlap.

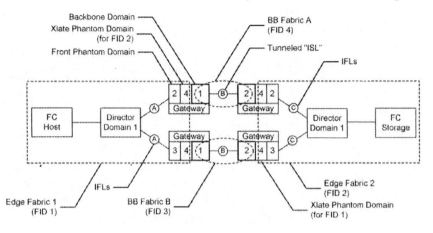

Figure 33 - FCIP Redundant Configuration

This example has four distinct fabrics. Each has a unique
fabric identifier (FID). There is one edge fabric at each site,
and a separate backbone fabric for each of the two FCIP tunnels. Like all FC-FC Routing Service applications, the edge
fabrics are connected to EX_Ports on the gateways and therefore use phantom topologies. This means that there are
multiple domain IDs per gateway: one front domain per
EX_Port, one shared xlate domain per remote fabric, and one
domain for the backbone fabric.

Note that each element has a unique domain ID within
each fabric. Domain duplication is allowed between different
fabrics by the router by using FC-NAT. Duplication within
a singe fabric cannot be supported (except for xlate phantom
domains) because this would break compatibility with existing Fibre Channel switches and standards.

For example, the gateway in the upper right corner of
Figure 33 uses domain ID 2 for both an FCR front domain
and its backbone domain. There is no problem with duplication since these are different fabrics. However, the gateway

could not use domain ID 1 at all, since that is already used in both of the fabrics it connects to. On the surface, it might seem that its use of domain 4 is a duplicate of the gateway below it, but this is an xlate domain. It isn't a duplicate domain; it is a shared domain and both routers use it to represent the same "thing." (I.e. the same remote fabric.) The use of the domain ID is synchronized between routers via FCRP, so the two routers on the left both use domain 4 to represent FID 2 (the remote site).[57]

Side Note

It is important to note that FCIP is not "all things to all people" for distance extension. Even the best IP networks usually have lower performance and reliability characteristics than are typically required for storage applications.

For example, to get a frame from a source port on an FC switch to a destination port on another switch across an ISL takes a small number of nanoseconds, or a small number of microseconds at worst. Even crossing an ISL consisting of 100km of dark fiber does not change latency appreciably: it adds a few hundred microseconds based on the speed of light, but even that is much faster than seek times on the fastest of disks. Typical IP WANs, on the other hand, take milliseconds or even multiple full seconds to traverse: many orders of magnitude slower than native Fibre Channel or WDM solutions, and – more to the point – in the same range as or even greater than disk seek times. This can have a negative performance impact at the application level...

Multipoint FCIP Networks

The previous example showed how two sites could be connected with the gateway. It is also possible to connect

---

[57] The fact that the two routers on the left use domain 4 to represent FID 1 is a coincidence.

many sites. Figure 34 shows an FCIP network connecting three sites.

This figure shows two sites (A and B) sharing access to storage at a third location (site C). For example, this could be a business continuance solution in which sites A and B both use site C for backups and mirroring, and perhaps can fail over to each other in the event of a major disaster.

Note that while it isn't absolutely *necessary* to combine the FCIP and FCR features, it is almost always *advisable*.[58] The following analysis of the example in Figure 34 assumes that FCR integration is used. In that case, the links indicated by labels D and E are IFLs, the FCIP tunnels through the IP WAN (links ABC) form a backbone fabric, and the three FC SANs at the bottom of the diagram are each edge fabrics. There are four unique fabrics in total.

Figure 35 shows how two of the Fibre Channel fabrics might look. It supposes that the fabric IDs were configured as FID=1 for site A, FID=2 for B, FID=3 for C, and FID=4 for the backbone.

The left-hand side of Figure 35 shows a possible topology of the site A (FID=1) fabric if it consisted of a single domain such as a SilkWorm 24000 director. The IFLs D and E each receive a Front Phantom Domain from the fabric principal switch, which in this case is certain to be the domain ID 1 director. Since domain ID 1 is already taken, the IFLs receive domains 2 and 3 unless the administrator has specified preferred domains for them. Each remote fabric for which LSANs are configured receives an xlate domain. In this case, there are two such fabrics, and – assuming that LSANs were set up to both– their xlate domains are assigned as 4 and 5. Note that the FID 2 and 3 fabrics could look identical to this, or could have radically different topologies and domain IDs.

---

[58] This is because FCR integration improves the reliability, scalability, and security of FCIP solutions, and does not have any offsetting downside.

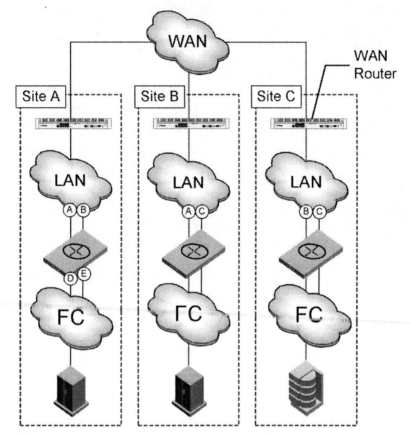

Figure 34 - FCIP Multipoint Physical Topology

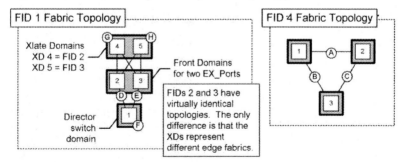

Figure 35 - FCIP Multipoint Fabric Topologies

The right-hand side of the figure shows a probable topology for the backbone fabric. Look at both Figure 34 and Figure 35. Note for example that more than one link has a label of A in Figure 34. These are really two halves of the same link, so the two A links are really one tunneled ISL. This can be seen in the right-hand side of Figure 35. When the tunnels form and the fabric converges, each gateway will receive a backbone domain ID through the usual assignment methods. Assume that the administrator had manually configured them such that site A had backbone domain 1, B had 2, and C had 3, or that the election process just happened to make those assignments. In this case, the fabric topology formed by the virtual ISLs would be as in the figure.

Figure 36 has a more complete representation of this. It is essentially a combination of Figure 34 and Figure 35, showing both the fabric topologies and the physical connections in one diagram. Note that the virtual ISLs each use different physical ports on the gateways, just as would standard ISLs. In this type of diagram, some physical ports of the platform are at the top of each platform block (i.e. the VE_Ports) and others (i.e. the EX_Ports) are at the bottom.

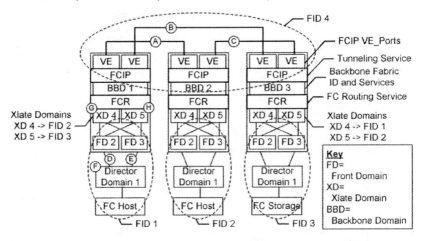

Figure 36 - FCIP Multipoint Meta SAN Topology

Redundant Configurations

There are several ways to build redundancy into an FCIP network. The correct approach depends on factors such as failure-case performance requirements and the criticality of the application. Briefly, the approaches involve scaling the number of IFLs and tunnels per gateway, the number of gateways per site, the design of the IP WAN (s), and the number and configuration of the tunneled backbone fabrics. Figure 37 uses a design with superior performance and availability over the design in Figure 34.

In general, this approach is preferred if uptime for the distance connection is mission-critical. Otherwise, a single component failure can cause an outage. The figure shows each site with redundant gateways, each with redundant IFLs and its own set of tunnels. As in Figure 34, there are three edge fabrics, but in this case there are two largely independent backbones: one formed by the ABC tunnels, and the other by the DEF tunnels.

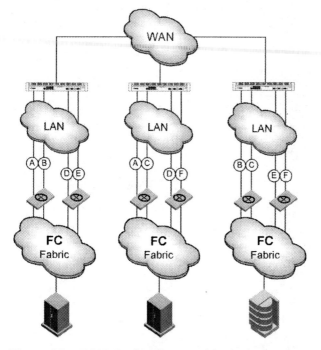

Figure 37 - FCIP Redundant Backbone Example

An even better approach is shown in Figure 38. This is similar to the previous example, but in addition each site now has two edge fabrics. The way the fabrics are attached to the

90

routers creates two entirely independent A/B Meta SANs. The total fabric count is now six edge fabrics plus two back-bones, divided equally into two Meta SANs. In addition, the IP networks are now redundant.

Of course, this approach may be too expensive for many customers. Redundancy and performance at each level can be scaled back to meet budgetary constraints. For example, if redundant WANs are not affordable, it would still be possible to achieve some redundancy at the WAN level. A customer could configure the routers with a protocol such as VRRP to provide redundancy between the platforms and a protocol like OSPF for redundant routes within the WAN.

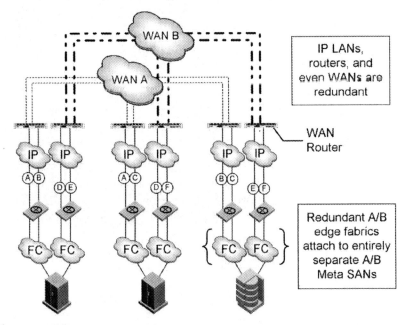

Figure 38 – FCIP Redundant Meta SAN Example

Ongoing Management

It takes very little effort to set up and manage the FCIP Tunneling Service. Configure a few parameters such as the IP addresses and default routes on both ends, and the tunnel will form automatically. Once it is online, it does not require daily administration any more than an ISL in a fabric would.

Of course, administering the IP network between the gateways may require additional effort. For example, this is where performance and reliability analysis and most trouble-shooting usually will be required.

WWN VE_Port Authentication

The FCIP service supports authentication of a remote gateway. This is configured using the CLI command portCfgFCIP. It is a one-step process on each gateway to configure the remote VE_Port's WWN, and this is generally executed as part of the port's initial configuration.

Side Note

Beware of salesmen bearing axioms... some vendors will use unsubstantiated buzz-word arguments such as, "To truly centralize information across a vast enterprise, you need IP." This turns out not to be true, as many customers can at-test, since major corporations and government agencies have truly centralized their information using Fibre Channel for years. Deploy IP SAN solutions from Brocade or other vendors only if there is a concrete *business reason why more mature SAN technologies like Fibre Channel will not work.*

Integrated vs. Third-Party FCIP Gateways

Some customers like to deploy "best-in-class" solutions, while others prefer a single-vendor approach. Brocade can support either of these models.

Brocade has strong partnerships with the leading providers of high-performance distance extension products such as CNT. For customers wishing to design networks with a "best in class" approach, it is acceptable and even recommended to use external FCIP solutions instead of the service integrated into the router. For example, a CNT Edge 3000 FCIP gateway could be used in combination with the FCR functionality of the router to solve any of the previously described SAN design problems, and would outperform the integrated FCIP solution.

As with most technology decision points, there are trade-offs to consider associated with using external gateways. For example, external gateways add some cost, lower system MTBF,[59] and have less integrated management.

Of course, these trade-offs may be perfectly acceptable. For environments in which performance is the top priority, an external gateway from a provider like CNT is recommended because they have value-added features like compression.[60] For customers where price sensitivity, manageability, and RAS are bigger concerns,[61] the integrated solution is better.

The bottom line is that both approaches work, and the decision usually comes down to network design philosophy. The Brocade router will work either way.

FCIP vs. SONET/SDH, ATM, and xWDM[62]

As the saying goes, you get what you pay for, and this is another case where decisions need to be made involving performance vs. cost tradeoffs. Just as with external FCIP gateways, SONET/SDH, ATM, and xWDM solutions for distance extension can work in conjunction with the router's FCR functionality.

---

[59] Mean Time Between Failures always becomes lower (worse) as you add more components to a system.

[60] which can be a compelling advantage on lower-bandwidth WANs, especially when transferring highly compressible data like text files.

[61] ...or who are transferring uncompressible / already optimally compressed data like JPEG images. Compressing a stream of already compressed data is rarely helpful. Similarly, if a customer already has compression in their IP WAN equipment, then FCIP gateway compression is not needed.

[62] xWDM refers to both coarse and dense wave division multiplexers.

Two things to consider are:

- Price. FCIP is usually less expensive for WANs, both in terms of deployment and ongoing network usage fees.
- Performance. IP SAN technology will have higher latency, lower reliability, and lower throughput than FC over SONET/SDH, ATM, or xWDM solutions.

FCIP is perfectly acceptable for applications such as off-site backup/recovery, since these may have relatively low performance sensitivity − compared to for example synchronous disk mirroring − and low reliability requirements − because if a given backup fails it is unlikely to cause application downtime.

However, the high latency and low reliability of most IP networks make them unsuitable for mission-critical and/or synchronous applications. While best in class FCIP vendors like CNT can handle network reliability issues in a graceful manner, IP technology is simply incapable of matching either native Fibre Channel or SONET/SDH gateway solutions. In general, the more critical an application is, the more likely that it is a candidate for SONET/SDH or xWDM. *Some* IP WANs are reliable and high performance, of course, but this is the exception, not the rule.

The bottom line is that IP SAN technology should not be considered from any provider for mission- or performance-critical applications unless end-to-end throughput, latency, and reliability are guaranteed, and more established, high performance, and reliable technologies are impractical for compelling reasons.

FCIP vs. iFCP

iFCP was developed to replace Fibre Channel fabrics with IP networks. iFCP still acknowledged the incumbency of Fibre Channel, since it provided no host or storage interconnect and required all nodes to use Fibre Channel. In a fully "native" iFCP solution, every Fibre Channel device needs to plug directly into a portal rather than a Fibre Channel switch, undergo a protocol conversion to IP, transfer to another portal, and be converted once again into Fibre Channel. This makes iFCP solutions extremely expensive, and far lower performance than their native Fibre Channel counterparts since every frame between Fibre Channel endpoints needs to undergo a double protocol conversion.

Prior to the invention of the FC-FC Routing Service, iFCP proponents[63] could claim that the technology had one advantage over FCIP in that it could isolate edge fabrics from WAN instabilities. Since FCIP gateways like the Brocade Multiprotocol Router now provide that isolation, this argument no longer applies.

While it was ratified as a standard, iFCP simply never caught on. At the time of this writing, only one vendor is shipping an iFCP solution, which they acquired in the process of buying another company for its iSCSI and FC-FC routing technologies. (The acquired company was not selling enough iFCP products to stay in business as a stand-alone entity, and was thus acquired at a loss to its investors.) The acquiring vendor also has an FCIP roadmap, as do all major SAN network infrastructure providers. Therefore the future viability of iFCP is doubtful at best: it seems likely that the protocol will simply go away in the near future, and that all iFCP products will become rapidly obsolete.

Detailed Walkthrough

This subsection goes through some of the more complex FCIP-FCR integrated usage concepts step-by-step. It is expected that most readers would require considerable time and effort to read this, and only readers seeking a deep understanding of the features need to make the effort. Figure 39 and Figure 40 are used for reference throughout this subsection. Text that appears in **bold** correlates to diagram labels.

---

[63] More accurately, *proponent* (singular). There was only ever one iFCP vendor .

The physical network topology shown in Figure 39 may seem overly complex at first. It is intended to illustrate several points, one of which is that the FCIP-FCR solution can solve complex design problems. Many real-world designs will be simpler than this.

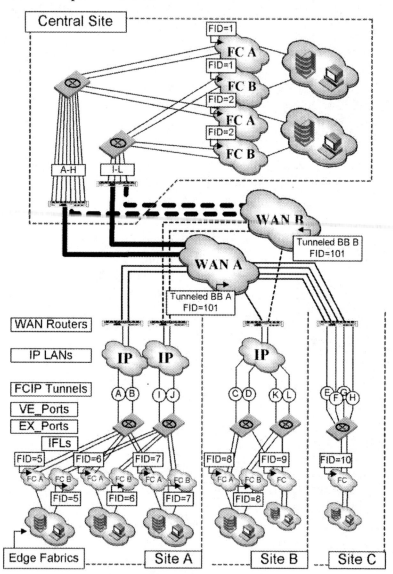

Figure 39 - FCIP Walkthrough Physical Topology

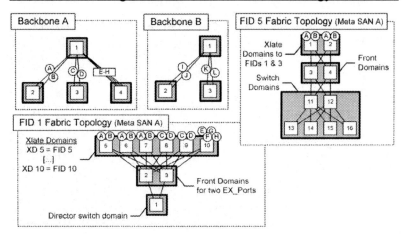

Figure 40 – FCIP Walkthrough Fabric Topologies

The example represents four sites with varying connectivity, performance, and availability requirements. **Site A, Site B,** and **Site C** are using the **Central Site** for off site backup / recovery and business continuance solutions. **Site A** requires the greatest possible redundancy, and approximately 1Gbit of throughput even in failure cases. **Site B** requires about half the performance, and occasional downtime potential is acceptable. However, because the IP WANs are less reliable (by storage network standards), it attaches to both. **Site C** requires high performance, but downtime for the WAN is not considered an issue, so it only attaches to one of the WANs and uses a non–redundant model at all levels. There is no traffic within the ABC site group: all traffic flows from those sites to the central site.

To support high availability requirements for some of the remote connections, two separate WANs are used. One might be a frame relay network and the other a native Gigabit Ethernet solution. For the purposes of this example it does not matter so long as high end-to-end connection quality and performance are assured. The central site connects to the WANs using "fat pipes" (i.e. multi-gigabit) while the remote sites use thinner connections (e.g. one gigabit per link). At the WAN level, connectivity is provisioned between each of the ABC sites and the central site.

The routers at each location have some number of **VE_Ports** facing the WANs and some number of **EX_Ports** facing their edge fabrics. The virtual ISLs (**FCIP Tunnels**) created by the VE_Ports attach between the ABC sites and the central site. They are arranged in two backbone fabrics. Because the EX_Port connections are kept separated, there are two unique Meta SANs. Each site has one router attached to **Backbone A** / Meta SAN A and another attached to **Backbone B** / Meta SAN B, except for **Site C** which does not require redundant WAN connections. Site C only attaches to Backbone A / Meta SAN A, so the backbone fabrics are asymmetrical. Figure 40 shows the fabric topologies of the two backbones.

In this example, the BB fabric domain assignments are 1 for the **Central Site** routers, 2 for **Site A**, 3 for **Site B**, and 4 for **Site C**. Note that the domain ID assignments in this example are the same between the two backbones, i.e. the Site A routers both have domain ID 1 for their backbone fabrics. This is a best practice to simplify ongoing management, but it is not required.

Similarly, FIDs are duplicated between the two Meta SANs such that both fabrics in a given A/B pair have the same FID. Just as domains only need to be unique within a fabric, fabric IDs only need to be unique within a Meta SAN. In addition to making administration easier by showing the correlation between the two fabrics, using the same FID for corresponding fabrics between the two Meta SANs prevents them from being accidentally merged.[64]

The VE_Port connections from the remote sites are illustrated in Figure 39 with circled labels **A – L** on the lower portion, and the corresponding central site links are shown in boxes in the upper portion. The circled **A** at **Site A** is a VE_Port that is configured to target the IP address of the

---

[64] Of course, this would also prevent the two Meta SANs from being *deliberately* merged without reconfiguration of the FIDs, but doing so would violate the redundancy model and almost always would not provide needed connectivity.

boxed **A** VE_Port at the **Central Site**. This physical to logical mapping is also shown in Figure 40. The **A** link between domains 1 and 2 represents the same **A** link as in the physical topology diagram.

While it would be theoretically possible to configure connectivity between for example sites A and B using the central site as an intermediate hop, this is not the intent of the solution and the design is not optimized for it. All LSANs have been configured from remote sites to the central site. As a consequence, each fabric at each remote site has two xlate phantom domains: one for each of the fabrics in its Meta SAN at the central site. The FID 5 block in Figure 40 shows the phantom topology of Fabric A at **Site A**. The circled AB labels at the top of that block indicate the links that could be used to reach the corresponding fabric for each xlate phantom domain.

The central site, however, needs to reach many remote fabrics. Indeed, the Meta SAN A fabrics at the central site need to reach three different fabrics at **Site A** alone. Each of the two Meta SAN A fabrics at the central site therefore has six xlate phantoms as shown in Figure 40. The Meta SAN B fabrics at the central site would lack the final domain, since **Site C** has no Meta SAN B connection. Examine the two diagrams and trace the physical and logical path from the director in FID 1 to the domain 16 switch in FID 5.

FCIP Tunneling Summary

For vendors who cannot afford do not have available higher performing and more reliable solutions like dark fiber, SONET/SDH, ATM, or xWDM solutions, FCIP offers an alternative method for extending SANs over distance. The FCIP Tunneling Service allows Fibre Channel ISL extension over an exiting IP infrastructure. It uses a transparent tunneling method rather than manipulating FC headers and payload. This improves efficiency and lowers risk. Each Fibre Channel frame is encapsulated into one or more IP packets and tunneled through the IP network, after which the gateway on the far end removes the encapsulation and re-stores the frame to its original condition.

When this technique is combined with the FC–FC Routing Service, fault isolation is provided between the sites, and also between each site and the IP Network. Administrators of each site have complete autonomy, with connectivity and dependencies only existing to the extent that the owners of separate fabrics agree to and explicitly configure them. This provides scalable performance, best possible reliability given the traversal of an IP network, a flexible and secure management model, and an attractive price point because the two technologies are fully integrated into the platform.

6: Technology Overview FAQ

Multiprotocol Router Platforms FAQ

Q: What SFPs are supported on the AP7420? (E.g. FC SWL, FC LWL, FC ELWL, and IP SWL.)

A: At this time, a variety of SFPs are supported in each of those categories. At this time Brocade has tested:

Table 2 - Platform SFP Support

Vendor	Type	Model
Finisar	SWL	FTRJ8519P1BNL-B1
Finisar	SWL	FTRJ8519-7D-2.5
Agilent	SWL	HFBR-5720L
Infineon	SWL	V23848-M305-C56
Finisar	LWL	FTRJ1319P1BTL-B1
Infineon	LWL	V23848-M15-C56
Finisar	ELWL	FTRJ1419P1BTL-B1

The list is likely to expand over time as more media are qualified, and support may vary between OEMs, so be sure to check with support providers for the up-to-date answer. Also try the *sfpSupport* CLI command.

Q: When will the platform be supported in Secure Fabric OS environments?

A: S-FOS integration is not available at the time of this writing, but it is being developed. While support from any given OEM cannot be promised, production quality code will be delivered for qualification in 2005.

Q: Will the router work with *xxx* vendor's external FC-to-*yyy* protocol gateway?

A: Possibly. It works with many FC distance extension products. Check the support matrix from the vendor as well as the relevant OEMs and support organizations to be sure.

Q: Does the AP7420 ship with SFPs? If so, are they all "tri-mode" capable? (Tri-mode SFPs can be used for 1G FC, 2G FC, and 1G ENet.)

A: It can certainly be delivered with tri-mode SFPs, and Brocade does encourage this approach since it gives the end user maximum flexibility. Default shipping configurations vary between different OEMs, so it is important to ask this question when ordering the router.

Q: When will OEM *xxx* support the router?

A: It is not possible for Brocade to commit OEMs to support dates prior to their own announcements. In general, customers need to ask their OEM sales representatives this question. At the time of this writing, several OEMs have completed qualification and announced general availability (e.g. CNT, EMC, HP, STK, etc.), and all others are somewhere along in the process.

Q: How many buffer-to-buffer credits can be configured per FC port on the AP7420?

A: The early access code on the platform was limited to 32 credits. The limit was expanded to **255** credits per port in XPath OS 7.3. The *architectural* limit is around five hundred per port or even higher, though it is not clear that there is a strong enough demand for such a configuration to justify development and testing. Note that credits are *not* shared among ports in a pool the way they are on other SilkWorm products: allocations on one port do not affect any other.

Q: What is a "Ports on Demand" license?

A: If the license is not installed, half of the ports on the platform will be persistently disabled. This allows Brocade to offer the 16-port platform at an 8-port price with the ability to add the other eight ports without changing hardware. It allows a "pay as you grow" approach. Not all OEMs support this feature.

Q: Is the Network Time Protocol (NTP) supported on the AP7420 when it is networked with other switches?

A: Yes. No caveats.

Q: Does the router have to be the principal switch?

A: No. The AP7420 platform is *capable* of becoming a principal switch on the backbone fabric, but it will *never* become the principal switch in any edge fabric. Part of the EX_Port services lite model precludes this.

Q: How is the platform serial port configured?

A: It is set to 9600/8/none/1/no flow control.

Q: With the virtual IP address on the management port, does the platform broadcast, for example, RIP routes?

A: No. Management interface failover is handled more like an HA server cluster than like an IP router.

Q: What is the speed of the ARMs in each port ASIC?

A: Each port ASIC in the AP7420 has three 133MHz ARM processors in addition to its fixed-gate logic. The ARMs are only required to operate on a small portion of certain frames. This gives the AP7420 great flexibility since the ARMs can be programmed independently, but also great speed, since the vast majority of operations are handled by optimized hardware in the ASICs.

Q: Does the platform support private loop nodes?

A: To some extent. Private loop devices cannot be directly attached to the router. When used as an FCR, private loop storage can exist in edge fabrics and communicate through the router to devices in other edge fabrics. When used as an L2 switch, private loop storage can communicate to hosts attached to the router. Private loop hosts require QuickLoop/FabricAssist. When used as an L2 switch, this will work *across* the router, but not to storage attached *to* the router. QL/FA is not supported across IFLs. (Brocade has observed that private loop HBAs are obsolete, and have been replaced in most SANs with public loop or fabric HBAs, so there is no apparent market drive to add QL/FA support to the router.)

Q: Does the AP7420 support hot code load and activation?

A: At the time of this writing, the platform supports hot code *load*, but not hot code *activation*. Hot activation is being considered for a future software feature release. The router is a "border" product, and redundant router topologies can support upgrading one at a time without network outage, so hot code activation is a lower priority than for other platforms.

Q: When will the router blade for the SilkWorm 24000 be available? When will it support multiprotocol routing?

A: Please refer to the appropriate sales channel for a non-disclosure agreement (NDA) discussion.

FC-FC Routing Service FAQ

Q: After reading the overview chapter, I sort of understand how the FCR service *works*, but not what it is *for*. Can you explain that?

A: The service makes it possible to support larger and more complex configurations, supports more flexible security models, delivers better fault containment, and simplifies many logistical problems that can otherwise cause day-to-day pain for SAN administrators. Section Two (the next set of chapters) illustrates many examples of business problems that the router solves, and explains why traditional solutions fall short.

Q: What happens if I add a switch to an edge fabric and it has a domain ID that is already being used by a phantom domain on a router?

A: This is the same as if the domain were already taken by a real switch. The phantom domain will keep its domain ID, and the real switch will either segment or receive a different domain ID, depending on its configuration.

Q: Do frames get "touched" by the platform CPU?

A: Not unless they are being sent to a fabric service like the name server. Data frames are handled by fixed gates on the port ASICs and by the three embedded 133MHz ARM CPUs within each ASIC.

Q: What prevents an EX_Port from becoming a principal switch on a rebuild, given that the router uses low WWNs for phantom domains?

A: The principal switch election process is described in the ANSI T11 documentation for FC-SW-*x*. The short version is that – in addition to the WWN comparison – a switch can either demand that it *must* become principal[65] by setting a high priority in the ELP frame, or demand that it *not* do so by e.g. not setting a priority at all. EX_Port phantom domains do the latter, so they really can't become the principal.

Q: How does the FCR handle different times existing on different edge fabrics? (I.e. the clocks on the FC switches are not in sync.)

A: It doesn't matter to the *FCR* service at all. Note that the *FCIP* service requires clock synchronization between backbone fabric domains for WAN_TOV enforcement to work, but that is all within one fabric. On general principal, it is advisable to synchronize all clocks with NTP, but this is unrelated to the FCR service.

Q: Can an FC router connect to more than one switch in an edge fabric? How does failover from one switch to another work? Is it active/passive, or active/active?

A: An FCR can be connected to multiple switches in an edge fabric. The redundant paths are active/active using FSPF. Failover works as if the phantom topology were built using real switches. See Figure 14 (p41) and the surrounding text for an example. In addition, redundancy can be configured on backbone fabrics. Each router can connect to its

---

[65] Which is a really bad thing to do, since – by definition – no two switches with that behavior can co-exist in a fabric. Fortunately, only one vendor is known to do this at the time of this writing. The rest of the industry has recognized this as an architectural flaw.

backbone redundantly, and different routers can have totally separate / independent backbones. See Figure 17 (p43) for a redundant BB fabric example.

Q: How many hops can the FCR service handle?

A: The *router* can handle up to 19 hops.[66] However, most *fabrics* are limited to 7 hops, and the end-to-end hop count should not exceed the limitations of the least capable network that a frame must traverse. This is rarely an issue since it is a best practice to avoid large hop counts in SANs.

Q: Do EX_Ports work with other vendors' switches?

A: Architecturally, yes. In fact, this has been tested to some extent with two other vendors at the time of this writing. A generally available version of this code is expected soon. In the mean time, Brocade is supporting multi-vendor deployments on a case-by-case basis. See "Chapter 11: Multi-Vendor Usage" for more information, or contact your Brocade sales team.

Q: I've heard that there is a limit on how many devices can be translated *per port* on the router. Are the xlate tables really loaded into every port? If so, how is this *not* a limitation on the entire edge fabric?

A: The tables are loaded into each port attached to the same FID, so it is a limitation per edge fabric, not per platform. In any case, it is not a practical limit. At the time of this writing it is possible to translate over a thousand devices into any given fabric. Since single-fabric scalability limits are only slightly more than that, and since presumably there will be devices located in the edge fabric, customers will run into limits on their fabrics before they do so on their routers.

Q: Where is FCRP from a standards perspective?

A: It is being offered to ANSI T11. Fibre Channel standards tend to take a long time to complete. (Although not generally as long as iSCSI.) It is too early to say whether or not it

---

[66] Remember that phantom links do not count as hops. Only ISLs and IFLs (both standard and tunneled) count.

will become the standard, though none of the other proposed methods have any support. In any case, the FC-FC Routing Service uses a programmable portion of the platform's ASICs, and upper-level routing protocols like FCRP run on the platform's main CPU, so if different standards are adopted, the platform hardware will be able to adapt.

Q: Does the Reliable Commit Service (RCS) work in edge fabrics, or does it need to be disabled?

A: FCR does not affect the RCS settings for edge fabrics. Phantom domains are largely passive, and participate in the edge fabric RCS only for zoning.

Q: What fabric-wide parameters need to be synchronized between edge fabrics?

A: Only data field size needs to be the same. Polls were conducted, and no users could be found who ever changed the default value, so adding support for different data field sizes is not considered a priority.

Q: If my edge fabrics are too large today to accommodate new devices coming in from LSANs, to what size should the edge fabrics be redesigned?

A: If you are already at the scalability limit for a fabric, importing more devices to the fabric will not work. In general, the edge fabric should be reduced to a size where its own devices plus those imported via LSANs will not exceed its SNS limit. As a place to start, see what would happen if the edge fabric were divided in half.

Q: How long does an xlate phantom domain remain after a device becomes inaccessible, either by dropping off or by having a path interruption?

A: Xlate domains are not removed unless the remote fabric is no longer reachable *and* the owner EX_Port goes down. Instead, the router adds / removes xlate PIDs from the phantom domain, as this is less disruptive. Note that if redundant routers are deployed it may be that one router will lose a path to the remote fabric while another router still has a path. In this case, both the xlate domain and xlate PIDs remain, but the router with no path removes its phantom FSPF route to that xlate domain.

Q: Why must LSANs use PWWNs and not NWWNs?

A: It is the only way to guarantee a unique name. Node WWNs can be duplicated in a fabric, so if an LSAN zone specified a Node WWN, the router would not know which port to export.

Q: If you remove a device that already has a Phantom PID assigned and insert a new device to the same physical port (PID), will it assume a different phantom PID in a given remote fabric?

A: The router does everything including xlate domain persistence by the WWN of a physical device, not by the PID. Unless the new device also has the same WWN as the device that was removed, the router will either (a) not translate the new device at all, or (b) if its WWN is configured in an LSAN to the same remote fabric, then a new xlate PID will be selected.

Q: Where would a frame get hard zoned out if it was incorrectly sent to a device?

A: At the switch port that the final destination device was plugged into. This is the same behavior as for all Brocade hard zoning.

Q: What is an "Owner IFL?"

A: An "owner IFL" is more properly referred to as an "owner front phantom domain." That domain "owns" the xlate domains that reside behind it. E.g. it is responsible for setting up the xlate domain's WWNs.

Q: Can the router connect to a Value Line switch?

A: Yes, but the switch needs to be upgraded with a full fabric license key. The discount pricing model for the VL switches assumed that they would be sold into market segments where they would be used as stand-alone platforms or in very small fabrics, *not* in environments where they would be networked into large Enterprise-class SANs or Meta SANs.

Q: What command allows you to see which port is the "Owner IFL?"

A: *fcrXlateConfig*

iSCSI Gateway Service FAQ

Q: Does the iSCSI gateway support redundant deployments?

A: Yes. It can do so either by using host-based configurations, or by configuring two gateways as an HA pair. However, at the time of this writing, most iSCSI nodes - including the Microsoft iSCSI driver itself - will not support HA configurations. Without support on the nodes, network-level HA is somewhat meaningless.

Q: iSCSI sounds very complicated. I thought it was supposed to be easy to deploy and not require any additional training. Isn't it "just IP" and therefore just like all of my other IP infrastructure? Shouldn't it be simpler to deploy and manage than FC, since my company has IP expertise?

A: This is a case of reality getting in the way of vendor hype. iSCSI is inherently quite a bit more complex to understand, deploy, and manage than Fibre Channel, which is one of many reasons why it has never gained wide market acceptance. Most of the complexity of a SAN is associated with higher level functions, not with the layers provided by IP and iSCSI. For example, it is almost unheard of to need to troubleshoot a Fibre Channel frame header; SAN professionals spend far more time troubleshooting end-point devices, which requires *storage* and *host OS* experience more than *Fibre Channel* expertise. Even if a person has senior-level expertise as an IP network engineer, they will require extensive re-training for iSCSI environments unless they are already storage experts, and also know iSCSI services inside and out.

Q: I have heard that the iSCSI market is "growing rapidly," but I cannot find even one example of a large iSCSI deployment in the real world. Can you give me a reference site?

A: Vendors often play games with statistics. If a company sold one unit of iSCSI product last year, and sold three this year, they might claim, "300% year-over-year growth." This sounds better than, "two more units." The reality is that iSCSI represents a miniscule percentage of the overall SAN installed base, and it is difficult to find large real-world iSCSI deployments because – in short – there are none.

Q: Is it possible to use a single network for both iSCSI and data network traffic?

A: It is *possible*, but it is almost always inadvisable. Doing this creates massive performance, reliability, and security issues for both the LAN and the IP SAN. Note that VLANs do *not* solve these problems: it is necessary to use a physically isolated network for IP SAN traffic to avoid the issues.

Q: I've heard that iSCSI is unreliable, and that there are no compelling business drivers for its adoption. What makes the Brocade solution different?

A: Brocade is using iSCSI to bring low-tier servers into existing production-quality SANs. iSCSI is not suitable for mission-critical applications, but not all hosts in a datacenter run such applications, and these hosts traditionally could not be attached to the SAN due to cost. Now, those hosts too can benefit from access to FC storage.

Q: There have been compatibility issues between FC devices in the past. Since iSCSI uses IP, won't all of these problems magically go away?

A: This is not the case. The compatibility issues still existent in the FC market have nothing to do with the network layers analogous to iSCSI. The FC industry has not had a frame-level compatibility problem since about 1995.[67] The challenges are all in other areas. For example, in some cases one vendor's multipathing drivers will not work with another vendor's storage controller. This has nothing to do with any

---

[67] That is, aside from proprietary VSAN tagging. This is done by just one vendor, but it does break compatibility with all other vendors' equipment at the frame header level. Oddly enough, the company in question solves the incompatibility problem by saying, "just turn VSANs off on ports that don't have our equipment." I.e. the way to fix the VSAN compatibility is to avoid using VSANs…

piece of the network, so changing the network will not help in any way. In fact, the iSCSI industry has not even begun to address the categories of interoperability and compatibility that are challenging the SAN industry today. For example, at the time of this writing there has not yet been a public demonstration of an iSNS server from one vendor communicating with an iSNS server from any other vendor, much less production support for this...

Q: How does the Brocade iSCSI solution compare to the offerings from vendor *xxx*?

A: It depends on the competitor and the customer requirements. At the time of this writing, the price to performance ratio is favorable to Brocade for most configurations starting from about fifty and going to many hundreds of software-driver iSCSI initiators. For customers who only have a few iSCSI hosts, or customers using accelerated iSCSI NICs, the router is less compelling unless they are also leveraging one of its other capabilities.

Q: How does the iSCSI gateway perform?

A: Much better than a typical host with an iSCSI software driver. So much so, in fact, that it requires several such hosts to saturate a single gateway port.

Q: Must zoning be implemented for iSCSI to present disks through the portal?

A: No. Zoning is required for FCR, and is strongly *recommended* for every SAN deployment, but not strictly speaking *required* for iSCSI.

Q: When does a WWN get assigned for an iSCSI host?

A: There are three possibilities: 1) When you create a zone using the router that includes the IQN of the host. 2) When the host first logs into the iSCSI portal.[68] 3) When the ad-

---

[68] If zoning is in use on the fabric, the host will not be able to communicate until step #1 is complete in any case. However, option #2 could be useful in that it could allow WWN zoning to be done instead of IQN zoning.

ministrator manually creates an assignment using *iscsiWWNAlloc*. Most often, the first option is the best.

Q: Can an unreliable iSCSI host cause a problem for an EX_Port–isolated edge fabric?

A: Not if the iSCSI host is being projected onto the backbone. If some ports on the router are being used for EX_Ports and some for iSCSI portals, this happens automatically. It is possible for a gateway to exist entirely within an edge fabric, in which case an iSCSI host could theoretically destabilize that entire edge fabric. (Note that this is not a special characteristic of either iSCSI or FC; it is a general characteristic of networks. This is a frequently asked question re: iSCSI because it is widely viewed as "bleeding edge" and particularly unstable at this time.)

Q: Can I project an iSCSI host onto an edge fabric if I want to take the risk of destabilization?

A: Yes. It requires placing a separate router into the edge fabric. As iSCSI becomes more stable, Brocade will support projecting iSCSI hosts into edge fabrics from a centralized router running FCR. This is not supported in the first release because it would risk contaminating stable production fabrics with unstable / experimental iSCSI devices.

Q: Is the iSCSI configuration saved by *configUpload* / *configDownload*?

A: Yes. Port configurations, WWN allocations, and CHAP secrets are all saved.

Q: Is the iSCSI service certified by Microsoft?

A: Yes. Brocade has passed WHQL Logo certification from Microsoft for the iSCSI Gateway Service.

Q: How many iSCSI servers can I connect per AP7420 running iSCSI Gateway Service?

A: The current maximum is fifteen ports[69] times eight sessions[70] equals 120 iSCSI hosts per gateway. As a practical

---

[69] Since at least one port needs to be going to an FC device.

matter there will be more than one FC port and some initiators will go to multiple targets, which would tend to lower the number slightly. Think of each gateway as supporting "about a hundred iSCSI hosts" in most environments. This may be expanded in a subsequent release depending on demand from end users.

Q: Sometimes I have trouble getting vendor support for more complex Fibre Channel solutions. Will iSCSI help with this?

A: Quite the opposite, in fact. Support for end-to-end solutions is not limited because Fibre Channel is complex; it is limited because storage networking is complex. Vendors like Brocade do a good job of hiding this complexity from end users through advanced software design, but it is there nonetheless. For example, it is possible for a network timing issue to cause a backup solution to fail. That is, if the network "goes slow" it can cause a tape under run, which may cause a backup to abort or at best go into a performance degraded mode which may exceed the backup window. For this reason, some vendors limit supported configurations for tape to SANs without the potential for performance bottlenecks. iSCSI networks are usually much slower than the FC networks which tape units were designed for, so the supported configurations for iSCSI to tape will be far more constrained than for Fibre Channel. Indeed, at the time of this writing there are no generally available and OEM supported iSCSI tape solutions at all. Similarly, vendors constrain end-to-end solutions when endpoints have not been tested with each other. This is because e.g. one vendor's multipathing driver may not work with another vendor's HBA driver. Changing the transport will not help with this. In fact, since iSCSI so-

---

[70] Assuming each host accesses one storage port. Note that the eight session per port limit is applicable to the router code available at the time of this writing, and that the router hardware is capable of expanding on this. However, there is evidence that the best practices will require relatively low per-portal oversubscription in any case.

lutions are so new to the market, they have the least testing and thus the least end-to-end support of any alternative...

Q: Does the service support iSCSI targets?

A: No. The platform hardware and software *architecture* can support iSCSI targets, but this has not been implemented yet due to a lack of demand.

Q: I understand that iSCSI doesn't have RSCNs. What happens when the virtual FC initiator representing an iSCSI host receives one?

A: iSCSI has an analogous mechanism known as an "iSCSI Asynchronous Event." The gateway translates RSCNs sent to portals and forwards them to the hosts.

Q: What is the definition of an iSCSI session?

A: In practical terms related to the Brocade gateway, a session is defined by one iSCSI host and one FC target port. The host can access as many LUNs on that single port as needed without creating another session, but if it needs to access a different storage port, another session will be used. This is important because all iSCSI products have a limit on the number of simultaneous sessions that can be supported.

Q: How do multiple gateways ensure that the IQN-to-WWN mapping for a host is consistent?

A: Using the Fabric Configuration Service. (FCS)

Q: What TCP port does the AP7420 use for the iSCSI Gateway Service?

A: Port 3260.

Q: What are "target portals," and how do they interact with IP addresses?

A: Each port has one iSCSI target portal, which may represent multiple FC targets. This is the bit of code that implements the translation between iSCSI and FC. Each port is assigned an IP address, which is used by iSCSI NICs to reach the portal.

FCIP Tunneling Service FAQ

Q: Does the FCR "connectivity with isolation" capability work across FCIP as well as FC-to-FC?

A: Not only does it work, it is the recommended deployment strategy. The FCIP VE_Ports become backbone fabric links between routers, with the fabrics at each site becoming edge fabrics.

Q: Is FCIP the recommended method for extending fabrics over distance?

A: No. It is one alternative, but from a technology standpoint, it is actually nearly the least attractive. (iFCP is less attractive than FCIP, given that it has all of the same issues plus it appears to be a dead end protocol.) The only situations in which extension over IP is appropriate are those in which alternative methods will not work.

Q: How does FCIP perform compared to other options?

A: It is the slowest. For example, a dark fiber link of around a hundred kilometers in length will never be slower than a few hundred microseconds, based on the speed of light through glass. Since nothing goes faster than light, it is not theoretically possible to design a faster transport. A similar IP WAN, on the other hand, typically has latencies several orders of magnitude slower than this, even when constructed with state-of-the-art equipment. It is for this reason that most IP network tools measure delay in milliseconds or even full seconds, rather than the microseconds or even mere nanoseconds typical of Fibre Channel solutions.

Q: Is the FCIP service tolerant of out of order delivery (OOD) in the IP WAN?

A: Yes. IP networks are prone to OOD, but FC devices require data in order, so gateways that tunnel over IP need to be able to reorder packets which are delivered out of order. The Brocade FCIP gateway has this feature. However, large amounts of OOD can affect performance.

Q: How frequently and for how long will the FCIP tunnel initiator attempt to connect to the far side?

A: It will retry every 20-25 seconds, and it will not give up.

Q: How does the FCIP service compare to other vendors' products like the CNT Ultra Edge 3000?

A: CNT has a special-purpose gateway that has been in production for quite some time. It is a strong product, and can be used in conjunction with the FCR service. This is appropriate if a customer needs CNT's value-added features (such as compression and tape pipelining) when a customer already has CNT equipment deployed, and when IP WAN distances are extremely long (many hundreds of miles) and/or WAN quality is low.

Q: How can I configure security for an FCIP tunnel?

A: Using *portCfgFCIP* *<port number> –w <WWN>* on each gateway will allow you to set the WWN of the switch that is allowed to connect to that FCIP port.

Q: How do I check to see if the service is working?

A: Use the *fcipShow <port number>* command. *portShow*, *switchShow*, *fabricShow*, *topologyShow*, and *supportShow* are also useful commands.

Q: Are buffer credits a concern for FCIP?

A: No, BB_Credits do not apply to FCIP. FCIP runs over TCP/IP/Ethernet, where the question for distance is whether you have enough memory at the port to hold frames across a bandwidth delay. Each port has lots of memory, so this is not the limiting factor for FCIP extension. The primary limiting factors are the delay and error rates of the IP network.

Q: How does FCIP as a protocol compare with e.g. FC over SONET/SDH, FC over ATM, or native FC?

A: It is less expensive and more widely available, but far less reliable and has much lower performance.

Q: Can the FCIP service support multipoint networks?

A: Yes. Simply configure one FCIP portal for each remote site. This is topologically like configuring separate ISLs within a single-site fabric. There are a number of clear availability and performance advantages to this approach. See Figure 34 (p88) and the surrounding text, and "Multipoint FCIP Links" starting on p169.

Q: What is a VE_Port?

A: FCIP tunnels form virtual ISLs. If these were real ISLs, they would have E_Ports at each end. Since they are virtual ISLs, they have virtual E_Ports at each end. (V.E.)

Section Two

Usage Cases

Section Topics

- Business Drivers for Each Service
- Implementation Mapped to Needs
- High-Level Deployment Examples
- Frequently Asked Questions

7: FC Router Usage

Business Drivers

The FC-FC Routing Service was created to solve the same business problems that drove Fibre Channel's creation. The main reasons to deploy SANs have historically been·increased asset utilization, centralized management, improved availability, better performance, and business continuity. Some examples of traditional SAN solutions include:

- Storage consolidation (disk or tape)
- Data migration (intra- or inter-site)
- High Availability clustering
- SAN-based system boot disks
- LAN-free backup and recovery
- Disaster recovery / business continuance
- Increased application performance

While Fibre Channel provides for all of those solution categories, the router *expands* such solutions significantly, delivering more fully on all value propositions of SANs. This chapter discusses how the router improves on some of these solutions in terms of:

- Scalability
- Reliability, availability, serviceability (RAS)
- Security
- Interoperability

It would be impractical to list all possible applications of FC routers vs. FC switches in much the same way that it would be impractical to list all possible applications of IP layer 3 switches vs. Ethernet layer 2 switches. Consequently, the examples in this section are intended to reflect broad *categories* of solutions, rather than being limited to specific configurations used in test labs. It can be assumed that these examples are *reasonable derivatives* of explicitly tested and supportable configurations.

Large Scale SANs

One of the drivers behind creating the router in the first place was SAN scalability. Metcalfe's Law broadly states that the value of a network grows exponentially as its size increases.[71] The larger a SAN becomes, the greater the value it provides to an organization. But it is also axiomatic that larger entities are harder to build and manage.

Data networks deal with this by breaking large networks into smaller, more manageable chunks using internetworking technologies such as routers and L3 IP switches. Scalability and manageability improvements are an inherent benefit of routed vs. flat networks. Network architects often create a hierarchy with subnets on the edge, routers or layer 3 switches at the backbone,[72] and connections to WANs still further out. The FCR allows a similar approach for designing large-scale SANs.

Figure 41 shows how a large Meta SAN could look when built around a redundant router backbone.

Because of the scalability and manageability advantages inherent to routed networks, customers planning large-scale deployments should follow the principles laid down by data

---

[71] http://encyclopedia.thefreedictionary.com/Metcalfe's%20Law

[72] The use of the word "backbone" in this context does not imply a *backbone fabric*, though optionally there may be one of those as well. Rather, "backbone" in this context refers to the relationship between routers and edge fabrics which is analogous to backbones and subnets in data networks.

network designers. Hierarchical networks tend to be designed from the backbone out rather than the reverse, and moving forward this is expected to be the method used to design scalable "green field"[73] SANs.

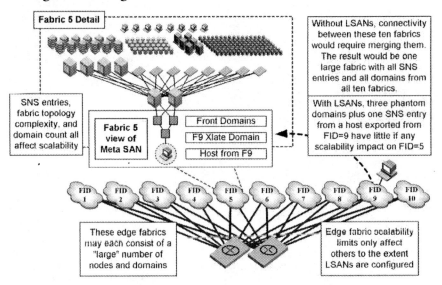

Figure 41 - Large Scale Meta SAN

In Figure 41, the designer started with a blank sheet of paper with two routers on the bottom and a set of hosts and storage on the top. They created the number and design of the edge fabrics last. Each edge fabric was limited to a maximum size. Perhaps the designer decided that e.g. 500 ports was enough for any given edge fabric based on their ability to manage that many devices in a single network. The number of hosts divided by hosts per fabric will yield the number of required edge fabrics.

Figure 41 also illustrates the scalability impact of the Meta SAN on Fabric 5, if one host from Fabric 9 were to be exported into Fabric 5. Even if every other edge fabric is as large and complex as Fabric 5, only a very small part of it is actually *seen* by Fabric 5. That fabric does not need to know

---

[73] "Green field" deployment means it is built from nothing, as opposed to built by modifying an existing production SAN.

abut zoning changes on other fabrics, or FSPF topology changes, or changes in the name server database. The router insulates edge fabrics from each other.

If, on the other hand, this network had been created as a single large fabric, every switch would require complete databases for all replicated fabric services. Things like zoning, FSPF, and the SNS could create timing and resource issues that could prevent the fabric from forming at all, or could create instability in some failure cases.

Table 3 - Large Scale SAN Solution Summary

Problem	Need to build large scale SANs
Traditional Fabrics	• Cannot scale as required • Would be unmanageable
FC Router	• Scalability problems are divided into smaller chunks • Manageability problems are contained within edge fabrics

SAN Island Consolidation

Millions of FC ports have been deployed in production environments. Some were deployed in large fabrics, but most were deployed in small unconnected fabrics referred to as SAN islands. In some cases this was deliberate; in others it happened as a side effect of the way switches were purchased.

There may be compelling reasons to link islands together. Sharing centralized resources, company-wide disaster recovery solutions, or indeed extending any of the solutions that drove the deployment of SANs in the first place may be causes to desire connectivity between islands.

Storage asset utilization in the pre-SAN datacenter was as low as 20%. For companies that moved to FC fabrics, this increased to 60% according to a recent survey of Brocade end users. This was a substantial improvement, but there still represented 40% unused space. Part of the reason was that many users had free space on different SAN islands vs. the hosts in need of it.[74]

Historically, storage administrators would solve this problem by merging SAN islands into large fabrics, but in many cases doing this would create an unsupportably large fabric. Even if islands could be merged without crossing fabric scalability limits, the process of doing so in a live production datacenter would be so logistically difficult and risky that it never would be considered by many customers.

The FC-FC Routing Service allows the interconnection of islands without needing to create massive fabrics, resolve domain conflicts, rework zoning configurations, or reconcile fabric-wide parameters such as Timeout Values (TOVs) and PID formats. Figure 42 illustrates one way that sixteen SAN islands could be interconnected with two FC routers.

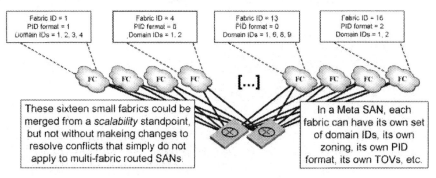

Figure 42 - Island Consolidation

This allows the sixteen fabrics to be connected without disruption. No software upgrades or configuration changes are required, and since routers never become principal

---

[74] The specifics of the statistical argument for SANs and Meta SANs depends on the survey used, which is usually the case with such arguments. For example, "The Storage Report – Customer Perspectives & Industry Evolution" shows an increase of 40% to 50% when moving from DAS to SAN. This was a joint report from Merrill Lynch and McKinsey published 19 June 2001. All industry reports agree that SANs greatly increase utilization; just the amount of the increase varies by analysis, as does the remaining inefficiency.

switches in an edge fabric, there will not even be a fabric re-configuration.

Table 4 – SAN Island Consolidation Solution Summary

Problem	Need to connect SAN islands
Traditional Fabrics	• Too hard to resolve conflicts • May not scale well enough
FC Router	• Makes conflicts irrelevant • Separates scalability between fabrics

Side Note

One of the business reasons frequently given for pursuing an island consolidation strategy is the need to "wire once."

Many customers have a large number of isolated fabrics, with 100% localization of traffic. This works very well until something changes in the environment. Perhaps an application needs more disk space than is available on its island, or needs to be moved onto a host on another island. Whatever the cause, 100% locality degrades over time and off-fabric connectivity is eventually needed. This progression of an environment away from its initial state order is known as "operational entropy," and it seems to be almost as inevitable in IT departments as is the principal of physics from which its name is derived.

Historically, the most common method of dealing with this involved having an administrator run down to a data center and re-cable the fabrics whenever cross-fabric connectivity was required. This could involve re-architecting and merging fabrics, with the attendant risk of downtime. With the router, it is finally possible for the connectivity to be wired into place ahead of time, and provisioned "on the fly" via LSANs... without needing to leave the administrator's desk.

Side Note

The light-weight EX_Port fabric services design in conjunction with FC-NAT allows router installation to be non-disruptive. If it attached to edge fabrics as a full member, subtle differences implementations could create compatibility issues requiring upgrades or unplanned downtime on edge fabrics. Without FC-NAT, domain ID conflicts would need to be resolved, as well as other conflicts like TOVs. The Brocade approach was designed from the ground up to attach to installed base production fabrics as gracefully as possible. An absence of FC-NAT or a presence of full participation in edge fabrics is a sign of architectural design flaws guaranteed to cause issues. One vendor has its "router" ports fully participate in edge fabrics and does not implement FC-NAT. Caveat Emptor.

Centralized Disaster Recovery

There are any number of business drivers that could cause an enterprise to implement a disaster recovery solution. It may be driven by fear of terrorism, by government regulations, or simply an understanding that natural and human disasters are part of life. Whatever the cause, if a company decides to build a disaster recovery site, it is generally necessary to move large amounts of storage data between that site and the primary location(s) on an ongoing basis. Storage networks provide an ideal solution for this problem.

However, creating one fabric that spans between the sites could be counter-productive. A disaster at one site could cause instability in the fabric at any other site. A problem at the disaster recovery site could *cause* a disaster at a production location!

The router keeps the production network separated from the disaster recovery network so that a disaster does not take down both sites at once. Figure 43 shows one way this could be configured.

127

This example connects four sites to a central site using SONET/SDH. It could just as easily use FCIP or *x*WDMs. Either way, the router would provide substantial advantages, and not just because of the FCR feature. With FCIP, the router could also be the gateway. With *x*WDM or native Fibre Channel over dark fiber, the large per-port buffer credit count would allow greater performance over distance.

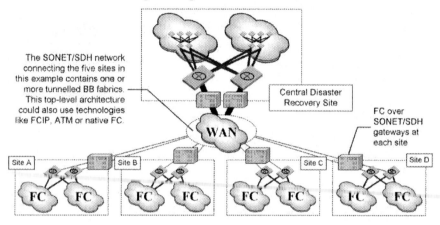

Figure 43 - Disaster Recovery Solution

Table 5 - Centralized DR Solution Summary

Problem	Need DR solution for company
Traditional Fabrics	• Sites have different management • WAN faults can affect production
FC Router	• Sites retain own management • Faults are isolated

Disk and Tape Consolidation

Some enterprise storage subsystems are extremely expensive. A single enterprise-class tape library or RAID array may cost in excess of a million US dollars. It is no wonder that one of the "killer apps" of storage networks is that they allow centralization and thus better utilization of storage and backup resources. IT organizations are interested in leveraging these capital investments across as many hosts as possible.

While Fibre Channel already provides for this category of solution, the router can extend the benefits through island consolidation, distance extension, and overall scalability.

For example, a datacenter may have many isolated SAN islands each with its own backup solution. Or perhaps the backup solution is centralized, but uses – and abuses – the primary LAN instead of the SAN. Using the router, the SAN islands can access centralized backup devices, thus reducing backup and restore times, administrative overhead, and the number of drives needed. The router allows each island to retain its own domain ID space etc.. Figure 44 shows how a tape consolidation solution might look.

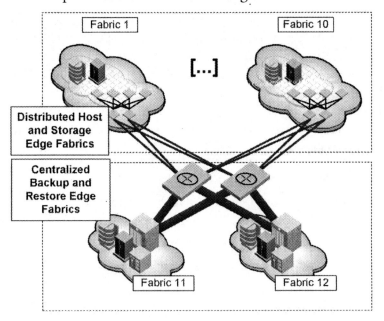

Figure 44 - Tape Consolidation

In this example, ten islands share a central backup/restore pool consisting of two fabrics and the attached storage subsystems. More edge fabrics could be consolidated using different Meta SAN topologies.

One advantage of this approach is that it does not tie together the management of the different edge fabrics, and does not allow connectivity between edge fabrics unless explicitly desired. This is important because the different SAN islands may not have a need for or derive any benefit from connectivity to anything except the central backup solution, and indeed might suffer if they were joined into a single management model. This is discussed in more detail under Inter-Island Security later in this chapter.

 ## Side Note

This example came from a real customer deployment. The customer calculated that they could save tens of thousands of dollars per month by consolidating tape libraries. Their backup software was able to consolidate whitespace on backups, which reduced daily tape consumption. In addition to buying fewer tapes, they needed to spend less money on off-site vaulting. The recurring high ROI of the tape consolidation solution more than covered the entire router infrastructure investment, allowing other FCR solutions to be implemented without additional cost-justification.

Table 6 – Tape Consolidation Solution Summary

Problem	Need to leverage tape resources across many fabrics
Traditional Fabrics	• Effort/risk to merge fabrics • Allows connectivity where *not* desired
FC Router	• Does not merge fabrics • Only provides connectivity where explicitly desired and configured

Large Buildings and CANs

Sometime there are geographical considerations other than distance that cause a routed network to be desired. In many enterprises, IT departments deploy hierarchical networks with subnets based on the floor of a building, or the building in a campus.

Campus Area Networks, or *CANs*, are distinguished from LANs because they tend to have thinner connections between buildings, tend to use optical rather than copper cabling to support longer distances, and tend to have intra-building locality. They are distinguished from *MANs* in that they have thicker connectivity, do not generally require devices like WDMs, and tend to have *less* locality. I.e. a CAN is somewhere between a LAN and a MAN in most ways.

Often this is done to facilitate manageability, but it also has performance and reliability implications. There is often a degree of locality in data networks, and the same can be true of SANs. Servers and their primary storage may be co-located within a building, but need network access to backup and disaster recovery resources in a central location. In this case, the local fabric would be isolated from performance or reliability issues on other fabrics, while still providing the needed connectivity. Figure 45 shows a campus SAN designed around a router backbone.

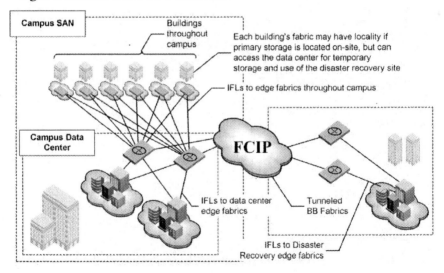

Figure 45 - CAN and Disaster Recovery WAN

In this example, the campus consists of seven buildings. The primary datacenter has two medium-size fabrics in a redundant configuration. Each of those fabrics is connected via IFLs (E_Port to EX_Port links) to each router. Additional

131

IFLs go to switches located in each other campus building. This allows servers and storage located throughout the campus to access resources in the datacenter.

The datacenter routers also use the integrated FCIP Tunneling Service to connect to a Disaster Recovery (DR) site. The tunneled connections are E_Ports, so the IP WAN contains one or two backbone fabrics depending on the configuration. At the far end, two more routers provide the other side of the FCIP link, and IFLs to the disaster recovery fabric(s). This means that all seven buildings in the campus also have access to the DR site.

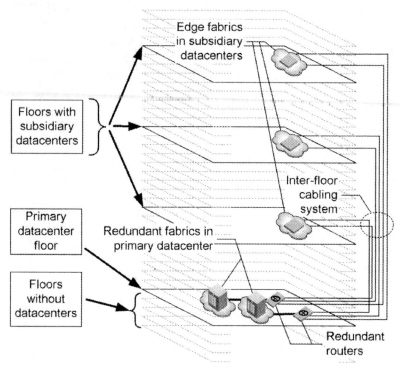

Figure 46 – Large Building Meta SAN

Similar examples can be made for large buildings. Figure 46 shows how a router could provide a backbone if datacenters were spread throughout the floors of a skyscraper. Like the CAN example, this is a technique that has been used in data networks for years.

This also shows a hybrid Meta SAN redundancy model. The subsection entitled Redundant Meta SAN Designs in the SAN Design chapter discusses redundant and resilient Meta SANs. This diagram shows the two primary datacenter edge fabrics connected as in one of the redundant models, while the edge fabrics in subsidiary datacenters are connected as in the resilient models.

Table 7 – Building / Campus Solution Summary

Problem	Connect fabrics separated by campus / large building distances
Traditional Fabrics	• Manageability domains are merged between datacenters • Inter-datacenter net may not be reliable·
FC Router	• Keeps manageability separate • Isolates fabrics between datacenters

Extended Distance Fabrics

As mentioned in the DR example above, creating one fabric that spans between production and DR sites could actually *cause* a disaster. This could happen if a WAN link were to become unstable, causing ISLs within the network to "flap," or if an RSCN storm in the DR site propagated to the production fabric. Furthermore, scalability limits associated with timing are exacerbated when high latency distance links are used. The router can be used to isolate the production SAN from the such problems.

It is possible to use the integrated FCIP capabilities of the Multiprotocol Router to extend distance, but it is sometimes better to use external gateways. For one thing, the performance and reliability of even the best IP networks cannot compare to native Fibre Channel connections. If a distance extension application requires better connection quality than IP can provide, it would be more appropriate to use link extenders, WDMs, or FC to SONET/SDH gateways. Attaching the router to these gateways is still beneficial because it provides inter-site isolation and scalability. Instabilities in the MAN or WAN will not cause instability on any edge fabric.

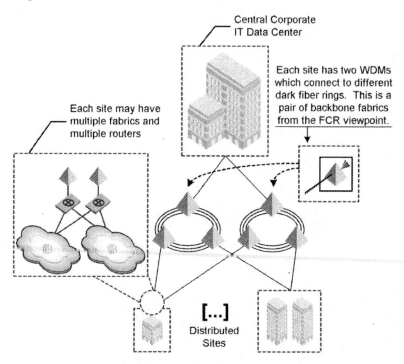

Figure 47 - MAN Using WDMs

Figure 47 shows how a MAN extension might look using *x*WDMs. In this example, several sites within a metropolitan area are connected with wave division multiplexers. These allow many optical signals to be carried over one physical cable by shifting the frequency of laser light. Each site has two routers. Each router has several E_Ports connected to the WDM mapped either to an A or a B backbone fabric.

This solution also takes advantage of the large number of buffer-to-buffer credits available on the router. It can achieve native Fibre Channel links near line rate at up to 300km, which is far beyond other similar solutions.

Table 8 – Extended Distance Solution Summary

Problem	Connect fabrics over wide distances
Traditional Fabrics	• MAN/WAN issues affect fabrics • Scalability of each site affects others
FC Router	• Backbone fabrics crossing MAN/WAN do not impact edge fabrics • Sites scale independently except to the extent LSANs are configured

Inter-Island Security

· There is an oft-quoted rule of thumb in network security that 80% of break-ins are internal. Using a SAN that is totally disconnected from general-purpose IP networks is a good start for security, but in some cases it is not enough.

For example, there may be SANs that belong to different departments. Perhaps payroll and accounting information is kept on one SAN island and manufacturing data on another. Different administrators are responsible for each SAN, and different access control procedures are in place for each. It would be against security policy for administrators of the manufacturing SAN to have access to the accounting databases. Since there is no need for servers from one SAN to access the other, one solution is simply not to connect the fabrics at all.

However, there could be a centralized IT business continuance solution to which both departments need access. Figure 48 shows this scenario. By using the router to connect the islands, administrative separation is maintained between edge fabrics while selective connectivity to the central resource is achieved. Even if one department's administrator were to make the router export a device without the cooperation of the other (which should be impossible) they would still be unable to access it, since zoning in the remote fabric would prevent communication from occurring. This is a "belt and suspenders" security model.

135

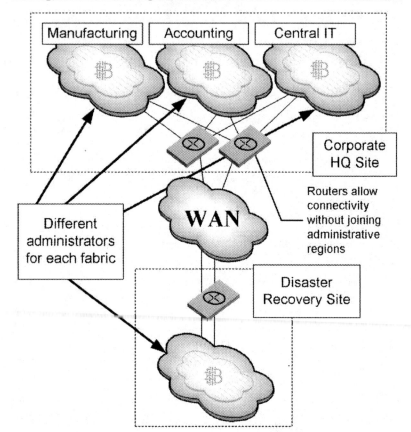

Figure 48 - Administrative Separation Meta SAN

Table 9 – Inter-Island Security Solution Summary

Problem	Connectivity but isolated management
Traditional Fabrics	• Must tie some degree of management to get connectivity • Solutions like VSANs and account rights do not solve the whole problem
FC Router	• Keeps administration *totally* separate between fabrics • Allows only connectivity that all administrators have agreed to configure

Data and Server Migration

Moving data is a full time job in many enterprises. Drivers for data and server migrations include:

- Storage arrays come off lease and/or need to be upgraded to newer technology on a continual basis
- Servers are obsoleted or repurposed
- Volumes fill and need to be moved to larger subsystems
- Corporate mergers and acquisitions or internal restructuring may require merging datacenters
- Application usage patterns change over time

Whatever the cause, it is frequently necessary to move data sets between arrays, or change the host to storage mappings. In environments consisting of separate fabrics, this is difficult or impossible. Merging fabrics on a temporary basis is one solution, but that entails administrative effort and risk.

The FC–FC Routing Service can solve the problem more effectively in two ways:

1. By consolidating islands in an enterprise on a permanent basis. This is a good approach for customers with recurring data movement. See Figure 42 (p125).
2. By consolidating only the islands that have data movement needs on a temporary basis. If an enterprise does not need to move data often, they may wish to buy one router and install it between different fabrics on an as-needed basis. Some may wish to outsource the operation. Many SAN consulting organizations own routers and can bring the hardware in as part of a data movement contract. Figure 49 illustrates this.

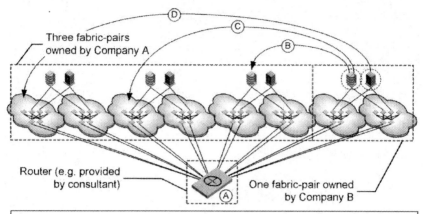

Each step of the migration process can be performed at leisure, a small portion at a time, rather that requiring a single large and risky step.

A. The router is installed and configured by the consultant, or temporarily allocated by the Company A storage group.
B. Data is copied from Company B's SAN to Company A's data center. The hosts at Company B continue to serve applications, but access their data across the router. This might be accomplished with host-based mirroring, so that both local and remote copies are available during transition.
C. Once data movement is complete, Company B storage arrays are repurposed in the Company A data center or are scrapped.
D. Finally, the Company B hosts are moved to the Company A data center. They may continue serving their applications or may be repurposed.

Figure 49 – Data Migration During Merger or Acquisition

Table 10 – Data and Server Migration Solution Summary

Problem	Need temporary connectivity while performing migration
Traditional Fabrics	• Disruption: resolve conflicts / reboot hosts • Risk: many changes at once
FC Router	• No need to merge • Spreads changes over time

Side Note

Not only do edge fabrics have limited visibility into each other, but the routers themselves know very little about edge fabrics. Such knowledge is not needed by the router because it is guaranteed to be on the border of a fabric.

For example, when an EX_Port receives a zoning update, the router scans for LSAN zones and discards everything that does not start with "LSAN_". If this were an E_Port on a regular FC fabric switch, it would need the complete zoning database, but as a router, it is certain that only LSAN zones are relevant. This means that the router does not need to have "infinite RAM and CPU resources," or similarly unrealistic characteristics in order to support many large edge fabrics in a Meta SAN. Optimizations are provided for all fabric services, which is why the router (a) is scalable and (b) has an EX_Port architecture referred to as "E_Port Lite." This approach also simplifies compatibility and quality assurance testing, since EX_Ports interact with edge fabrics in a limited way.

This is a key advantage for the Brocade approach. One other vendor has their "router" ports fully participate in all fabrics, which obviates most of the advantages of moving to a routed architecture. They give each fabric its own daemon set, but they all run the same daemon versions, use the same CP, RAM, and underlying OS, and this OS needs to know everything about every fabric. This does not address scalability, compatibility, rolling firmware upgrades or fault containment. This same vendor retains inter-fabric dependencies like domain ID uniqueness which prevents nondisruptive installation in the installed base, uses proprietary VSAN tagging to ensure maximum hardware-level incompatibility with all other FC vendors, and has not provided the required support for FC-NAT technology.

Caveat Emptor.

8: iSCSI Gateway Usage

Business Drivers

As discussed in the chapter entitled "iSCSI Gateway Overview," the iSCSI protocol had a rocky start in the industry. Recently, a number of iSCSI vendors either have been acquired at a loss to their investors or have simply gone out of business. In one well-publicized case, both happened: an iSCSI vendor was acquired by a large data networking company, and the acquiring company was then forced to close them down due to a lack of sales.

While the SCSI over IP concept seems simple in principal, practical difficulties have prevented it from gaining traction. For example, the price to performance ratio of iSCSI TOE-accelerated HBAs is not compelling compared to Fibre Channel HBAs: at best iSCSI over Gigabit Ethernet can attain half the throughput of 2Gbit Fibre Channel, and the gap is increasing. At the time of this writing, 4Gbit Fibre Channel at cost parity with 2Gbit FC is close on the horizon. And the iSCSI promise of using a single network for all data and storage traffic has proven to be illusory, since performance, security, and reliability considerations dictate separating data and storage networks whether running FC or iSCSI.

On the other hand, some servers are worth less than the cost of either a traditional Fibre Channel HBA *or* TOE accelerated iSCSI NIC. Even low cost Fibre Channel HBAs may be too expensive, and some hosts may not even have a free slot to install one in. But such a host might have one or more built in and unused Ethernet interfaces.

141

As a result, the "killer app" for iSCSI seems to be providing connectivity for hosts not deemed valuable enough to warrant Fibre Channel connections. End user demand for just this usage case drove the creation of the Brocade iSCSI Gateway Service.

Low-End Storage Consolidation

Many IT organizations classify servers into tiers. Top-tier servers are mission critical: downtime can cost millions of dollars an hour. Perhaps a manufacturing line is dependant on a top-tier server. Lower down are servers for which limited downtime is inconvenient, but for which there is a less direct financial impact, such as a workgroup email server. Below this are servers that may have duplicated services, such as DNS, WINS, or NIS. Downtime for individual servers may not be noticed, but the *services* are critical. Finally, there are servers for which downtime is simply no issue. Examples include personal web servers, or business applications that are used only rarely. [75]

Even for the lowest tier applications, there may be a benefit from consolidating storage onto centralized subsystems. For example, this may facilitate backup, disaster recovery, and capacity planning. Figure 50 shows one way that the iSCSI gateway can allow stranded servers access to Fibre Channel fabrics.

This customer has a pair of fabrics with perhaps 500 nodes each. These are used for storage consolidation. There are perhaps 100 more servers that could benefit from connections to the fabrics, but for which HBAs would be too expensive. The user calculated performance and resource requirements to determine how many links were needed, and found that one gateway would suffice. They chose to deploy

---

[75] Note that low-end storage consolidation is already a large market served well by Fibre Channel technology today. iSCSI would be more properly considered appropriate for lowest end storage consolidation.

redundant gateways to ensure that a single outage would not impact all 100 servers.

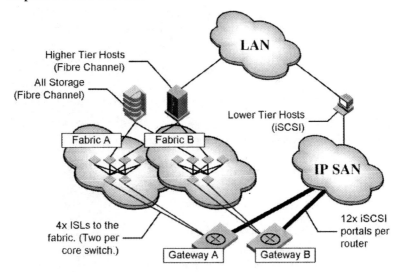

Figure 50 - iSCSI Storage Consolidation

Table 11 – Low-End Consolidation Solution Summary

Problem	Provide access to Fibre Channel disks for lowest-tier hosts
Traditional Fabrics	• Fibre Channel HBAs are too expensive and may require unavailable PCI slots • Fibre Channel performance and reliability aren't needed for these servers
FC Router	• Can use "free" Gigabit Ethernet ports already on motherboards • Allows isolated IP SAN approach to provide sufficient reliability

Low-End Distance Extension

For customers with stranded servers, FCIP will often provide good performance and the most economical method for integrating the stranded servers into the SAN. However, in some cases there will be very few servers in each of many different locations, and the servers will not have high-performance or high-reliability requirements. In these cases, iSCSI may provide a more practical solution.

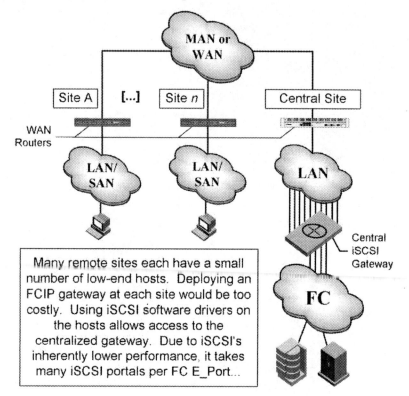

Figure 51 - Low-End iSCSI Distance Solution

This example shows many stranded sites, each with just a few low-priority hosts. Rather than install HBAs and FCIP gateways at each site, this customer installed an iSCSI gateway at the central site and used software iSCSI drivers at the remote sites.

Note that there are availability considerations with this design in addition to the cost vs. performance trade-offs: if an iSCSI driver malfunctioned at one of the remote sites, it could potentially impact the larger IP network. This design technique should therefore be approach with caution.

Table 12 – Low-End Extension Solution Summary

Problem	Connect many small low-tier sites to a central Fibre Channel SAN
Traditional Fabrics	• Dark fiber may be unavailable, and hosts may not warrant FC HBAs • FCIP requires one or more gateways at each site, and FC HBAs in all servers
FC Router	• Can use IP network if reliability and performance are sufficient • Only needs a gateway at the central site, not at the distributed sites

Low-End Disaster Recovery

Low-end servers that might be iSCSI candidates are often not considered important enough to warrant elaborate disaster recovery solutions. However, in some cases they are protected just for the sake of completeness. Figure 52 shows how such a solution might look.

In this example, a customer has a primary datacenter ("Production Site") with an FCIP disaster recovery solution already in place for the mission-critical applications and tape backups. That datacenter also has a number of lower-tier applications that could be included in the DR solution if possible. In addition, they have satellite offices each with a small number of lowest-tier applications.

To solve the connectivity problem, gateways are installed in the existing DR fabric at both the primary datacenter location and the DR site. iSCSI hosts at any site can access DR-protected storage through either gateway, so if a disaster causes them to lose access to the production site gateways they can continue to serve their applications through the DR site gateways.

Note that there are technical issues associated with using the iSCSI protocol to access tape drives. Tape solutions simply do not react well to the network performance issues inherent with iSCSI. Unless answers are found to these problems – which is by no means certain – the DR solution must involve RAID or JBOD storage, rather than tape.

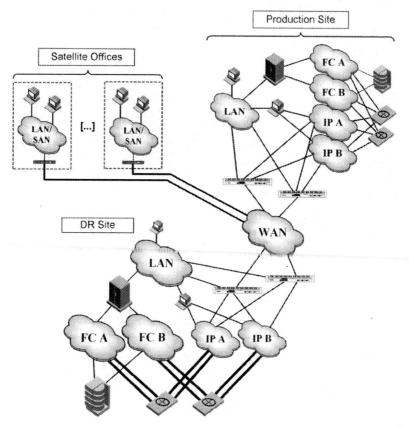

Figure 52 - iSCSI DR Solution

Table 13 – Low-End DR Solution Summary

Problem	Connect low–end hosts to DR solution
Traditional Fabrics	• Hosts do not warrant HBAs from perform-ance or reliability standpoints • May be in locations without dark fiber
FC Router	• Uses existing NICs • Uses existing wiring

Low-End Cluster Server

This is another case where the performance and reliability vs. cost tradeoff could be made entirely in favor of cost. This customer has a large number of cluster servers running middle-tier applications. Since the servers duplicate functions, the reliability of any individual server is not a priority. Since they are running middle-tier Windows applications, performance is not a consideration. Figure 53 illustrates how the architecture might look when using an existing Fibre Channel SAN to provide storage for these clusters.

It was critical that all members of the cluster not lose access to storage simultaneously – perhaps due to a broadcast storm on the IP SAN or some other common denial of service event – so this customer used their IP LAN as a secondary iSCSI network.

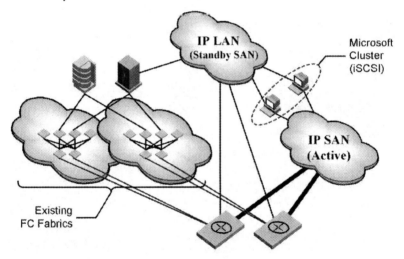

Figure 53 - iSCSI Cluster Solution

This would not be a good approach for sustained usage because the iSCSI solution could harm the production LAN or vice versa, but in this case the LAN would be used only in extreme failure cases. Note that careful consideration would need to be paid to security on the LAN to prevent hackers from bypassing security measures on the servers. In environments where security is a concern, it would be preferable to deploy a second iSCSI SAN, as illustrated in Figure 54. A similar network is also shown in Figure 27 (p66).

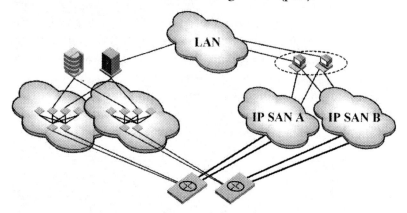

Figure 54 - iSCSI Cluster Solution Improved

Table 14 – Low-End Cluster Solution Summary

Problem	Allow nodes in cluster to share disk
Traditional Fabrics	• Too expensive for low-end clusters • Will take downtime to install HBAs
FC Router	• Uses cheaper components across the board • GigE interfaces already in hosts can be configured without downtime

9: FCIP Tunnel Usage

Business Drivers

In the wake of recent global events, corporations and government agencies alike have been focusing more on disaster recovery and business continuance solutions. In some cases, such solutions are driven in fiduciary duty, while in others regulations mandate their presence. Storage networks that span distance are a natural fit for such deployments.

In addition, recent economic trends have caused IT departments to find ways to do more with fewer resources. Better utilization of enterprise-class storage systems has been a driving force behind SAN growth, and distance extension technologies allow these benefits to span sites. These same trends have caused some companies to look at mergers or acquisitions and datacenter consolidation, which has created demand for site-to-site data migration solutions.

The preferred approaches for extending Fibre Channel over distance are based on higher performance and reliability technologies such as dark fiber, xWDMs, ATM, or SONET/SDH gateways. However, there are cases where these solutions are either unavailable or prohibitively expensive. If a high performance IP network with a high reliability service level agreement is available, FCIP can be used instead to solve these business problems.

Disaster Recovery

Disaster planning includes strategies like disaster tolerance or recovery and off site backups. FCIP facilitates this by al-

149

lowing solutions to span wider areas than native Fibre Channel can support. FCIP/FCR integration further facilitates these solutions by preventing WAN or remote fabric instabilities from affecting production fabrics. Figure 55 shows a centralized off-site backup and recovery solution using the router, with data replication as well.

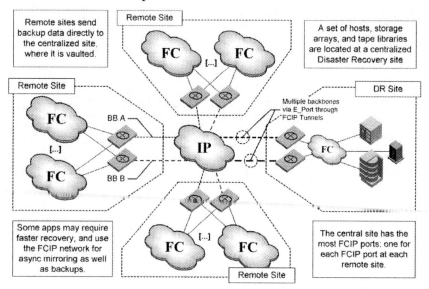

Figure 55 – Disaster Recovery with FCIP

There are three or more sites, each with two or more fabrics using the centralized site for disaster recovery. Applications at remote sites mount tape drives at the central site and write backups directly to the off site location for vaulting. Some applications use the DR connections for volume replication so that they can quickly recover to a "last transaction" state to servers at the central site. The routers at the central site have an FCIP port for each remote FCIP port, forming two backbone fabrics. All site fabrics are edge fabrics. See Figure 40 (p97) for similar fabric topologies.

Table 15 – Disaster Planning Solution Summary

Problem	Need disaster recovery
Traditional Fabrics	• Instabilities at other sites could *cause* a disaster at the production site • Other WAN technologies may be too expensive to deploy
FC Router	• FCR integration isolates sites from each other and the WAN • Integrated FCIP lowers TCO

Site Consolidation

FCIP can be used when SANs must be connected over distance, but higher performance and more reliable solutions such as Fibre Channel over dark fiber or WDMs are unavailable. Such connectivity might be needed for site-to-site consolidation. FCIP solutions can facilitate consolidations during reorganizations, facilities relocations, and equipment reallocations. Figure 56 illustrates such a solution.

When the company in this example was growing rapidly during the late 1990s, they acquired several startups and smaller companies in the same state, but in different cities. Each had their own buildings, IT infrastructures, and organizations, so the company now has several legacy datacenters throughout the region. To save on facilities and operational costs, they have decided to consolidate their datacenters down to just two: one primary site and one for disaster recovery.

However, it is not possible for them to shut down operations at the remote datacenters for extended periods of time to perform an offline migration because they are serving mission-critical functions for their business units. A massive simultaneous migration would also require considerable use of temporary contractors for IT staffing, and would be risky.

151

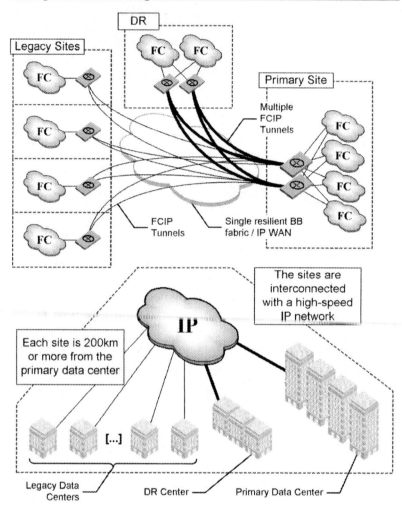

Figure 56 - FCIP Site Consolidation

The company therefore will use the router to connect the SANs at each site so that one application at a time can be migrated opportunistically over whatever overall time period is required. The routers will continue to be used after the migration to provide disaster recovery connectivity and to route between fabrics at the two remaining sites.

Note that this example uses a single resilient backbone fabric across the IP network. If the network were being used for mission-critical traffic, a redundant backbone would be preferable.

Finally, note that connectivity between the primary and the disaster recovery sites is "thicker" than between the primary and the legacy sites. This is to support ongoing data replication and backup applications. There might be just one FCIP tunnel between each primary router and each legacy site, but two or more from the primary to the disaster site routers.

Table 16 – Site Consolidation Solution Summary

Problem	Migrate data between sites during consolidation process
Traditional Fabrics	• Different sites may have incompatible fabric parameters such as domain IDs • Large scale simultaneous changes involve too much risk to production
FC Router	• FCR feature allows domain conflicts • Allows migration procedures to spread changes out over time

CAN/MAN Resource Utilization

In CAN or MAN environments, it may be desirable to use FCIP to gain better utilization of storage resources in much the same way that native Fibre Channel fabrics are used for storage consolidation.[76] The difference is that FCIP solutions tend to employ a high degree of locality on each end of the link. Provisioning of storage across the link is done to satisfy temporary provisioning requirements, to allow access to production data for development servers, to provide scratch disks, and for other similar low priority tasks.

---

[76] Due to the inherent performance limitations of any IP SAN solution (i.e. they degrade over distance much faster than other approaches) using WANs in this way is not advisable.

For example, there may be an excess of free storage in one datacenter within a campus, and a critical shortage in another. Waiting until more storage can be added to the second datacenter is not acceptable due to the critical nature of the shortage and the length of purchasing cycles. The traditional solution would be to merge the fabrics in the different datacenters using dark fiber. The router's FC-FC Routing Service can improve on dark fiber solutions as shown in Figure 47 (p134) through Figure 46 (p132), and many similar examples. However, if dark fiber is *not* available between the datacenters, FCIP may solve this problem, as shown in Figure 57.

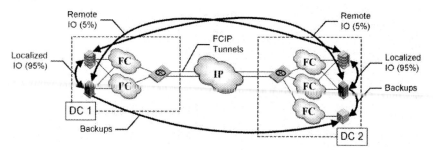

Figure 57 – Resource Sharing Across Campus with FCIP

The campus in this example has two large datacenters. The geographical separation is a result of how the campus IT environment grew; it does not imply separation of function or administration. Each center has roughly the same number of hosts and storage arrays, they are administered by the same people, and they serve the same kinds of applications to the same user community. If dark fiber were available, the administrators would simply share fabrics.

Since dark fiber is *not* available, the datacenters are connected with routers and FCIP. The administrators can still manage the Meta SAN from a single point by using Fabric Manager or a similar external multi-fabric aware management application.

They will continue to employ locality within each datacenter: each host and its primary storage will be on the same

154

end of the FCIP link. By connecting them as in the figure, the SAN administrators gain several advantages. For example, they can:

- Temporarily allocate storage between centers.
- Facilitate data migrations between the centers.
- Consolidate backups for the two datacenters.

Table 17 – CAN/MAN Sharing Solution Summary

Problem	Share storage array resources between sites separated by CAN/MAN distances
Traditional Fabrics	• High locality means that 2Gbit Fibre Channel performance is excessive • May not have dark fiber available for native Fibre Channel links
FC Router	• Lower performance IP links sufficient and potentially less expensive • FCIP uses existing IP infrastructure, while FCR keeps IP instabilities separate from edge fabrics

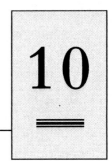

10: Combined Services Usage

Business Drivers

It is possible to combine the different router functions within a single platform.[77] There are many reasons a user may want to do this. For example:

- One service can enhance another. Take the FCR/FCIP integration in the Multiprotocol Router. The two services solve very different problems, but when combined, both are improved: FCIP allows Meta SANs to span longer distances, and FCR allows FCIP to be more reliable and scalable.

- Platforms have overhead built into them in the form of power, cooling, management interfaces, chassis mechanicals, and the CP complex that runs the operating system. If this is leveraged across more functions, the total cost tends to be lower.

- More integration means less equipment: Fewer things to manage, fewer support contracts, fewer vendor relationships, less rack space and power used, and fewer training requirements.

Certain combined usage cases have been discussed in previous chapters. Many examples throughout this book show combinations of FCR and FCIP, and some combine FCIP and iSCSI. This chapter discusses those combinations, but

---

[77] Some limitations may apply. As always, contact the appropriate support provider before deploying complex configurations.

also includes all other combinations and the reasons to consider using any of them.

Combined iSCSI/FCIP Solution

Some environments require SAN over IP extension for both high and low tier applications. For example, a datacenter might provide services to a remote site for disaster recovery of mission-critical UNIX systems and to branch office sites for lowest-tier Windows systems. This solution type is shown in Figure 20 (p54).

In addition, it is possible for one environment to need an FCIP distance solution and also have low-end hosts that can benefit from SAN access, not for distance, but to provide cost effective *local* connectivity. Figure 58 shows this category of solution.

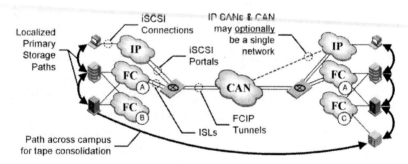

Figure 58 – FCIP and iSCSI Combination

In this example, a campus has two production datacenters, each with a redundant pair of Fibre Channel fabrics. There is no dark fiber available between them, but there is a reliable IP network. The SAN administrators have used FCIP to merge the "A" fabrics from the two datacenters to consolidate backups. The "B" and "C" fabrics remain separate to prevent IP SAN instabilities from affecting both of the redundant fabrics at the same time. As a result, there are really three fabrics: one isolated in each datacenter and one spanning between the two. The iSCSI hosts access Fibre Channel storage locally within their datacenters using an IP SAN for fan-in. (They may or may not be connected to the

IP campus network. For highest reliability, they should not be connected unless traffic patterns truly require it.)

There are two traditional solutions to this problem:

1. Use Fibre Channel HBAs for the low-end hosts. Historically, there were cost barriers for HBAs that might make iSCSI attractive despite its performance, reliability, and security flaws. This is not always the case now, as HBA prices are dropping rapidly, so be sure to check for availability of low cost HBAs before deploying iSCSI.

2. Use separate special purpose iSCSI and FCIP gateways. The cost of deploying separate gateways is likely to consume much if not all of the savings on HBAs, so the value proposition of this is suspect.

Table 18 – iSCSI/FCIP Solution Summary

Problem	Need both to connect low-end hosts and extend fabrics
Traditional Solutions	• HBAs may be too expensive • Multiple external gateways for iSCSI / FCIP hard to manage and expensive
FC Router	• iSCSI uses built-in GigE ports • Combined solution saves on TCO

Combined FCIP/FCR Solution

It is of course unacceptable for a disaster recovery to cause downtime for a production environment. However, without isolation between production, pre-production, and remote disaster recovery fabrics, exactly that can happen. It is axiomatic that IP links are less reliable than Fibre Channel links, and IP WAN links still less so. Since disaster recovery solutions are inherently wide area in nature this can introduce an unstable element into an otherwise reliable network. By combining the distance extension capabilities of FCIP with the fault isolation characteristics of FCR, this can be avoided.

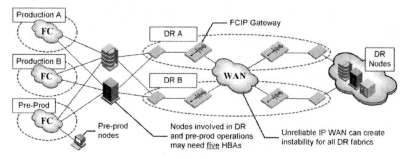

Figure 59 - DR *Without* FCIP/FCR Integration

In the example in Figure 59, a company has solved the problem by using completely separate A/B fabric pairs for their production SAN vs. their disaster recovery solution, and another totally separate fabric for pre-production.

While this does guarantee that a disturbance on pre-production or disaster recovery fabrics will not be disruptive to the production SAN, this does not provide easy sharing of resources. There is no connectivity at all between fabrics unless at least some or all hosts and storage arrays have five SAN connections each. It also requires the use and management of expensive external FCIP gateways.

Figure 60 shows a better approach. Using the router with both FCIP and FCR licenses installed, a dual redundant Meta SAN is implemented.

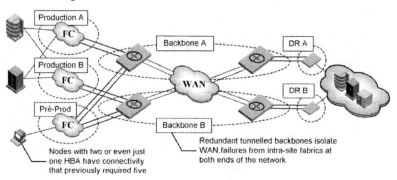

Figure 60 - DR *With* FCIP/FCR Integration

160

This solution provides the required fault isolation between each fabric, retains the fully redundant A/B model, but still allows connectivity to be configured as needed. Hosts and storage can communicate across all fabrics, but now only need two HBAs for fully redundant operation. There are still five fabrics, but the FC routers allow cross-fabric communication, and also save cost by eliminating the need for external gateways. In short, this solution provides better connectivity with equal fault isolation for substantially less cost.

The traditional solution – using special-purpose external FCIP gateways – can be combined with the FCR service as well. This is recommended if performance is critical on each FCIP link, the WAN has performance and stability issues, or extremely long distances are being covered. In this case, the router does not use its own FCIP capabilities: it connects to external gateway (s) using E_Ports, and the external gateway(s) can handle the protocol tunneling.

Table 19 – FCIP/FCR Solution Summary

Problem	Extend fabrics over distance
Traditional Solutions	• WAN or remote fabric instabilities can affect all sites, and different sites administered by different people • Cost of external gateways plus routers excessive both to buy and manage
FC Router	• Isolates faults and admin domains • Integrated solution saves cost both initially and on an ongoing basis

Combined iSCSI/FCR Solution

Customers can deploy production-quality solutions using FCR and try out less trustworthy iSCSI solutions on the same platform without risk to production environments. The router places virtual initiators for iSCSI hosts onto the *backbone fabric* of the router. Production edge fabrics are isolated from this by EX_Ports, so instabilities on the backbone do not propagate to edges. By attaching a few ports of a multi-port Fibre Channel array to the backbone and the rest to production edge fabrics, iSCSI hosts can get access to the same array as the production servers using a totally different fabric and a different set of array ports. When the IP SAN or iSCSI drivers on the hosts have problems, no part of the production data path will be affected. Figure 61 shows this solution. Note that the storage ports could potentially be connected directly to the gateways: an external FC fabric switch is not necessarily required for the backbone.

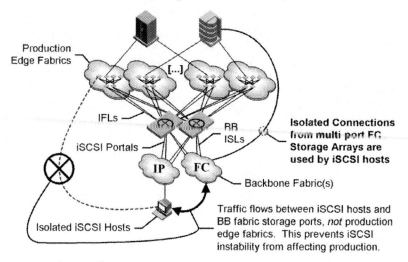

Figure 61 - iSCSI/FCR Integration

This further leverages the investment that was made in the platform primarily for the FC-FC Routing Service. This customer wanted the FCR capability to solve a pressing business need, and wanted iSCSI to test in an isolated way due to concerns about its potential negative impact on production applications. Using an external iSCSI gateway would be possible, but would take more rack space, power, cooling, etc.. It also would require additional management software and expertise, additional vendor relationships and support contracts, and would be a wasted investment if iSCSI were deemed unviable after the evaluation period. Indeed, the value proposition of saving money with iSCSI would be difficult to make given the cost of multiple external gateways.

162

By using the dual-purpose routers, there is little if any additional investment to justify since the iSCSI license and iSCSI drivers for hosts are both free.

After further maturation for iSCSI standards and products it may be desirable to have the iSCSI hosts' virtual initiators projected directly onto edge fabrics, or to allow FC-NAT connectivity between the backbone and the edge fabrics. The router's hardware and software architecture allows this to be connectivity to be added with a software upgrade if iSCSI manages to gain market traction. (See the Future Directions subsection below for more details.) Note that it is possible to have iSCSI initiators participate in edge fabrics today by using multiple router platforms for users willing to take these risks or for customers using the iSCSI hosts with pre-production fabrics.

Table 20 – iSCSI/FCR Solution Summary

Problem	Connect existing FC storage to iSCSI hosts without risk to production
Traditional Solutions	• Connecting gateway directly to production edge fabric adds risk • Single-purpose iSCSI gateway adds cost and management complexity
FC Router	• Router isolates iSCSI hosts from production fabrics, but still allows connectivity to multi-port arrays • Single platform to buy and manage

Combined iSCSI/FCR/FCIP Solution

It is possible to use all three services at once on a single platform. Perhaps a customer has a production need for an FCIP distance extension solution for off-site backups, using FCR to share that solution with several administratively separated fabrics and to isolate edge fabrics from WAN failures, while simultaneously providing low-tier hosts with isolated iSCSI access. Figure 62 illustrates this usage case.

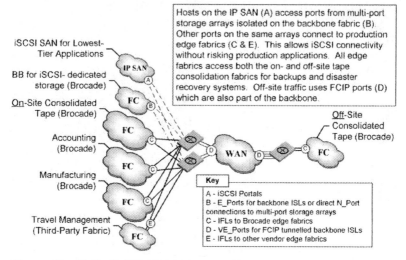

Figure 62 - FCR/FCIP/iSCSI Integration

A traditional solution would be to use different special-ized gateways for the two IP solutions, and either merge fabrics or use a third platform for fabric-to-fabric connectivity and isolation. If the fabrics were merged, then unreliable iSCSI hosts could bring down production fabrics, and either way separate gateways would add initial and ongoing cost and complexity.

Note: Figure 62 also shows a second switch vendor. Such scenarios are covered in the next chapter.

Table 21 – FCR/FCIP/iSCSI Solution Summary

Problem	Need solutions in all three categories
Traditional Solutions	• External gateways from different vendors expensive and hard to manage • No fault isolation between production fabrics and bleeding edge iSCSI hosts
FC Router	• Greatest management and cost leverage of any option • Isolates iSCSI from FC while still providing needed connectivity

Future Directions

This subsection discusses ways in which the router *could* evolve to support additional usage cases over time. It is not a comprehensive list of possible future features; it only lists some of the features that might affect major usage cases. All features in this subsection are supported by the platform hardware, and could be enabled by software upgrades. Of course, any forward looking statement about future directions for a new technology must be taken in the correct context: that of a conceptual discussion of what *might possibly* occur, rather than definitive statements about what *will* occur. Only when the router has been in production for longer will Brocade be able to prioritize which of these additional capabilities to add and in what timeframe. Check with the appropriate channel for availability and timing of these features.

End-user feedback is a key part of the feature prioritization process. If these or other features are required to solve real-world problems that the router cannot currently address, please communicate that to Brocade through the appropriate sales channel or by registering on the *SAN Administrator's Bookshelf* website: http://www.brocade.com/bookshelf.

Edge to Backbone Routing

At the time of this writing, it is not possible to configure FC-NAT connectivity between edge and backbone fabrics. Figure 63 shows this currently unsupported configuration.

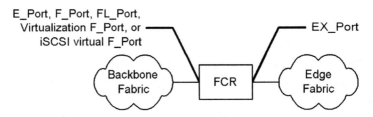

Figure 63 – Backbone to Edge Fabric Routing

In general, this configuration is not needed, and there are scalability advantages to keeping this separation. However, there are two limited cases where it might be useful.

165

The virtual Fibre Channel initiators for iSCSI hosts appear on the backbone fabric of a router. If the iSCSI protocol ever becomes mainstream it may be desirable to support FC-NAT routing between iSCSI hosts and production edge fabrics. Today, it is possible to achieve the same effect in several ways. For example, a user could have iSCSI hosts communicate with edge fabrics by using a separate router platform within an edge fabric (i.e. that has no EX_Ports), or the same connectivity can generally be achieved using multi-port arrays that span fabrics. Because there are several workarounds and iSCSI is unlikely to be combined with production solutions any time soon, this usage case is not considered a high priority.

Another application for edge-to-backbone routing involves virtualization applications. At the time of this writing, there are no production fabric virtualization applications available, but when this changes it may be desirable to combine them onto platforms also running as multiprotocol routers. It is likely that virtual devices will at least initially appear as N_Ports on the backbone fabric, so accessing them would either require separate platforms or backbone to edge routing.

More Complex Topologies

In general it is desirable to keep storage network topologies simple and low radius, i.e. using as few hops end-to-end as possible. This helps performance and reliability considerably, and is one of the major reasons that the core/edge fabric topology has dominated SAN design. The current embodiment of the FC-FC Routing Service is designed to support low radius designs exceptionally well, but is not designed to handle arbitrarily large hop-counts or arbitrarily large numbers of intermediate router hops. For example, edge fabrics currently need to be *leaf* networks (i.e. must have one of the traffic flow-end-points) and cannot be intermediates like a backbone fabric. Conversely, backbone fabrics must be intermediates and cannot be leaf networks. Figure 64 shows an unsupported traffic pattern since it traverses an intermediate edge fabric.

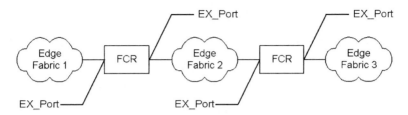

Figure 64 - Intermediate Edge Fabrics

Note that this is not an entirely unsupported topology. Devices on Fabric 1 could get to devices on Fabric 2, and devices on Fabric 2 could reach others on Fabric 3, but devices from Fabric 1 could not communicate with any on Fabric 3 because they would need to cross an edge fabric in the middle to do so. If Fabric 2 were connected with E_Ports, it would become a backbone fabric, and Fabric 1 to Fabric 3 communication would be possible, but devices on Fabric 2 could not then reach Fabrics 1 or 3.

At the time of this writing, there is no evidence that arbitrarily complex topologies are required or even desired for Meta SANs. However, the router is architecturally capable of supporting such configurations if demand should arise. Support has not yet been added simply because it has not been requested. It may be added to a future release even in the absence of explicit demand simply to achieve a more architecturally complete solution.

EX^2-IFLs

An Inter-Fabric Link (IFL) is formed by connecting an E_Port to an EX_Port. This is therefore sometimes called an EX-IFL. An EX^2-IFL would be formed by connecting two EX_Ports together. (These might be referred to as EX^2_Ports.) Figure 65 shows what this currently unsupported configuration would look like.

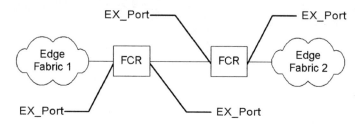

Figure 65 - EX^2-IFLs

There are certain cases where this could be useful. For example, if a router is the only platform at one end of a DWDM MAN link and has nodes directly attached to it, that side of the connection would have better fault isolation if the MAN link were an EX_Port instead of an E_Port. (Otherwise both the nodes and the E_Port would be part of the backbone fabric.) Since the far-end link might also be an EX_Port, this would require EX^2-IFLs. It is also possible that EX^2-IFLs could be used to connect redundant A/D fabrics together in a more reliable manner than EX-IFLs, however it is rarely advisable or beneficial to connect redundant fabrics together in any way at all.

VEX_Ports and VEX^2_IFLs

VE_Ports are virtual E_Ports contained within an FCIP tunnel. VEX_Ports would be virtual EX_Ports inside an FCIP tunnel. Similarly, VEX^2_IFLs would be virtual IFL tunnels formed by two such ports. Figure 66 shows what this would look like.

This could be useful in a similar context as the EX^2-IFL: if one end of an FCIP WAN link consisted of a single router with nodes directly attached, VEX_Ports would allow superior fault isolation.

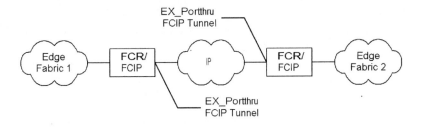

Figure 66 - VEX_Ports

Multipoint FCIP Links

At this time, each VE_Port must be associated in a 1:1 manner with a physical port on a switch. A connection between two switches through an FCIP network is much like a physical point-to-point link between them. It would be possible to create multiple virtual E_Ports on a single physical FCIP port as shown in Figure 67.

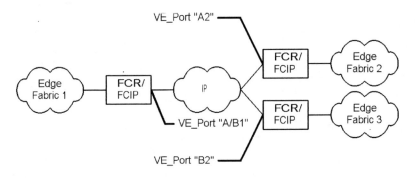

Figure 67 - Multipoint FCIP

However, this would have negative performance and reliability implications, and IP SAN solutions are already inherently lower performance and less reliable than traditional Fibre Channel SANs. For example, a single SFP failure would then affect multiple links, and each link would have to share IP-network-limited bandwidth with all others.

In any case, the same network topology can be supported using multiple physical VE_Ports, as shown in Figure 68. This approach does not have the performance or reliability issues mentioned above. As a result, "virtual FCIP sub-

169

interfaces" is not a high priority feature to add. Look from Figure 67 to Figure 68. The only difference between the two figures is that one additional port is used on the router at the Fabric 1 site, which prevents Fabric 2 failures / perform-ance requirements from impacting Fabric 3 and vice versa.

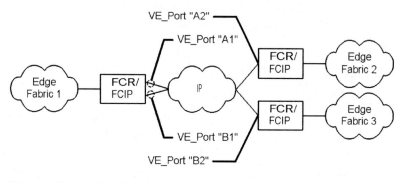

Figure 68 - Multipoint FCIP Corrected

11: Multi-Vendor Usage

The router is architecturally capable of connecting to Fibre Channel switches from other vendors, and there are a number of situations in which this can be beneficial. Most multi-vendor usage cases map to similar Brocade-only usage cases, the difference of course being that the customer would have some Brocade switches and some from another vendor. For example, a user who has a Brocade-only installation may want to use the router for scalability reasons in an island consolidation solution, and a user with both Brocade and another vendors' switches may want to deploy the router in exactly the same way for exactly the same reasons.

The router can also address some compatibility issues that exist between different vendors' fabrics by isolating the upper level fabric services that pose the greatest challenges for interoperability. It is inherently easier to link heterogeneous fabrics with an "E_Port lite" architecture than for a large mixed fabric to achieve and maintain compatibility.

Brocade has deployed the router this way at a number of production sites to date with OEM support. However support for this feature may or may not be *broadly* available from any given channel. This is a matter of testing priorities, end user demand, and market timing. As always, check with the appropriate vendor to determine the supportability of any given multi-vendor configuration before attempting a deployment. If there is a compelling business case for multi-vendor support in any customer site, contact a Brocade sales person directly if standard support channels are unavailable.

Tape Consolidation

In some large-scale enterprise environments, more than one vendor's switches have been deployed to support different applications. For example, Brocade switches may have been used for storage consolidation, while another vendor was deployed in a separate backup/restore fabric. In order to allow a tape consolidation solution to work optimally, hosts on the Brocade fabrics must be able to access tapes on the other fabric.

Merging these fabrics would create disruption to the environment, would require a "lowest common denominator" approach to features, may break management applications, and could violate support agreements. All of these issues could potentially be addressed by the router. Figure 69 illustrates this.

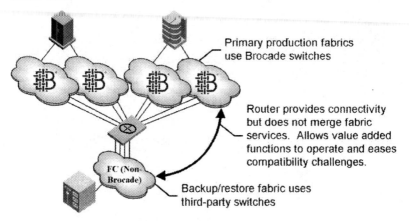

Figure 69 - Multi-Vendor Tape Consolidation

Island Consolidation

There are many benefits to connecting previously isolated SAN islands. Better resource utilization, facilitating migrations, centralizing storage pools and disaster tolerance solutions, and all other SAN benefits are enhanced by the larger connectivity models that island consolidation can allow.

However, there are many challenges for island consolidation even when all edge switches are from a single vendor, and these are compounded if the islands use switches from different vendors. Even if the different vendors' switches have a lowest common denominator compatibility mode, it is certain that this will preclude the use of certain features and will involve running untested / unsupported configurations. In addition to resolving fabric parameter or configuration mismatches, the router acts as a buffer even between fundamentally incompatible fabrics. This is because EX_Ports can have different personalities on different edge fabrics, even within the same router.

In addition to feature set, supportability, and manageability issues, some vendors have used the Fibre Channel address space in an unnecessarily limited way.[78] One vendor can only address up to about thirty domains in a fabric. Since the router can hide entire fabrics behind single domains, this allows it to scale far beyond even the theoretical maximum configurations that these vendors could support.

Figure 70 shows an island consolidation solution that allows provisioning storage between fabrics for short notice demands. It provides connectivity that would not be possible for merged fabrics with the different switch vendors. There are three vendors involved: Brocade, Vendor X, and Vendor Y. The total number of domains in the Meta SAN exceeds Vendor X's capabilities, there are devices to which Vendor Y hosts need access that cannot attach to Vendor Y switches due to their firmware limitations, and all edge fabrics are running incompatible firmware versions. Yet all nodes can communicate as needed through the router.

The ability to configure off-fabric storage is particularly critical, since Vendor X's domain count limitations preclude

---

[78] To be fair, Brocade did something like this on the first switches Brocade shipped. (The SilkWorm 1000 series). However, no Brocade switch shipped in this century has been so limited. The strange thing is not that other vendors *did* this, but that they *still* do it at the time of this writing.

further scalability of their network, and Vendor Y – being new to the SAN market – has compatibility issues that prevent their fabrics from working at all with most storage nodes.

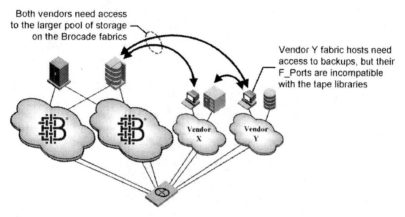

Figure 70 - Multi-Vendor Island Consolidation

*x*WDM and FCR

At the time of this writing, the Multiprotocol Router can allocate up to 255 buffer-to-buffer credits per port, and is architecturally capable of allocating even more. (Requires XPath OS 7.3 or higher and the Extended Fabrics license. Earlier versions supported 32 credits per port.) This is makes the Multiprotocol Router a superior platform for distance extension solutions using native Fibre Channel over dark fiber or *x*WDM. With FCR integration to isolate faults and management between sites, the router is doubly useful in this context. It can be used to facilitate distance solutions in either Brocade-only or multi-vendor environments.

For example, a user may have non-Brocade switches that they wish to use in a high performance disaster recovery solution. Their switches may not be capable of allocating enough credits to sustain throughput. In addition, different sites may have standardized on different vendors' switches. Using a Brocade router to connect the sites ensures optimal performance and solves many compatibility problems. Figure 71 illustrates this approach.

174

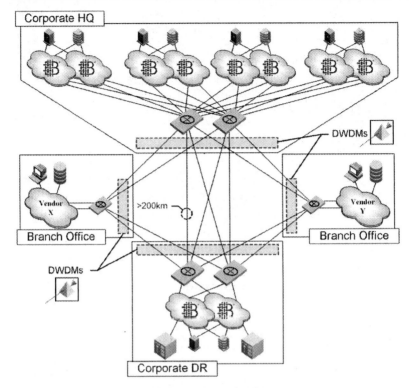

Figure 71 - Multi-Vendor xWDM and FCR

In this example, one company has four sites. Their head-quarters has several Brocade fabrics, as does their disaster recovery site. These are located between 200km and 300km apart. There are two small branch offices that use non-Brocade switches. The HQ site needs access to the DR site, and the two branch offices need access both to the DR site and to the HQ site. All four are connected with a xWDM solution. Routers are placed at each site with EX_Ports connecting to the existing fabrics, each EX_Port individually set in the appropriate compatibility mode. The xWDMs are configured to create a partial mesh as in the figure. These links form a backbone fabric. Brocade's standards-compliant tagging mechanism allows each backbone link to carry traffic from any edge fabric while still maintaining compatibility with existing switches.

The routers' large buffers allow high performance on the long distance links, and the FC-FC Routing Service keeps management at each site totally separated, resolves compatibility problems between the different vendors' operating systems, and allows selective LSAN access to be configured as needed.

FCIP and FCR for CAN Resource Sharing

It is possible that more than one vendor's switches may be used within the same campus, or even in the same datacenter. Users may wish to share resources between these fabrics for any of the same reasons that they created storage networks in the first place. If so, the router may be used to provide these benefits between fabrics that previously could only be attained within single homogenous fabrics. Figure 72 illustrates this scenario.

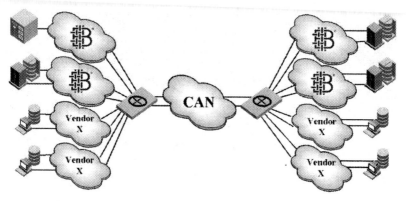

Figure 72 - Multi-Vendor CAN

In this example, one campus has two datacenters, each of which has two Brocade fabrics and two from another vendor. The customer would like to have a single network to achieve optimal resource utilization, and to facilitate certain recurring operations like data migrations between arrays on different fabrics. The customer uses two Brocade routers to solve the connectivity problem.

Even after the routers are in place, nearly all traffic will be localized within the existing fabrics. As a result, only one

176

router per datacenter is used. (If either router fails, connectivity will be lost temporarily, but this may be considered acceptable depending on the priority of the applications traversing the CAN.) Since traffic between datacenters will be rare and low priority, FCIP is used instead of dark fiber to connect the two routers together.

Low Impact Vendor Migration

Some customers have switches from other vendors with which they are unsatisfied. They want to migrate to a homogenous Brocade environment so that all fabrics have the same value-added features, run the same code, use the same support and supply channels, take the same spare parts, and leverage the same expertise.

Unfortunately, it is often difficult to change switch vendors without major disruption. It may require extensive reconfiguration of hosts, downtime for applications, and in all cases requires taking risk. To migrate an entire fabric at once may take more effort and risk than even the many benefits of an all-Brocade solution would justify.

The router can mitigate these problems. A router can be put into place between the Brocade fabric (to migrate to) and the other vendor's fabric (to migrate from). Devices can be moved one at a time as convenient, thus minimizing disruption, effort, and risk. Only when all devices have been moved will the legacy (other vendor) switches be retired. Figure 73 illustrates the steps taken to perform a low impact migration from a mixed Brocade / Vendor X multi-fabric environment to an all-Brocade solution.

The customer in this example starts with two completely independent fabrics, to which the customer adds at least one router. The number of routers and the number of ports per router depend on the length of time the migration is expected to take, and their performance and availability requirements during the migration process.

There are a set of hosts and storage devices on the Vendor X fabric communicating as indicated in the upper left quadrant of the figure.

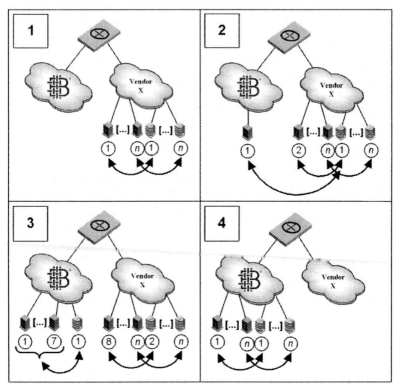

Figure 73 - Multi-Vendor Migration

When convenient, the user schedules one host or application at a time to be moved.[79] This is shown in the upper

---

[79] This may or may not be disruptive to that one host, depending on the capabilities of its HBA drivers. Migrations are complex topics due to the number of possible scenarios that need to be discussed, and therefore generally warrant dedicated procedure guides.

At minimum, access will be lost while the cable is moved, and potentially the host will need to be reconfigured or rebooted. It depends on whether or not the host can handle changes to its storage port's PID gracefully, and whether or not the xlate domains can be set up to "clone" the PIDs that the devices had in their real fabrics. For example, if a storage device is attached to domain 10 in its source fabric, and domain 10 is free in the fabric its hosts are being migrated to, then the router admin could manually configure domain 10 as the preferred xlate domain for the storage port's fabric, and manually configure the storage port to appear as right. After it is moved to the Brocade fabric, it continues to access the same storage ports as before, even though they are still located on the Vendor X fabric and are still serving hosts on that fabric.

Eventually, all of the hosts associated with a given storage port will have been moved to the Brocade fabric. In this example, there were seven hosts accessing storage port #1. When convenient, time is scheduled to move the storage port over, as shown in the lower left panel.[80]

This process is repeated as necessary over as long a period of time as necessary until all applications / hosts and storage arrays have been relocated. At that point, the Vendor X fabric is empty as shown in the lower right panel, and their equipment can be retired.

This is essentially the same procedure that would be used to migrate hosts between two Brocade fabrics if one fabric needed to be retired. For example, one fabric might be using older 1Gbit Fibre Channel switches. This method would be applicable if the user wanted to migrate to newer 2Gbit or 4Gbit Brocade switches using a low-impact procedure.

Note that there are many variations on this procedure. The essence of the solution is that routed connectivity between the fabrics allows data migration to take place one host, storage port, or application at a time, rather than needing to coordinate downtime schedules for all at once. This can have substantial benefits in large, complex, or tightly change-controlled environments.

---

the same PID on that domain. All that said, this is mostly an historical note, since most HBA drivers today can be moved without this kind of special effort.

[80] This also may be disruptive to the hosts that access it, as in the previous note. The rule of thumb is that if a host can withstand its storage array being moved to a different port in the same fabric without disruption, then this operation will also be non-disruptive.

12: Usage Cases FAQ

FC-FC Router Usage FAQ

Q: What are some of the business drivers that caused Brocade to create the FCR service?

A: The FCR does not enable categorically new SAN solutions. It enables improved network infrastructure, in much the same way that IP routers and NAT firewalls did so for data networking. This extends the benefits of existing SAN solutions. There are many areas in which the FCR provides concrete business benefits. Some examples include the need to support:

- Scales to larger configurations than flat FC fabrics
- Connecting SAN islands without changing domain IDs and other fabric-wide parameters
- Less complex data migration procedures
- Improved solutions for backup/restore and disaster recovery: tighter integration and higher reliability
- Separate administrative domains with selective connectivity: edge fabrics remain entirely separate administratively, and connectivity needs to be allowed by consensus of all fabric administrators.
- Simplified interoperability between different Fibre Channel switch vendors' products
- Fault containment between networked fabrics

181

Q: What advantages does the FCR service provide over traditional fabrics?

A: The service improves scalability, reliability, availability, serviceability, security, and interoperability

Q: Does the router increase any-to-any scalability?

A: It increases any-subset-to-any-subset scalability. That is, you can configure a large network, but at any given time only a subset of devices will connect to each other across fabrics. Exporting all devices to all fabrics would not have scalability benefits. Since this is not really needed in SANs, (e.g. hosts don't talk to each other, so they don't need to be zoned together), this has the same effect as any-to-any connectivity.

Q: You mentioned tape consolidation. Will the router work with xxx tape library? That is, can the library exist in one edge fabric and the server in another?

A: It certainly should, provided that the tape library is supported on the fabric. If you attach *any* FC node to a switch in an edge fabric, unless it is a private loop host, it should be able to work across the router just as well as it could work within its edge fabric. If it doesn't, it is either a misconfiguration, or a defect in the node's FC drivers or in the router.

Q: Does the FCR support extended distance native FC links, as in the Extended Fabrics feature on other Brocade products?

A: Yes. The configuration would typically involve the intersite links being backbone fabric E_Ports, with EX_Ports going to the fabrics at the local site. E_Ports on the router should support 255 or more credits. This requires XPath OS 7.3 and higher, and the Extended Fabrics license.

Q: If an administrator on one edge fabric exports a device in an LSAN, and the administrator of another fabric doesn't import it, what happens?

A: Nothing happens. Both fabrics need to have LSAN zones containing the device's port WWN or the router will not provide a mapping.

Q: How do EX_Ports help scalability?

A: They have a light-weight version of fabric services that does not cause fabrics on different EX_Ports to merge. This eliminates the "n^2" scalability problem caused by all domains needing to know everything about all others. It also limits the number of domains that FSPF must be aware of, and the number of nodes that the SNS must register and respond to. In addition, the "services lite" architecture limits the amount that any router needs to know about any edge fabric, so the routers themselves do not become a scalability bottleneck.

iSCSI Gateway Usage FAQ

Q: All of the iSCSI solutions look like they could be built using Fibre Channel. Am I missing something?

A: No. At a high level, iSCSI does not do anything that Fibre Channel doesn't already do. The difference is that some components of an iSCSI solution might be cheaper, assuming that you use built-in NICs and commodity Ethernet switches instead of enterprise-class IP gear or iSCSI/TOE cards.

Q: Is there an inherent limit to the distance supportable in a DR solution with iSCSI?

A: Yes and no. As a practical matter, performance and reliability degrade as distance is increased in real-world IP networks. Since SANs require extremely high, or at the very least, extremely deterministic performance and reliability, outside of totally controlled experimental environments, IP SAN technology should not be used over long distances. At the time of this writing, this means something in the range of 200 miles, provided that the IP network is highly reliable and has extremely low delay.

Q: What amount of delay and what error rates are acceptable on an IP network to run iSCSI?

A: This is application and distance dependant. In general, there should be less than **one millisecond** of end-to-end delay on average and less than one second delay during peak periods. Error rate + packet loss should be no greater than greater than **0.01%**. While higher values can be *supported*, they can result in at least an order of magnitude reduction in performance, if not more.

Q: I've heard that there are a bunch of different and incompatible versions of the iSCSI standard. What iSCSI versions are supported on the gateway?

A: At the time of this writing, it is based on draft #20 of the IETF standard. The Brocade implementation is designed to be adaptable, so as the standard and industry de-facto implementation continues to change, Brocade can keep pace.

Q: Does the gateway work with *xxx* iSCSI HBA?

A: Brocade's research indicates that there is almost no market for iSCSI HBAs at this time, and probably not in the future either. Customers seem to be using iSCSI software drivers exclusively, though the market is so small it is hard to be sure.

Q: Does the gateway route iSCSI storage to FC hosts?

A: Not at the time of this writing. There does not appear to be much iSCSI storage in the market, and what little is available tends to be more expensive than FC storage. The gateway is capable of doing this with a software upgrade if the iSCSI market ever materializes.

Q: Saving cost is good, but I don't want to lose my data. That would be a whole new kind of expensive. I'm just not comfortable with iSCSI today. Will there ever be a place for iSCSI in mission-critical datacenter environments?

A: Maybe. For now, it is on the fringes of the datacenter, and iSCSI adoption rates have consistently missed analyst projections for years. However, there is no guarantee that these trends will *not* change if the protocol ever becomes stable, and if the iSCSI value proposition stops eroding.

FCIP Tunnel Usage FAQ

Q: Is there an inherent limit to the distance supportable in a DR solution with FCIP?

A: This is the same as with iSCSI. The supportable distance is a function of network delay and reliability.

Q: What amount of delay and what error rates are acceptable on an IP network to run FCIP?

A: In general, there should be less than **one millisecond** (1ms) of typical-case delay and less than one second delay at worst-case peak. Error rate + packet loss should be no greater than greater than **0.01%**. Even at these levels, performance will be reduced vs. any other distance extension technology. The way to benchmark a WAN is to compare its latency to the speed of light, which is about 5µs/km. This is what you would get with native FC or an *x*WDM. If a 200km IP WAN has 1ms of end-to-end of delay, then it is doing well; if not, the use of IP is a bottleneck, and other distance extension solutions should be evaluated.

Q: Will the FCIP service interoperate with the vendor *xxx* FCIP gateway?

A: No. The FCIP standard has just been ratified, but no two gateway vendors can interoperate at this time. This is generally true of most IP SAN technology. However, FCIP is the protocol of choice in the industry for distance extension, and it is clear that multi-vendor interoperability is on the horizon. (Note: This is true of FCIP, but not iFCP.)

Q: When should I use a third-party gateway?

A: When it has required value-added features that the Multi-protocol Router lacks, e.g. tape pipelining. Be sure to evaluate the real benefit of such features before deployment. For example, if the network will be carrying binary, encrypted, and/or already compressed data – common with many backup and replication solutions – then gateway compression will not generally improve performance. Many environments already have some form of compression on WAN links, and it is likely that compression on the FCIP gateway would *reduce* performance in these cases.

Section Three

Deployment Guide

Section Topics

- SAN Design Theory and Practice
- Installation and Configuration Tips
- Ongoing Management Tips
- Troubleshooting Tips
- Frequently Asked Questions

13: Meta SAN Design

Basic Networking Models

Before discussing which SAN design strategy to use under various conditions, it may be beneficial to review the basic networking models that are supported by the router. The generic simple-case network designs for each of the three services can be distilled down to a few abstract block diagrams.

For example, the simplest case for the FC-FC Routing Service is connecting two fabric switches with one router, using one IFL to each switch. This is shown in Figure 74 and again in Figure 75 as a block diagram.[81]

Figure 74 - Most Basic FCR Design

---

[81] The block diagrams throughout this chapter often use a single device icon (such as the single FC switch icons in Figure 74) to show a simple case. Almost all deployments will be more complex, but analogous. For example, the FCIP sequence starting with Figure 80 (p192) shows an Ethernet switch icon for the FCIP network. In most cases, a real deployment would consist of many switches, connected to several routers, potentially connected to multiple WAN service providers. At a high level, all of that infrastructure would occupy the same place in the block diagram as the single switch.

189

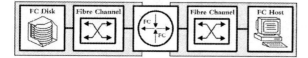

Figure 75 - Most Basic FCR Design - Block Diagram

Look at the two figures and see how they correlate with each other. The light grey boxes in the background of Figure 75 each represent a separate fabric. Notice how the router sits partially on each fabric, joining them for connectivity but preventing them from merging. Of course, each block in this diagram could be repeated *n* times: there could be many routers, many storage and host blocks, many switches in each fabric, and many fabrics. In fact, in almost all real-world applications, there *will* be many more devices than are shown in the figure.

In configurations involving many fabrics[82] or geographical separation between fabrics,[83] it may be desirable to use one or more intermediate backbone fabrics. The degenerate case of a backbone fabric Meta SAN is shown in Figure 76.

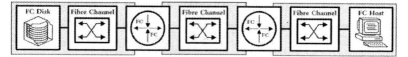

Figure 76 - Most Basic FCR Design with Backbone

The backbone block in the center of this figure could be anything that would normally form a fabric between two switches. For example, it could be a standard FC switch or fabric of switches, or one or more FCIP tunnels (VE_Port), or one or more ISLs (E_Port, not EX_Port) directly connecting the routers.

---

[82] I.e. more fabrics than there are ports on an individual FCR platform. More than sixteen fabrics if using the AP7420.

[83] E.g. if large distances separate fabrics, then the router can be useful due to its high per-port buffer count and its ability to administratively separate different sites. Also, it may not be possible to attach ISLs from remote edge fabrics directly to the router at a central site.

Backbone fabrics allow more scalability and flexibility by networking routers together at a higher level than Fibre Channel fabrics.[84] While there are limitations to the complexity of backbone fabric Meta SANs supportable at the time of this writing, the router backbone architecture does solve all currently proposed design problems.

In real world backbone fabric deployments, there would almost always be more than two fabrics connected by more than two routers, with two or more IFLs to each fabric. While the figure above is not very realistic, it does illustrate the basic network model in a straightforward and clear manner. Real world deployments build upon that basic model, as shown in Figure 77.

Note the use of four edge fabrics, four routers, multiple IFLs per router-fabric connection, multiple routers to each edge fabric, and two separate backbone fabrics each with multiple ISLs.[85] This is a design template upon which an enterprise-class Meta SAN could be built. In mission-critical environments, this topology would be duplicated (A/B) with hosts and storage being connected to each network.

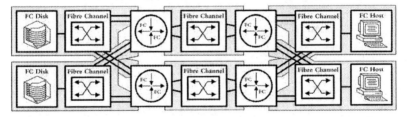

Figure 77 - More Realistic FCR Design

The iSCSI Gateway Service can be represented in its simplest form by showing one fabric connected to one iSCSI network using one ISL and one portal respectively, as shown

---

[84] That is, in a hierarchical network, FC routers are "higher up" than switches.

[85] The switches shown between the routers could either be expanded into multi-switch fabrics, or collapsed down to direct router-to-router ISLs or FCIP tunnels. This applies to *all* backbone fabric examples, not just Figure 77.

in Figure 78.[86]   The light grey box still represents an FC fabric while the darker grey box represents an IP network.

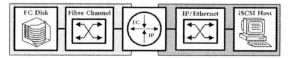

Figure 78 - Most Basic iSCSI Design

Again, this is not very realistic. There would almost certainly be many more iSCSI hosts, connected to multiple portals on multiple gateways. This is shown in Figure 79.

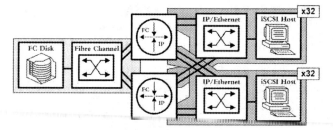

Figure 79 - More Realistic iSCSI Design

The FCIP Tunneling Service in its simplest form allows one fabric to span two sites using a router at each end. The routers connect to their fabrics with a single ISL each, and connect to each other using a single virtual ISL tunneled through an IP network[87] as shown in Figure 80.[88]

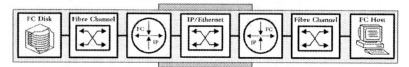

Figure 80 - Most Basic FCIP Design

---

[86] Actually, the *simplest* design is to connect nodes directly to the router.

[87] The IP network could involve different topologies and technologies. Some options include point-to-point links - though there is little application for this - a switched Gigabit Ethernet network, or a technology like ATM or SONET/SDH.

[88] As in the iSCSI example, it would be possible to collapse the node connections directly to the router . If this were done, the two FC**Error! Bookmark not defined.** switches would be eliminated. Note that in this case the FC-FC Routing Service cannot be combined with FCIP, because that would be a case of edge to backbone routing. This is planned for a subsequent software feature release.

The previous examples show the usage of each service in isolation. In the case of the FCIP Tunneling Service, it is expected that almost all deployments will involve integration with the FC-FC Routing Service. When used in this manner, the connections to the fabrics are IFLs instead of ISLs, and the tunneled connection between the routers is a backbone fabric virtual ISL. This is shown in Figure 81.

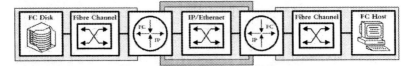

Figure 81 - Most Basic FCIP Design with Backbone

The difference between Figure 80 and Figure 81 is fairly subtle. There are three light grey boxes representing fabrics in Figure 81, with the darker grey IP network box surrounding the middle one, while there is only one long light grey box in Figure 80 that is surrounded at one point. This shows that the FCR service separates the network into three fabrics, so that – for example – if the IP WAN experiences a reliability problem like a flapping link, the fabric-level disturbance would be limited to the backbone. Thus, site-to-site traffic could be affected, but traffic within either of the sites would continue without impact.

Again, this is a good illustration of the *degenerate* case usage of the FCIP service, but is not of a *typical* case. At a minimum, there usually would be multiple IFLs to each edge fabric and multiple backbone fabric virtual ISL tunnels between sites as shown in Figure 82.

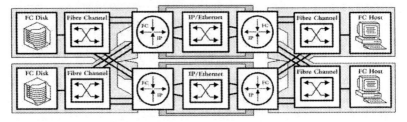

Figure 82 - More Realistic FCIP Design

This figure also shows a redundant backbone case. The two routers in each row are connected to each other, but not to those in the other row. This would be beneficial if multiple IP networks were available: if one or the other IP network became unstable, it would destabilize only one of the two backbone fabrics.

The preceding figures represent the basic building blocks for routed storage networks. The remainder of this chapter builds upon those core concepts.

Core/Edge Networking Extended

While multiprotocol SAN routers are recent innovations, neither SANs nor routers are new. The most popular designs using SAN routers will employ a blend of switched SAN and routed data network methods, the dominant being an adaptation of the Core/Edge (CE) approach. Just as in standard fabrics, other topologies can be supported, but – also as in standard fabrics – CE variations are likely to be the most popular for large-scale deployments.

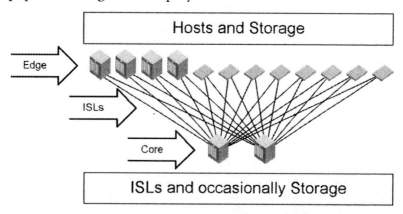

Figure 83 - Traditional Core/Edge Fabric

Figure 83 shows a standard CE Fibre Channel fabric. In such a fabric, the switches that form the core serve to interconnect many edge switches. Devices attach mostly to the edges, but may be connected to the core if it is built using high-port-count directors such as the SilkWorm 24000.

CE designs have dominated the enterprise SAN architecture space for many reasons. Networks built using this approach are:

- Well tested, since most large fabrics in production take one core/edge form or another, as do most fabrics in switch vendor test labs

- Well balanced, since the symmetrical design takes full advantage of FSPF for load sharing and redundancy

- Economical, having options to support differing cost-to-performance ratios

- Easy to adapt and modify over time, since each core is duplicated and edge switches are interchangeable

- Simple. Easy to document, troubleshoot, and understand

- Easy to scale without downtime by adding more edge switches or migrating to higher port-count core switches one at a time

CE Meta SAN – CE Fabric Analogy

The same advantages apply when using the router in an analogous manner. To show how the analogy works, Figure 84 has a generic block diagram of a CE fabric, while Figure 85 has a similar diagram of a CE Meta SAN.

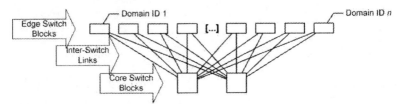

Figure 84 – Generic CE Fabric Block Diagram

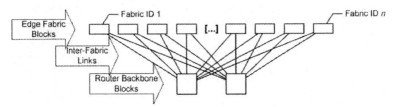

Figure 85 – Generic CE Meta SAN Block Diagram

195

The edge fabric blocks in the second diagram could contain any reasonable fabric design, including CE fabrics. That is, a CE Meta SAN may contain *n* CE fabrics. In effect, Figure 85 could contain Figure 84. See Figure 86.

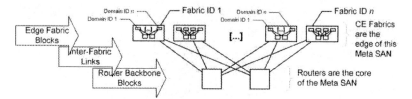

Figure 86 – Generic CE Meta SAN with CE Edge Fabrics

CE Meta SAN Approaches

Broadly, there are two ways in which CE design can be applied to the routed SANs:

- By attaching the router to the core of an existing fabric and viewing the routed backbone as being another *level* of core. There would be three levels to the design: fabric edge, fabric core, and Meta SAN core. The first two levels together form an edge fabric. This is the approach likely to be used to add routers to installed base environments. See Figure 87, and indeed many of the other Meta SAN diagrams throughout this work.

- By using the router as a core and attaching one tier of edge switches to it. This is a superior design for green field networks using high port-count edge switches that localize traffic mostly within each edge switch. It can also be appropriate for tying together environments that previously consisted of isolated directors, or very small non-CE networks. In this case, the fabrics are still referred to as edge fabrics, but may have no internal hierarchy of their own. See Figure 88 through Figure 91.

196

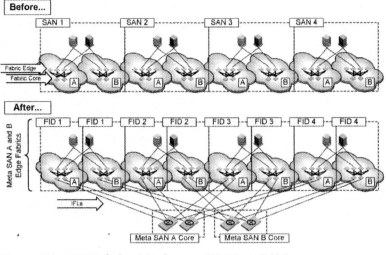

Figure 87 - CE Fabrics Moving to CE Meta SANs

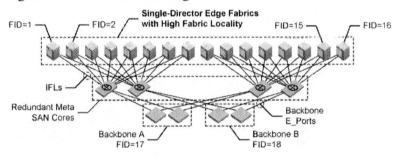

Figure 88 - Director-Based CE Meta SAN

This approach is well-suited for Meta SANs comprised of high-port-count platforms because they are more likely to have high traffic localization, so having a thin matrix of IFLs will provide adequate performance. Depending on the number of directors, and the performance and geographical requirements, the design could even be accomplished without backbone fabrics as shown in Figure 89.

Figure 89 - Collapsed Director-Based CE Meta SAN

In general, whenever a simpler design like this is possible it should be used. As long as locality is high, there should be no need to use more than two IFLs (for redundancy) per edge fabric, each going to a different router. The rule of thumb is that if the number of edge fabrics is equal to or less than the available port count of each router, in the absence of geographical dispersion or abnormal performance requirements, it should be possible – and indeed preferable – to "flatten" the design this way.

If the objective is to interconnect an existing environment consisting of a large number[89] of small isolated islands, then it is likely (a) that backbone fabric(s) will be required, and (b) that few IFLs per edge fabric or ISLs per backbone fabric will be needed. This means that a flattened network probably will not work, but that the design still can be relatively straightforward. This could be true in a datacenter that started out with forty-two individual switches or small fabrics. Figure 90 shows an example of the "after" environment.

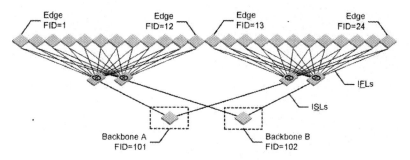

Figure 90 – CE Meta SAN with Many Small Edge Fabrics

The BB fabrics in this example could consist of standard FC fabric switches as shown, or could use any other method that would form a fabric between the routers. For example, direct ISL connections between routers would work, even if they were long distance connections. Similarly, FCIP tunnels or SAN other extension methods would be fine.

---

[89] I.e. larger than the port count of a single router. In the case of the AP7420, this is sixteen.

One possible variation on this theme is to have a Meta SAN connecting many isolated fabrics as in Figure 88, Figure 89, and Figure 90, but with a few larger and more complex fabrics as in Figure 87. This might be used, for example, to tie many isolated fabrics (each consisting of a small number of small switches) into a centralized backup / recovery fabric (consisting of a few larger switches). Figure 91 shows an example of a similarly complex design. Note that Meta SANs of this complexity are likely to be the exception rather than the rule in the real world.

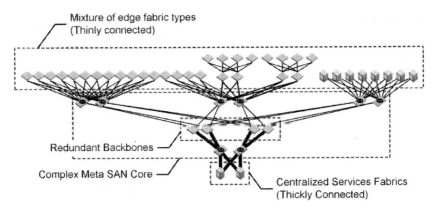

Figure 91 - Complex CE Meta SAN

CE Design for IP Networks

The essence of the CE design philosophy is to create *low-radius* networks. This means that there is as short a "distance" – i.e. as small a number of hops – as possible from the middle of the network – the core – to the farthest node – attached to an edge switch.

An IP network may not be a pure CE design and yet still be true to the *essence* of CE networking. Indeed, data network engineers pioneered this approach, although they usually called their architectures by other names, like "star topology" networks.

The topology of the IP network turns out not to matter directly to the router. However, it does matter very much how reliable the network is, and how well it performs: delay and packet loss at the levels typical in IP networks can have a dramatic impact on SAN performance. Low-radius networks tend to outperform and have better reliability than high-radius networks, so they tend to be more appropriate for SANs. This stands to reason: the fewer hops between end-points, the less potential for congestion, latency, and failures. The "CE Essential" design goal for IP SANs should therefore be to keep as small a hop-count as possible between multi-protocol router ports in an FCIP network, or multiprotocol router ports and hosts in an iSCSI network.

Non-CE Designs

At the highest level, only CE designs and their variations are supported by the FC-FC Routing Service at this time. That is, there must be a router tier in the middle, with only one optional tier of backbone fabric(s), and edge fabrics surrounding this. It is not currently possible to e.g. have traffic cross more than one backbone in series end-to-end. (See the "More Complex Topologies" on page 166.)

At the next level down, however, there can be quite a bit of variation. Building a CE Meta SAN does *not* mean that each edge or backbone fabric needs to be a CE design, and very often they will not be. The backbones between routers in most of the CAN/MAN/WAN examples in this book are cascaded or meshed in some way. Many of the immediately previous examples in this chapter use single-domain edge fabrics. Even if the existing fabrics are full meshes or arbitrarily complex partial meshes, the router can connect to them.

The two IP SAN services support radically different top-level topologies - indeed, they are really unaware of the IP network topology – but it is rarely necessary to make things more complicated than some variation on a CE layout.

The thing to keep in mind when building a Meta SAN in which subnets and/or fabrics have complex, high-radius topologies is that a high hop count may impact application performance, especially when using IP SAN technology. This may be a necessary trade-off if existing fabrics or

CAN/MAN/WAN geography dictate a complex topology. If not, it is always best to use a simple topology. Always use Occam's Razor[90] when configuring networks: if you can make a network smaller in radius and simpler in design, it is best to do so.

Meta SAN Locality

SAN Locality Basics

The best performance in a network can be attained by understanding its traffic patterns. If these are well enough understood, it may be possible to *localize* traffic by putting ports close together if they communicate often with each other. This concept is known as *locality*. For example, in a CE network it may be possible to attach hosts and their primary storage ports to the same edge switch. This allows most IO to follow an efficient path, never leaving the switch, rather than traversing a set of ISLs. In a Meta SAN, the same technique can be applied at the edge fabric level.

Although locality has been used in data networks for decades, SANs are inherently better suited to this kind of analysis and design. For example, in most data networks, true any-to-any traffic patterns may occur and must be accounted for. On the other hand, in almost all SANs it is predictable that hosts will only ever communicate with storage ports – not other hosts – and that certain storage will be used most often by any given host. Indeed, SANs can be viewed as having "any subset to any subset" traffic, rather than true "any to any" patterns.

The vast majority of real-world storage networks are not so performance-sensitive that high locality is even required. However, in addition to improving performance, locality im-

---

[90] William of Occam (or Ockham) was the medieval European philosopher who is credited with first thinking of the principle of parsimony. In science, this means that one should not make more assumptions than the minimum needed to explain an observation. It is often stated as, "the simplest solution is usually the best." Phrased this way, it has broad applicability to computer science...

proves RAS. If traffic patterns are localized to some extent, the impact on applications of network failures is more limited in scope. Locality also implies that there are fewer components in the network – reducing cost and improving reliability numbers like MTBF – and it facilitates trouble-shooting, since there are fewer components to examine in a localized flow that is experiencing problems.

In many enterprise SANs, locality is also a function of time. When a SAN is initially deployed, it may be a migration from Direct Attached Storage (DAS). DAS inherently has 100% locality, so when moving from DAS to SAN it is possible to maintain much if not all of this localization initially. However, as the SAN matures, traffic patterns will likely move away from locality as nodes are added, moved, or decommissioned, or repurposed for new applications.

Locality and the Router

Locality in the context of the Multiprotocol Router means using knowledge of traffic patterns to keep a significant portion of traffic contained within a fabric, rather than crossing IFLs. Since a fabric can be a fairly large entity, this should be easy to achieve for most designers.

Indeed, in most cases, each edge fabric tends to have locality implied without any special design effort: a Meta SAN may be built from existing 100% localized SAN islands, or different departments, or there may be geographical separation between fabrics with strong intra-site localization. Any of these could yield high traffic locality at the fabric level.

Just as in traditional SANs, Meta SAN locality is often a function of time. Some factors that drive high initial fabric localization may degrade over time as the network matures. For example, if the Meta SAN is built out of initially 100% localized islands, any use of inter-island links *at all* will reduce locality. There is a strong tendency for traffic patterns to change in this way over time. This principal is known as "operational entropy," and is one of the primary reasons for FC routers to exist: even if a SAN can be designed with

100% fabric locality initially, it is likely that changing business needs will result in a requirement or at least a strong preference for inter-fabric traffic at some point.

Bands of Locality

Locality is not an all-or-nothing technique. It may be that some locality occurs within a fabric in a Meta SAN, some within a switch in that fabric, and some within a blade or port group inside that switch. The degree and scope of locality is application-dependant.

In general, the greater the performance and RAS requirements of an application, the greater the degree of locality that should be employed, and the narrower its scope. The highest performance and RAS will occur when localization is done within a small port group on a single switch in a single fabric. However, designing for and maintaining such a high degree of locality is time consuming, tends to counter the benefits of networking, and in many cases is actually impossible to achieve. Therefore this degree of localization is generally reserved for connecting hosts to their primary storage arrays in mission-critical applications, or for cases where the SAN is used as a subsystem for a single massively high performance application like a parallel supercomputer, a data mining cluster, or a real time satellite imagery download and analysis pipeline. Such applications generally require either large single fabrics, or Meta SANs with many routers and many IFLs.

Locality can be thought of as a set of bands moving outward from the traffic source port, as shown in Figure 92, with the highest RAS and performance being closer to the center and easier to create SAN designs being further out.

In more complex Meta SANs, locality can occur between edge fabrics co-located on a given router vs. fabrics that must be reached by crossing a backbone fabric. Figure 88 and Figure 90 show Meta SANs where this is the case. This may also occur between sites in a CAN, MAN, or WAN as in Figure 55 and many similar examples. In these cases, a site can be considered either an area of a fabric (no FCR) or an area of the backbone (with FCR).

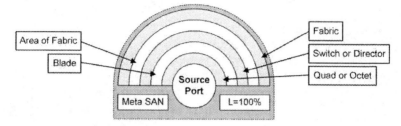

Figure 92 – Bands of Locality

> ### ✓ Side Note
>
> *Few of the fabrics that Brocade has assessed have perform-ance characteristics that require locality. On the other hand, few have traffic patterns that would make localization difficult. Except in the highest performance environments in the world, the decision of how much if any attention to pay to locality almost always comes down to the philosophy of the SAN designer, rather than being driven by technical impera-tives such as real-world application performance needs.*

Locality within the Meta SAN itself will always add up to 100%. Each band below that level may have any portion of traffic localized.

If *all* traffic flows across IFLs, then the lower bands will have 0% locality. If *no* traffic flows across IFLs, then the bands will add up to 100% locality. More often, the break-down will be something like Table 22.

The center column refers to the percentage of traffic lo-calized at that level but not any level above or below. The right-hand column shows the traffic localized at that level *and* all previous levels. For example, if traffic flows between two ports on the same quad or octet, it is implied that it is also lo-calized within the blade, director, area of fabric, fabric, area of backbone, and Meta SAN. Traffic localized within the blade but explicitly *not* within an octet is shown in the center column. Traffic localized within the blade *including* traffic localized within octets is shown in the right-hand column.

Table 22 – Utilization of Bands of Locality

Locality Band	Locality %	Running Total
Quad/Octet	5%	5%
Blade	10%	15%
Switch/Director	40%	55%
Area of Fabric	25%	80%
Fabric	10%	90%
Area of BB	5%	95%
Meta SAN	5%	100%

The result is that localization closest to the source port (e.g. port group level) tends to be a low percentage because it is difficult to design for and maintain. Except in the most performance-sensitive of applications[91] it is rarely worth the effort of pursuing localization at the port group or blade level. Localization at the switch level is easy to design for and yields a good return for the effort. If a fabric is complex, it is often possible to keep traffic within a thickly ISL-ed area of it, so only a relatively small percentage of traffic is really any-to-any within a fabric.

In fact, there is so much "built in" localization at the edge fabric level that the traffic that must leave an edge fabric tends to be very small. Except in corner cases, locality is easy to achieve and provides benefits at the switch, fabric, and backbone area levels, so administrators do not actually *design* for it: it just *happens*. The locality distribution across bands most often has a shape somewhat like a bell curve, with the vast majority of traffic being localized before leaving a fabric. This fact should be kept in mind when provisioning IFLs.

---

[91] For example: real time satellite imagery download and analysis, data mining operations, or online video editing.

IFL Provisioning

Provisioning of links in any network is a matter of matching network bandwidth to application-driven load. To put is simply, how many Inter-Fabric Links to configure for any given edge fabric depends on how much traffic will be placed on them. To determine this, several methods could be used. This subsection discusses three approaches.

Provisioning for Peaks

In some cases, it is appropriate to provision the network for its worst-case, or *peak* utilization. This is generally the most expensive approach, but can be appropriate for environments in which the impact of a slow network is similar in scale to the impact of a down network. Real time applications such as satellite imagery download and analysis might qualify, for example, because if the network cannot keep up with incoming data, it will be lost. Similar situations can occur in large scale data mining operations, parallel supercomputer clusters, video editing workgroups, or television broadcast applications, to name just a few.

To determine the peak utilization for all of the IFLs going to/from a given fabric, find the total number of nodes on the fabric that may need to use those links at the same time.[92] If historical performance data is available for those nodes, take the highest utilization level from each and add them together. If not, add up the maximum speeds of their interfaces.

For example, an edge fabric may have 100 hosts and 15 storage ports. At any given time, most traffic may be localized within the fabric, but two of the storage ports will be mirrored across fabrics in a disaster tolerance solution, and two of the hosts will use IFLs for off-site backups. Assuming that real performance data were unavailable and that all ports were 2Gbit Fibre Channel, then peak usage would be as-

---

[92] If you have already decided how LSANs are to be configured and have an idea of how the applications using the LSANs behave, this will be straightforward. If not, you will need to make an educated guess.

sumed to be (2x storage ports + 2x hosts) x 2Gbit = 8Gbits/sec. of throughput. Four IFLs would be required to handle this load.

For applications that warrant an even more conservative approach, a designer would allocate an additional "fudge factor" to handle short-notice future requirements, IFL failures, and other unplanned events, as well as occasional imbalanced utilization of the IFLs. It might be appropriate to configure six or even eight IFLs to the edge fabric in this case.

<u>Provisioning for Averages</u>

In most environments, configuring IFLs for peaks is not necessary. Traffic flows do not often peak at the same time, do not do so for sustained periods even on those occasions, and there is no real business impact even if overlapping peaks are sustained. For this typical-case environment, provisioning should be done based on projected *average* utilization.

In the previous example, it might be determined that on average the two mirrored storage ports are relatively inactive, using only an average of 0.5Gbits between them. Perhaps backup speeds are constrained by the tape drives, and can only sustain 1Gbit between the two hosts. Perhaps backups are done during off-peak hours, so they rarely intersect with high usage periods for the storage arrays. The average utilization would be something less than 1Gbit in this case.

This number has to be viewed through another filter, however. Backup traffic is sustained for the duration of the backups, so the bandwidth provisioned must not be less than the largest sustained application requires. In addition, when a tape drive is starved for data, it may cause the backup to fail or go into a degraded "start/stop" mode. It still would be possible in this case to sustain full performance on the solution using a single IFL, but in other cases this consideration could increase the provisioning.

The conservative approach would be to configure two IFLs for redundancy and future-proofing, but configuring up to eight as in the peak method would be excessive.

Provisioning Based on Rules of Thumb

In many cases, a designer will not know all of the usage cases for the network ahead of time. Once connectivity is set up, more uses tend to present themselves. It may be possible to determine that a set of IFLs must have *at least* a certain capacity – for example using an average utilization method – but not so easy to say that they will need *no more than* a given amount. However, configuring for 0% locality (i.e. assuming simultaneous peak usage of the IFLs by every device in the fabric) is prohibitively costly, and almost never accurate. (See the previous subsection on locality.) It is more effective to use the minimum utilization as a baseline, and to provision above that level using rules of thumb.

One approach is to use the ratio of hosts to storage for the overall Meta SAN. This is a method often used for ISL provisioning in traditional core/edge fabrics, and is a good number for that because it is lower than the peak provisioning approach and is likely to be correct because hosts generally only "talk" to storage ports. However, in Meta SANs the degree of localization within a fabric is likely to be much higher than switch-level locality in a fabric, so this number can be safely reduced still further.

Look again at Table 22 (p205). Notice the running total in the fabric row. As a rule, something on the order of 90% of traffic can be expected to remain localized on an edge fabric, if any effort is made to localize traffic at all. Reasonable IFL over-subscription ratios therefore can be much higher than ISL ratios, even when specific performance data and LSAN configurations are unavailable.

The rule of thumb method for IFL provisioning therefore can be stated this way:

1.   First configure for all *known* IFL utilization.
2.   Then add at least one additional IFL for redundancy and to support unanticipated needs.
3.   In the absence of other traffic pattern knowledge, increase this number based on the ratio of initiators to

targets in the Meta SAN modified by the anticipated localization percentage. If a Meta SAN has 1000 hosts and 100 storage ports, the ratio is 10:1. If an edge fabric has 100 hosts, it would require 10 IFLs, reduced according to the level of fabric locality. If 90% of traffic is localized, then the fabric would only need one more IFL added to the IFLs from rules 1 and 2.

To put it yet another (more obscure) way, IFL provisioning could be calculated according to the formula:

```
IFLs = ( known_traffic + 1 ) + ( fabric_hosts /
h:s_ratio ) * ( 1 - fabric_locality_percent ) )
```

Of course, this need not be followed as an axiomatic rule. If all storage in a Meta SAN is located on one fabric, and the hosts on another, then most of the IFLs must be configured going to the storage fabric. As always, rules of thumb are *aids* to intelligent SAN designers, not *replacements* for them.

Redundant Meta SAN Designs

This subsection provide example of some of the ways redundancy can be designed into Meta SANs. The methods used here are direct extensions of current storage network best-practices. Of course, there are many possible variations on the following techniques. It is possible that part of a Meta SAN will use one model, and another – perhaps less critical – section may use a different model. The bottom line is that the redundancy model should be tailored to the requirements of the business application, and should almost always be used end-to-end between the server running the application and all of its storage devices.

Resilient Meta SANs

The defining characteristic of a *resilient* SAN is that there is no single point of failure within the connectivity model. Each link has one or more alternates; each core switch is likewise duplicated. It is possible to lose an edge switch, which would impact all nodes attached to it, but critical nodes are connected to at least two edge switches.

In a resilient Meta SAN, each edge fabric that exports devices must have at least two routers providing paths to every other relevant edge fabric. Nodes generally would be connected to A/B redundant fabrics within this model. Figure 93 shows an example of this style of deployment.

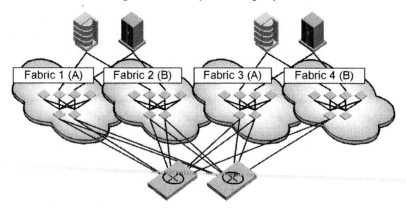

Figure 93 – Resilient Meta SAN

This is a highly reliable network design. It has the advantage of being able to route between A/B redundant fabrics, which can facilitate complex failover models. It can also allow single-attached hosts to gain some degree of network-level multi-pathing when storage ports are redundantly attached to different fabrics in the Meta SAN. Finally, this can be useful when tape drives are single-attached to one or more backup fabrics, but hosts are dual-attached.

However, this is not a fully redundant solution. This is because catastrophic failures on the routers could – at least in theory – impact both the A and B edge fabrics simultaneously. High availability guidelines for mission-critical deployments require a fully redundant Meta SAN.

Fully Redundant Meta SANs

Figure 94 shows an example of a fully redundant design. A fully redundant SAN duplicates the entire connectivity model. In a dual redundant *fabric* design, there are two com-

210

pletely separate fabrics. Similarly, in a dual redundant *Meta SAN*, there are two completely separate (A/B) Meta SANs. Critical hosts and storage arrays are dual attached, with at least one connection to each Meta SAN. This provides the greatest possible fault isolation. For example, it prevents a misbehaving HBA on one Meta SAN from being able to interfere with nodes on the other.

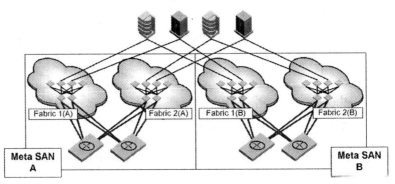

Figure 94 - Redundant Meta SANs

There are many variations on this theme. For example, the design might not be symmetrical. Perhaps Meta SAN A would have attachments from all nodes, while Meta SAN B would only be used for mission-critical nodes. Or perhaps the existence of two Meta SANs would lighten the resiliency requirements within each Meta SAN: perhaps the second core switches would be removed from each edge fabric, or the second routers and the duplicated EX_Port connections could be dispensed with. See Figure 95.

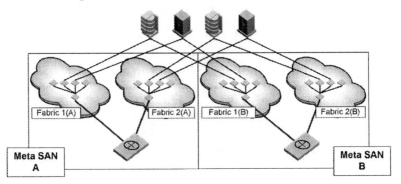

Figure 95 - Redundant Meta SANs – Variation

In general, it is best to design in redundancy at each level as long as budget constraints will allow. Just because redundant core switches within edge fabrics *could* be eliminated does not imply that they *should* be eliminated. Like many other things in network design, the decision about how much redundancy to build into each level of the network comes down to site-specific tradeoffs between price, performance, and RAS.

Backbone Fabric Meta SANs

The Backbone Fabric architecture is used to achieve scalability beyond the port count of an individual router, and to allow optimal behavior when routers are geographically separated, such as in a disaster recovery solution. One or more routers are connected to each edge fabric via EX_Ports, and are connected to a centralized backbone fabric via E_Ports. This is depicted in Figure 96. (Also see Figure 12 on p33.)

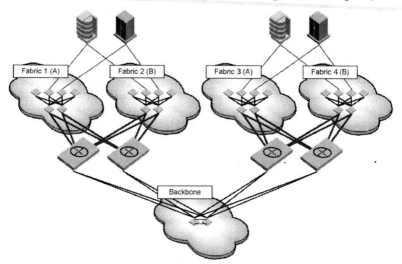

Figure 96 - Backbone Fabric Meta SAN

If an LSAN is configured between two fabrics attached to the same router, traffic on that LSAN will *not* use the backbone. However, if an LSAN spans between fabrics attached to different routers, traffic will flow across the BB fabric.

LSAN zone data and xlate configurations are exchanged across the backbone using FCRP. The BB fabric can be constructed with any standard Brocade switches or using ISLs between the routers, and is even architecturally compatible with other vendors' switches. Use of BB Fabric Meta SANs can be combined with either of the redundancy models described above, and with the iSCSI Gateway Service and FCIP Tunneling Service.

Parallel Redundant BB Fabric Meta SAN

It is possible for resiliently deployed routers to use separate backbones. This works much like the single backbone case, but has greater availability and scalability. An entire backbone fabric can fail without causing loss of connectivity across any LSANs, which eliminates certain failure modes. A redundant backbone Meta SAN is shown in Figure 97.

Note that each router can have as many connections to its backbone fabric as are desired for appropriate performance and reliability, but any given router can be attached to only *one* backbone fabric. You cannot cross connect a single router to BB-1 and BB-2. Attempting to do so will either fail (segment) or will merge the two backbones into one fabric. Therefore deploying redundant backbones requires also deploying multiple routers.

Figure 15 (p43) through Figure 16 show a redundant backbone configuration in great detail. Figure 7 (p24) shows a degenerate case[93] of the redundant backbone architecture. This shows that even when a router has no E_Ports, it still has backbone fabric. That fabric consists of one domain: that of the router itself. If two routers are connected as in Figure 7 (p24), there are two independent single-domain backbone fabrics. In that example, the backbone fabrics are purely internal to the routers, since they do not have any nodes or other switches on them.

---

[93] Degenerate Case: Being mathematically simpler than the typical case. (From the Encyclopedia Britannica.)

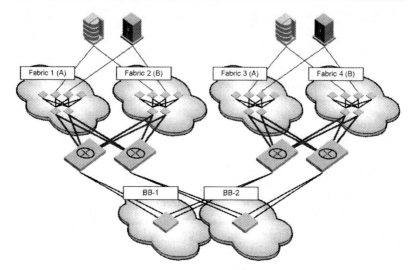

Figure 97 - Redundant BB Fabric Meta SAN

Parallel redundant backbone fabric Meta SANs can be combined with the other redundancy models discussed above. For example, Figure 94 (p211) shows a degenerate case of this method combined with fully redundant Meta SANs. Figure 98 shows an expanded example of this.

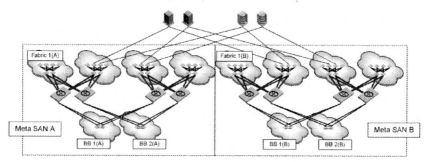

Figure 98 - Redundant Meta SAN + Redundant BBs

Finally, note that Figure 43 (p128) and most of the other distance extension examples use redundant backbone fabrics, though these are not specifically called out in most of the illustrations. In many of the FCIP examples such as Figure 127 (p293), redundant backbone fabrics are tunneled through the IP network. This is an example of FC-FC Routing Service integration with the FCIP Tunneling Service, and is the best practice for redundant WAN deployments.

IP Network Redundancy

There are many more approaches to building highly available networks than could fit in this book. This subsection gives several models to illustrate broad categories of solutions. It starts with the simplest models to illustrate basic concepts, works up to more redundant and complex, or "pure" models that show ideal goals but often have prohibitive cost, then scales back to more realistic approaches.

Logical Separation of Networks

At minimum, building a highly available IP SAN solution means designing for total separation between data and storage network traffic. This can be logical separation using software like VLANs, or (better) physical separation using different network equipment for IP SAN and data traffic. Figure 99 has one example of logical separation and Figure 100 has another.

For WANs, MANs, and sometimes CANs, IP SAN links are usually lower priority than intra-site FC links because high locality is employed at the site level. That is, if data network instabilities were to take down the IP SAN connection between sites, there would be *exposure* since, for example, a disaster recovery solution would be down, but this may not by itself cause an *application outage*. If this is the case, "separation" may mean using technologies like VLANs and QoS, but still running IP SAN and data network traffic on the same *physical* links.

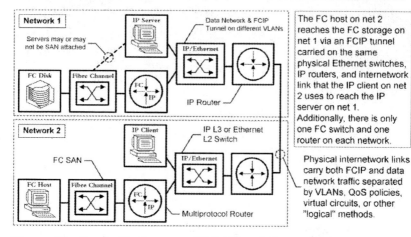

Figure 99 – Logically Separate IP SAN and Data Nets

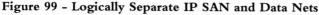

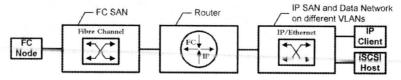

Figure 100 – Combined iSCSI and Data Network

Figure 99 has two networks separated by IP routers. Each network location has one Fibre Channel switch and one Brocade Multiprotocol Router being used as an FCIP gateway between the two networks. In addition, one location has a server running an IP-based application (such as email) and the other site has a client of that application. A single Ethernet switch and IP router set is used at each location to carry both the client/server traffic and the FCIP tunnel. The Ethernet switch is configured with VLANs to separate the IP SAN and client/server traffic, while the IP router-router link might use a WAN technology like virtual circuits in frame relay. The connection between the routers may reasonably be a WAN, MAN, or CAN link. If the networks were separated merely by LAN distances, FCIP probably would not be needed: native FC would be used instead.

Figure 100 shows a similar design using iSCSI instead of FCIP. The iSCSI host uses one NIC for both iSCSI and data network traffic. This is plugged into an Ethernet switch that it uses both to reach IP servers for a client/server application, other IP clients for peer-to-peer networking, and to reach the iSCSI gateway. The traffic may be separated using VLANs: the iSCSI portal could be a member of one VLAN, the IP servers and clients on a different VLAN, and the iSCSI NIC a member of both. In this case, not only are failure modes tied together, but performance may also be an issue if iSCSI traffic floods the data network, bringing down other applications.

The important point in each case is that both IP SAN and data network connections use the same physical switches, routers, and links, so that in many cases a failure of either the IP SAN or data network will cause a failure of both. This is only an acceptable approach in environments where occasional failures of either network or both at the same time is considered acceptable, and in which lowest possible cost is the only concern.

Physical Separation of Networks

Even moderately higher priority applications should use a physically separate IP network as shown in Figure 101 and Figure 102.

These figures could be thought of as "corrected" versions of the previous two. This is the only reliable way to protect against rogue devices attached by end users, network-aware viruses, broadcast storms, and the myriad of other problems that affect IP networking.

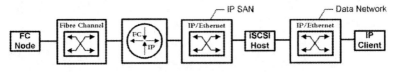

Figure 101 - Separate iSCSI and Data Networks

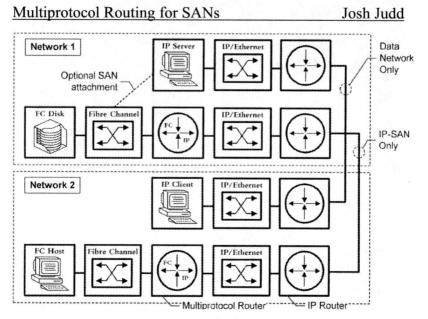

Figure 102 - Physically Separate IP SAN and Data Nets

Fully Redundant Networks

While the network separation approaches discussed above each have a positive effect on availability – the second especially – neither are completely redundant. True redundancy requires two or more physically separate IP SANs with redundant node connections. This is the IP SAN equivalent of the dual redundant A/B fabric or Meta SAN models.

Within the A/B IP SAN model there is considerable room for variations. Figure 18 (p53), Figure 21 (p56), and Figure 28 (p78) show some possibilities. Figure 103 and Figure 104 illustrate this another way.

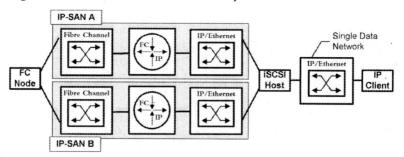

Figure 103 - Redundant IP SANs

218

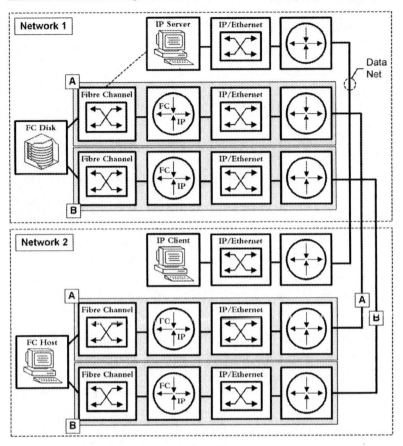

Figure 104 - Separate & Redundant IP SANs/Data Nets

In these examples, there is not only a physical separation between the IP SAN and data network applications, but there is also a physical separation between two A/B IP SANs. The important points are that no single failure can take down both the A and B IP SANs, no failure of either IP SAN can impact the data network, and vice versa.

It may not always be possible to achieve this degree of physical redundancy, but it is always a good idea to use this model as the design target, and scale down from there to meet budget constraints. On the other hand, even this model is not the pinnacle of redundancy: it is also possible to scale *up* from this point, as the next subsection demonstrates.

219

Redundant/Resilient IP SANs

The previous examples provided redundancy between A/B IP SANs, but not *within* each IP SAN. Redundancy can also apply at this level. In the Fibre Channel world, this is often referred to as *resilient* network design. In a core/edge fabric, using multiple ISLs between edge and core switches and using multiple separate core switches are examples of resilient design techniques. This prevents minor single failures within a fabric from causing a network-wide event.

Even when resiliency is employed, redundant A/B networks are still recommended for mission-critical applications since some events – like Ethernet broadcast storms in the IP SAN space – can have network-wide scope, but resiliency can be used on top of redundancy to prevent small failures – like a single SFP laser burning out – from causing a large scale failover to the second network.

In high availability design, it is always best to catch failures lower down on the stack, and using redundant pairs of resilient networks accomplishes this. It is analogous to using redundant power supplies in a server that is part of a cluster: just because it *could* fail over its applications to another cluster node does not mean that it *should* do so except under extreme failure conditions. If a power supply failure could be handled without a cluster failover, then it should be handled that way. Similarly, the best HA designs for SANs use both redundant networks and resilient paths within those networks.

In the context of IP SANs, this means designing each network with any or all of:

- Multiple router ports per IP SAN
- Multiple router ports per Fibre Channel fabric
- Multiple routers between each IP SAN and FC fabric

For example, if a redundant/resilient iSCSI solution is desired, it could be configured as in Figure 105.

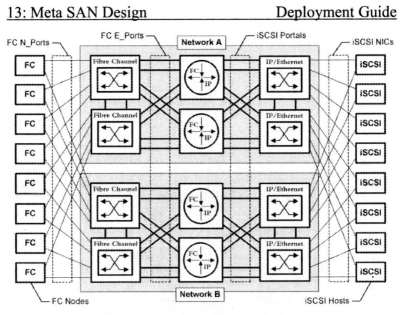

Figure 105 – Redundant/Resilient iSCSI Solution

This shows two entirely separate networks, each of which has two Fibre Channel switches and two IP/Ethernet switches connected using two separate iSCSI gateways, each of which has multiple ports to its fabric and multiple ports to its IP SAN. The Ethernet switches would use a method like Spanning Tree Protocol and/or Ethernet trunks on their redundant links, the Fibre Channel switches would use FSPF and/or trunking, and the gateways can be configured as a redundant pair using the Brocade Fabric Configuration Server and/or using manual configuration on iSCSI hosts. All hosts and storage arrays are redundantly connected and use multipathing software to coordinate usage of the different paths.

Figure 106 shows a similar approach but uses FCIP: each site has access to two Meta SANs, each of which has two Multiprotocol Router platforms with resilient IFLs to the edge fabric and resilient virtual ISLs in separate BB fabrics.

Of course, Figure 106 is unrealistic for most customers due its high cost and complexity. The design goal from an availability standpoint should be to get as close as possible to this architectural template without violating budget constraints. If it is necessary to compromise, a designer may trim

221

out redundancy. For example, it might be acceptable to set-tle for separate ports on a single router in each of the SANs. This is illustrated in Figure 107.

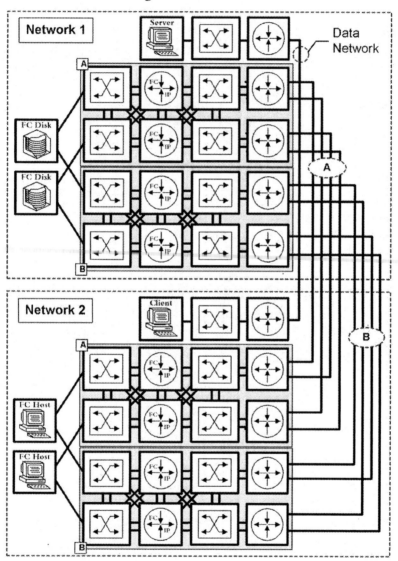

Figure 106 – Fully Redundant/Resilient FCIP Solution

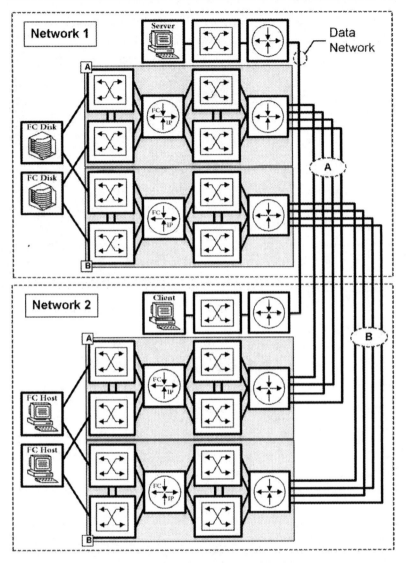

Figure 107 – Partially Resilient / Fully Redundant FCIP

While Figure 107 is not *entirely* resilient within each of the A/B SANs – a single router failure causes an A/B failover event – this compromise solution does allow for individual link failures to occur without causing a larger scale failover event. If even further cost savings were required, the eight A/B internetwork links could be collapsed into two physical links with a protocol like OSPF providing failover. This illustrates that a reasonably resilient and totally redundant design with separation of data network and IP SAN traffic can be accomplished with substantially less equipment than as previously shown in Figure 106.

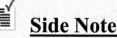

Side Note

Another way to achieve a compromise between full redundancy and cost effective deployments is to use a separate network for all active IP SAN traffic, and configure nodes to use the data network as a standby IP SAN path. While this asymmetrical approach is lower performance, less secure, and less reliable than a separated solution, it does provide many of the benefits at about half the cost.

Note that the use of multiple parallel FCIP tunnels in the previous examples is also related to performance. Both IP SANs and long distance solutions are by their very nature far lower in performance than Fibre Channel solutions, and running IP SANs over distance can only compound this issue. It is therefore necessary to configure several virtual ISLs using FCIP to achieve equal performance to a single native Fibre Channel ISL or IFL, so the redundant and resilient backbone design technique not only improves reliability by taking a "belt and suspenders" approach, but is also necessary in many cases to meet minimum performance requirements.

The tunnels use separate, resiliently connected IP networks. Furthermore, all of the IP SAN traffic is kept entirely separate from all data network traffic. Try to trace one of the tunneled backbone fabrics through the diagram. See how different backbones remain on physically separate links from end to end. This approach has the advantage of being "pure," meaning that it illustrates redundancy at every level without compromise. It makes a useful model for HA network design, and in cases where budget is not an issue, this is the "right" way to design for maximum performance and availability. For the most part, however, it just shows that anything can be taken too far.

Rightsizing Fabrics and Subnets

After experimenting with large, flat Ethernet segments, data network designers converged on a hierarchical approach with smaller subnets interconnected by routers. It is likely that the Fibre Channel market will follow a similar evolution now that FC-FC routers are available. The remaining question is how large each edge fabric will be.

For layer 2 switched Ethernet networks, most engineers seem to have decided that the right maximum size of a subnet is about 250 ports, or one Class-C IP subnet. Between these segments, layer 3 switches or routers are used.

This would seem on the surface to indicate that the right size of a Fibre Channel fabric might also be in that range, and in some cases this is likely to be true. However, there are differences between Fibre Channel and Ethernet protocols and usage cases that must be considered.

For example, the primary scalability issue that flat switched Ethernet segments faced was caused by excessive broadcasts, caused by for example ARPs. However, the analogous scalability concern for Fibre Channel – excessive RSCN propagation – is already addressed by zoning in Brocade fabrics. Furthermore, SAN traffic patterns may require larger high-performance regions than Ethernet networks require. This also argues for larger edge fabrics.

Scalability challenges remain, but these are associated with Fibre Channel's higher-level intelligent fabric services, such as the storage name server, FSPF, or zoning database exchanges. These have already been solved approximately to the two thousand port level at the time of this writing for networks built using modern Brocade directors like the SilkWorm 24000, and this is still being expanded. Practical limitations below that level are often related to manageability, fault containment, use of older and/or smaller switches, and vendor support matrices. But just because a fabric *can* scale much higher than an Ethernet subnet does not mean it *should* do so.

The right size of any given edge fabric can be determined using three rules. Each fabric should be:

1. No larger than the **support provider** has **qualified**. This may include factors such as firmware versions, switch types, topology, domain-count, and port-count.
2. No larger than the **customer** can **manage**. Large fabrics can be challenging to change-control, and some management tools have scalability limitations.
3. No larger than the largest **outage** a **customer** could **withstand**. If the entire fabric went down, what would be the business impact? Even for customers deploying redundant fabrics, having all hosts simultaneously fail over to a second fabric may not be a desirable event.

Once these factors are considered, a maximum size a fabric "should" reach will become apparent. It will likely be somewhere between the Ethernet limit (about 250 ports) and the fabric limit (up to about 2000 ports at the time of this writing). There is not yet an industry-wide rule of thumb analogous to the one that IP/Ethernet converged on, but it seems likely that it will be in the range of no more than 500 to 1000 ports per fabric in most environments, beyond which manageability, change control, and fault isolation may to become difficult for customers.

For dedicated iSCSI SANs connecting to a gateway as in Figure 21 (p56), the right size of a subnet will generally be "as small as possible." This amounts to the number of iSCSI hosts fanning in to an iSCSI portal on the gateway, or the size of a single Ethernet edge switch, *not* the ~250-port Class-C "rule of thumb" limit. There is no need to configure connectivity between different iSCSI NICs: all IO will flow from the NICs to the gateway iSCSI portal ports. Creating a single large iSCSI SAN would add cost, risk, and complexity, but would not provide a counterbalancing benefit.

14: Guidelines, Tips, & Caveats

This chapter provides guidelines, tips, and caveats related to deploying multiprotocol routers. It goes beyond the product user manual and the firmware release notes. It is not, however, a "superset" list that *substitutes* for these documents; rather, it is intended to *supplement* to them.

The guidelines in this chapter are also not intended to be viewed as vendor support constraints. Check with the appropriate support provider for those. Rather, this chapter is intended to give both support providers and end users a starting point from which to develop more complete guidelines and, eventually, best-practices. When multiprotocol SAN routers have been in production for a longer time, this book will be updated to reflect the way industry best-practices and vendor supported configurations have developed.

Since caveats, tips, and guidelines tend to be based on production usage of a product, and change as the product is enhanced with new features, it is almost certain that content in this chapter will be updated frequently. It is strongly recommended that readers register online to receive free updates, and to gain access to other manuals and whitepapers. (**http://www.brocade.com/bookshelf**)

FC-FC Routing Service General Tips

Limiting Dependencies

The FC-FC Routing service limits dependencies between edge fabrics, or between sites when also using the FCIP service, or between unreliable iSCSI hosts when using the iSCSI service. However, it only does so when reasonable zoning policies are followed, and when some degree of fabric-level locality is used.

In order to get the most out of the service, only configure off-fabric connectivity using LSANs for devices that actually need the connectivity. For example, do not create large any-to-any zones that translate all devices in a fabric to all other fabrics just in case connectivity is needed at a later date. This will remove many of the scalability and fault-containment benefits of the service.

LSAN Zoning

Aside from starting with "LSAN_" and containing only port WWNs and their aliases, LSAN zones are indistinguishable from regular zones. This is useful because it allows existing management applications to operate on LSANs, which allows SAN administrators to use familiar tools and management paradigms.

It also means that LSANs can be configured with great flexibility. It is possible to create LSAN zones that overlap with other LSAN zones or with regular zones. One WWN alias could be a member of a local "regular" zone and also a member of an LSAN zone.

Alternately, a single zone could be used to provide both intra- and inter-fabric connectivity. An LSAN zone could allow connectivity between nodes on the *same* edge fabric and to nodes on a *different* edge fabric. Indeed, a single LSAN zone could provide intra-fabric connectivity and also inter-fabric connectivity to *multiple* remote fabrics. There are situations in which this might be a desirable scheme, for example during data migration when nodes within an LSAN might move between fabrics with regularity.

However, for most applications it is simpler to keep inter-fabric LSAN zones separated from regular intra-fabric zones. In combination with a structured LSAN zone / alias naming scheme, this makes it easier to analyze inter-fabric dependencies for change control, and to tell at a glance which nodes are shared between what fabrics.

✅ Side Note

In some cases, a router will be connected to one or more fabrics that have no active zoning policy in place. It is necessary to activate zoning on edge fabrics before LSANs can be created. From a security standpoint, the use of zoning is a best-practice in all cases, so this is not a bad thing. The ideal approach would be to use the router installation as an opportunity to create a meaningful zoning policy for all edge fabrics, reflecting the connectivity that is truly required. However, in some cases this would be too time consuming and/or could be considered an unacceptable risk from a change management standpoint. If so, it is possible to create one "catchall" zone that has the [domain,port] of all devices in the fabric. This is effectively like having no zoning in place within the fabric, but still allows LSANs to be created.

LSAN Naming

When creating the name of an LSAN zone, it is a good idea to indicate the remote FID to which it is connecting as well as a functional description of the zone's purpose.[94] This way, if an outage is scheduled for the remote FID it will be easy to see which zones will be affected.[95] Similarly, WWN aliases for remote nodes should specify the both the node name or function and its fabric location or function.

The generic LSAN zone name format could be:

---

[94] This could be specified by FID or functional name. For example, if the FID=1 fabric is being used for disaster recovery, a zone on FID=2 that accesses it might as easily be called "LSAN_FID_001_backup" or "LSAN_DR_backup". Again, the exception is Meta SANs in which nodes move between fabrics frequently. These should be named by function alone.

[95] In UNIX terms, you would "grep" the zoning configuration for the string "FID*xxx*" where *xxx* is the FID of the fabric that will have the outage. Or, if not specifying by FID, grep for the remote fabric's functional name.

LSAN_FID[*xxx*]_[*function of zone*]

...or...

LSAN_[*remote fabric name*]_[*function of zone*]

The generic LSAN WWN node alias could be:

[*name or function of node*]_FID[*xxx*]

It important point is not that one of those two particular formats must or even should be used. Rather, the point is that *some* kind of meaningful and structured format should be in place so simplify ongoing management.

LSAN Overlap

It is usually cleaner to create multiple LSAN zones that overlap with each other and with regular zones rather than creating large zones that serve both inter- and intra-fabric functions. Similarly, if possible it is desirable to create different LSAN zones for different remote fabrics. That way, an administrator can tell at a glance which nodes will be impacted by inter-fabric events such as an outage for a router.

This also improves fault management by containing RSCNs generated by remote fabrics to the greatest extent possible. It *is* desirable for devices that are communicating with remote nodes to be notified if, for example, those nodes are powered down – which is the purpose of RSCNs – but it is *not* desirable for local nodes to be notified if they are *not* communicating with remote devices. Since Brocade fabric zoning acts as an RSCN containment mechanism, smaller zones with more focused membership result in smaller and more appropriate RSCN notifications. If a node is in a zone unnecessarily, it may receive unnecessary RSCNs.

LSAN Zoning Example

Figure 108 shows a Meta SAN providing connectivity for disaster recovery between two fabrics: FID=1 and FID=2. FID=1 is the DR fabric and FID=2 is at the primary site. There is one storage port on FID=1 that needs to be accessed both by a host on FID=2 (the primary database server) and by a host on FID=1 (the disaster recovery database server). There is a storage port on FID=2 that only needs to be accessed by the FID=2 host. Once the connectivity is configured, the FID=2 host will mirror all writes to both storage ports. In the event of a disaster, the FID=1 host will take over the database using up-to-the-instant data on the FID=1 storage port.

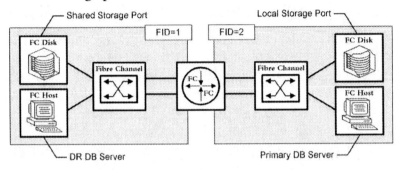

Figure 108 - LSAN Zoning Tips Example Topology

An administrator on FID=1 could configure this connectivity using a single zone that started with the string "LSAN_" and contained the WWNs or aliases of all four devices.[96] This is illustrated in Figure 109.

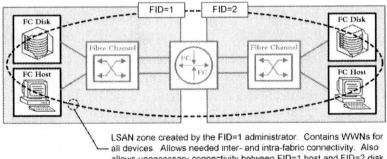

LSAN zone created by the FID=1 administrator. Contains WWNs for all devices. Allows needed inter- and intra-fabric connectivity. Also allows unnecessary connectivity between FID=1 host and FID=2 disk.

Figure 109 - LSAN Zoning Tips Example - Single Zone

However, this allows more inter-fabric connectivity than needed: it creates a superfluous dependency between the DR

---

[96] It almost goes without saying that the administrator on FID=2 would need to configure a similar zone.

host and the primary disk. It exports the FID=1 host into FID=2, even though it never needs access to FID=2 storage. Also, it would be hard to tell from looking a the zoning data-base which devices were *really* using the inter-fabric links.

It would be cleaner to create two different zones: one for intra-fabric traffic and another for inter-fabric connectivity. The first zone would follow the existing zone naming con-ventions, and would contain both the FID=1 storage and the FID=1 host. This would not export the FID=1 host unnec-essarily. The second zone would follow an LSAN naming convention, and would contain both the FID=1 storage and the FID=2 host. This method is shown in Figure 110.

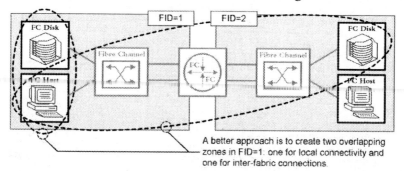

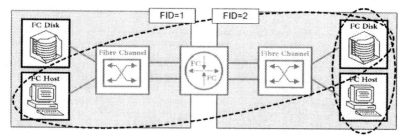

A better approach is to create two overlapping zones in FID=1: one for local connectivity and one for inter-fabric connections.

Figure 110 - LSAN Zoning Tips Example - Two Zones (FID=1)

Note that the FID=2 fabric would have a similar but slightly different zone set. It would have the same LSAN zone, but would have a different intra-fabric zone set, as shown in Figure 111.

Figure 111 - LSAN Zoning Example - Two Zones (FID=2)

Side Note

It may be tempting to name all zones in all fabrics with the LSAN_ prefix in order to eliminate the need to change zone names if devices move between LSANs later. This is not recommended, since it limits the scalability of the router. Each router can only process a certain number of LSAN zones. While this is a large number (thousands), it is still a limited resource and therefore should be conserved wherever possible. As a best practice, only use the LSAN_ prefix for zones that will actually span fabrics.

Meta SAN Management Applications

Broadly speaking, there are three categories of SAN management applications that relate to the router:

- Element Managers – These manage the router platforms themselves. The CLI and WEB TOOLS are examples.

- Single-Fabric Managers – These perform operations on or display information about fabric-wide services like zoning, FSPF, or SNS. Many can display fabric topologies graphically. WEB TOOLS and the SAN Health™ tool are examples.

- Multi-Fabric Managers – These perform the functions of single-fabric managers, but in addition they can be used to manage many fabrics at once. The Brocade Fabric Manager and the SAN Health tool are examples.

To manage Meta SAN network infrastructure (i.e. switches, routers, and LSAN zones) it is necessary to have element management and either single- or multi-fabric management tools.

The router comes with its own GUI and command line element management interfaces, and after initial setup there is generally little that needs to be done to the router itself on a regular basis. A single administrative group should be the owner of each router: if the site security model requires dif-

233

ferent administrative groups to be able to configure the router from an element management perspective, then multiple routers should be used and networked together using a backbone fabric.

Edge fabric management can be done by a single administrative group or a different group for each fabric.

If different administrators are responsible for different edge fabrics, then single-fabric management tools are appropriate. The zoning configuration from Figure 110 would be created by the FID=1 administrator, and a similar action would be taken separately using the same or different single-fabric management tools by the FID=2 administrator. Once these two actions were complete, the router would automatically configure LSAN access.[97]

On the other hand, if the same administrative group owns both edge fabrics, it may be more productive to use a tool that is aware of multiple fabrics. The latest version of the Brocade Fabric Manager (FM), for example, can see both the FID=1 and FID=2 fabrics at once, and can configure the LSAN in one operation instead of two. FM versions 4.2 and later provide an LSAN configuration wizard under [Tools][Share Devices]. Figure 112 and Figure 113 show the wizard being used to create a new LSAN.

Using the wizard, it is only necessary to enter a unique LSAN zone name and click the device(s) to be shared across the router. Fabric Manager will then create matching LSAN zones in each fabric. Note that this wizard cannot perform *all* possible LSAN operations; it may still be necessary to use standard zoning tools for more complex LSANs.

---

[97] When selecting a single-fabric management tool for LSAN environments, it is necessary to ensure that the tool can accept manually entered WWNs. If, for example, the tool only allowed selection of WWNs from a pull-down menu derived from the fabric SNS database, then it would not be possible to enter the WWN of a device on a remote fabric. Fortunately, almost all fabric management tools allow users to manually input WWNs.

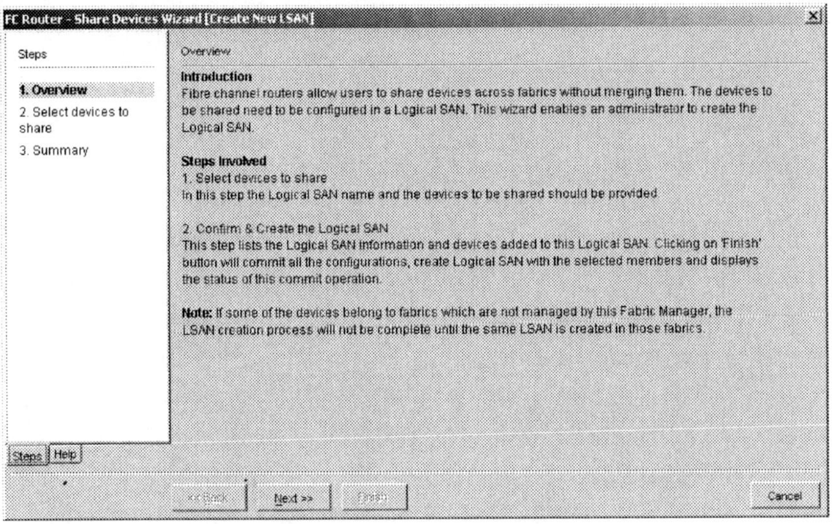

Figure 112 - FM LSAN Creation Wizard (First Screen)

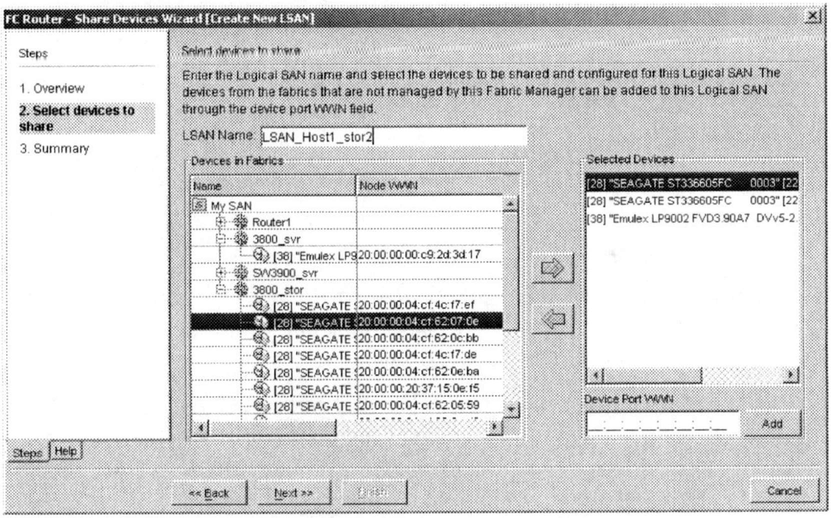

Figure 113 - FM LSAN Creation Wizard (Second Screen)

At the time of this writing, Brocade partners are still in the process of updating their management tools to be LSAN-aware, so in some cases third-party multi-fabric mangers may require multiple operations to create LSANs. When evaluating third-party tools, look for the following features:

- Multi-fabric knowledge is key. Look for the ability to discover and display many fabrics at once.

- Knowledge that there can be connectivity between them if routers are in place. This is important so that the tool can manage zoning properly.

- Ability to display physical Meta SAN topology including the routers. (This is applicable only if the tool is designed to output network diagrams.)

- Ability to display the logical (fabric and phantom) topologies of each edge and backbone fabric.

- Knowledge that a port WWN can exist in more than one fabric, and may have different PIDs in these fabrics. Some tools may index nodes by PID, which are not unique in multi-fabric environments, or may only have the ability to associate a given WWN with one PID, which will not work for exported devices.

SCSI Extended Copy and FC-NAT

Extended Copy (or *xcopy*) is one method vendors have defined to enable serverless backup applications, and at the time of this writing, it is the only technology known to have a possible *innate* compatibility problem with FC-NAT. It is theoretically possible for an xcopy application to specify Fibre Channel Port IDs (PIDs) in the *payload* portion of a frame. (Normally PIDs are only used in the *header* of a frame.) While Brocade has not ever seen this occur in testing, if it did happen, xcopy would not work between edge fabrics.

To determine if this issue will affect a given application, use the following criteria. If any answer below is "no," then this caveat will not apply.

1. Does the environment use serverless backups?
2. Does that application use xcopy?
3. Does that application span fabrics using the FCR?

4.   Does its implementation of xcopy embed PIDs in the *payload* portion of frames, as opposed to the header?[98]

The platform hardware (XPath ASICs) that is used to implement FC-NAT in the router would allow the it to translate PIDs in the payload of xcopy frames as well as in the headers. However, this caveat has not been proven to have any real-world applicability at all, so adding this feature has not been a priority. If a real-world case is found where PIDs are used by an application in the payload of FC frames, please report it in detail to **bookshelf@brocade.com**.

iSCSI Gateway Service General Tips

Session Limits

As mentioned in the iSCSI Overview chapter, each connection between an iSCSI host and storage port – known as a session – takes up resources such as CPU time and RAM on both the host and storage sides. No iSCSI device can support an infinite number of sessions – this is an inherent limitation of the protocol – and it is important to understand what the limitations are prior to designing an IP SAN.

When using the Brocade gateway, the storage side of the session is the gateway portal, a.k.a. the iSCSI port on the multiprotocol router, rather than the actual FC storage port. There will be session limits that apply to the gateway portal(s) and to the host(s).

At the time of this writing, the iSCSI service can support eight sessions per port. That means it is possible for eight iSCSI hosts to share a single portal if they each only access one storage port. If each host accesses two storage ports, then four hosts could share a portal. Accessing multiple LUNs on

---

[98] Short of using an FC**Error! Bookmark not defined.** analyzer, it may be easier to ask the vendor this question. The more likely alternative is that it would embed WWNs. (This is the "right" way of doing it even in environments without FC**Error! Bookmark not defined.**-NAT, since PIDs can change as devices move around in a fabric or domain IDs change.)

a given storage port does *not* take up multiple sessions. This limit is intended to be expanded in subsequent firmware releases, but requiring resources on a per-port basis for sessions is an inherent problem with the iSCSI protocol itself, so it will never be possible to design an iSCSI device that does not have *some* kind of session limit. Whatever the limit may be in the future, it will always be possible to use multiple portals on the gateway or multiple gateways if it is necessary to configure more sessions than a single portal can handle.

Distance Limits

There are no fixed limitations on how great a distance can exist between an iSCSI host and a portal on the gateway. However, there are *practical* limits. This is because greater distances result in greater delay, and usually in lower reliability as well. To work correctly, any storage networking solution must be able to ensure a good response time and connection quality. Even minimal packet loss rates[99] can have a large impact on performance, and latency on the orders of magnitude that IP networks experience can rival disk seek time as a performance limiting factor.

While only a detailed analysis of the network can yield a definitive answer about the supportable distance for iSCSI, the rule of thumb is that it should not be configured for more than a few hundred miles even when running over the fastest and most reliable of IP networks. If the network has high·latency[100] or low quality,[101] then the distance will fall rapidly, so it is critical to use IP networks with high service level agreements (SLAs) for long distance IP SAN connections.

---

[99] That is, minimal by IP standards. *Zero* frame loss is considered the baseline for real–world FC**Error! Bookmark not defined.** networks, and equivalent reliability is basically unattainable outside of a lab environment for IP networks.

[100] E.g. greater than one millisecond is "high" latency.

[101] E.g. greater than 0.01% [packet loss + error rate].

iSCSI + FCIP Distance Caveat

Sometimes a site will have both iSCSI connections and FCIP tunnel(s) to another site. This can work well, provided that the iSCSI hosts access storage at the remote site in *parallel* with the FCIP link, rather than *through* it. Figure 114 and Figure 115 show an incorrect and correct configuration.[102]

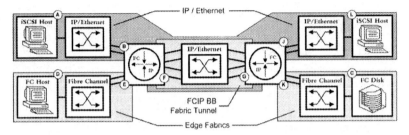

Figure 114 - Incorrect iSCSI + FCIP WAN Usage

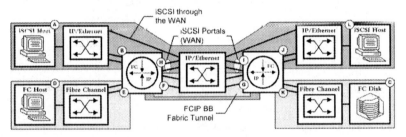

Figure 115 - Correct iSCSI + FCIP WAN Usage

If the connections were configured in the *incorrect* manner, then each packet from an iSCSI host (A) would need to be converted from IP to FC by the near-side gateway (B), back to IP for the FCIP tunnel (F), and back to FC by the far-side of the tunnel (G,K) for delivery to the disk (C). While it is *possible* to configure the network that way, it would be – to say the least – an inefficient process, and would further reduce the supportable distance and further reduce the

---

[102] The figures in this subsection are somewhat misleading. They show iSCSI to edge fabric connectivity, which is a case of backbone to edge routing and is not currently supported, though it is planned for an upcoming release. (See Figure 63 p165.) A similar architecture is supported today which involves connecting a storage port to the backbone. (Figure 61 p162) Alternately, the FCR feature could be deactivated, in which case all fabrics in effect would be on the backbone.

already severely degraded performance and reliability inherent in any IP SAN solution.

A better approach is to use near-side portals only for in-tra-site IO, and using iSCSI portals on the remote gateway directly for inter-site IO. When the WAN is set up this way, each packet will only be converted from IP to FC just once.

Configuring the WAN properly in this example means having WAN-facing iSCSI portals at each end.[103] On the near end, the portals would be used by the iSCSI hosts to ac-cess local storage ports, so the iSCSI host on the right (L) would use its local portal (J) to reach its local disk (C). The hosts would be configured to go directly to the portals on the remote gateways to access remote storage, so if the iSCSI host on the left (A) needed to access the storage on the right (C) it would use the WAN-facing iSCSI portal on the right-hand gateway (I) *instead* of its local portal (B). Both iSCSI and FCIP packets would flow across the WAN in parallel.

iSCSI vs. FC Performance

Under no conditions can 1Gbit iSCSI match Fibre Chan-nel performance. At best, 1Gbit iSCSI running over TOE- and iSCSI-protocol accelerated NICs to accelerated iSCSI-native storage can achieve half the performance of a standard 2Gbit Fibre Channel connection, and with 4Gbit FC on the way the gap will double again. The most popular iSCSI con-figurations by far are even slower still: they involve non-accelerated built-in Gigabit Ethernet NICs running software drivers. These are typically limited to just a few megabytes per second in real-world deployments.[104] See Figure 22 (p57) and the surrounding text for a further discussion of this.

---

[103] In other usage cases this may not be needed. For an example, see Figure 51 (p144) and the surrounding text.

[104] iSCSI storage or network equipment vendors will often demonstrate higher performance by not running any applications on the host. Applications take up CPU cycles that are needed to make software iSCSI stacks perform well. Cus-tomers who do not run applications on their hosts will benefit from this testing.

For customers deploying such limited iSCSI solutions, the key to performance on the gateway is how may hosts each portal can support simultaneously.

Given the session limits at the time of this writing (eight) it has only been possible to test up to eight software iSCSI hosts per portal, and these have only been able to drive up to about 400Mbits/sec. of throughput to a given port. As the session count increases, per-portal throughput is also expected to increase. Check manuals, release notes, and documentation available on the Brocade website for current performance benchmarks.

FCIP Tunneling Service General Tips

WAN_TOV

Fibre Channel standards require that switches limit the lifetime of a frame from end to end. Of course this includes the time spent traversing switch internals or sitting in port buffers, but it also includes the time a frame spends in transit on switch-to-switch links like ISLs, IFLs, and FCIP tunnels. The time that a frame sits on even a long distance native Fibre Channel link is so minimal that it does not generally need to be accounted for, but due to the high latency inherent in IP solutions, this is not the case with FCIP tunnels.

The Brocade FCIP service is capable of accounting for the time frames spend in transit across the IP network. This feature is known as the wide area network timeout value, or *WAN_TOV*, and it is always recommended that this feature be enabled.

The gateway does this by putting a timestamp into the encapsulation header on one end, and checking it against the gateway clock on the other side. When de-encapsulating a frame, the receiving gateway will calculate the difference between the time in its own clock and the departure time

---

Unfortunately, *most* real-world deployments require applications as well as iSCSI drivers to run simultaneously.

recorded in the frame header. If the transit time exceeds WAN_TOV then the frame will be discarded. Otherwise, the frame will be de-encapsulated and forwarded.[105]

For WAN_TOV to work, it is necessary that the gateways on each side have tightly synchronized clocks. To allow this, the gateways support the Network Time Protocol (NTP).

To enable FCIP with WAN_TOV, first enable NTP on both switches. Use the *tsClockServer* command to do this. Then stop the ports that are to be configured for FCIP using the *portStop* CLI command. Configure the port for Gigabit Ethernet and set basic IP parameters using *portCfgGigE*, then restart the port using *portStart*. If it is necessary to change from the default value for WAN_TOV, this can be done using the *configure* command. It should be no lower than 1,000ms. (That is, one second, but all TOV values are configured in milliseconds.) Use *portCfgFCIP* on each gateway to enable FCIP. This includes an option (-t) to activate WAN_TOV enforcement. Once the tunnel is configured, use *fcipShow* to monitor the state of the tunnel.

See the appropriate man pages or printed manuals for details on command usage.

MAN/WAN Technologies

There are many technologies for transporting storage traffic over metro and wide areas. Some examples include:

- **FC Over Dark Fiber**. In this case, native Fibre Channel traffic – usually running on E_Ports or EX_Ports – is carried over a dedicated optical connection between sites. If the dark fiber is leased, the owner does not provide ser-

---

[105] While using WAN_TOV is always recommended, it is an optional feature. If it is not enabled on the sending gateway, the timestamp fields will not be set, in which case the receiving FCIP will de-encapsulate and forward the frame without checking the transit time.

vices on the line.[106] This is left entirely to the customer. FC over dark fiber is highly reliable and high performance, as it minimizes equipment that could fail, does not require protocol conversions, and the bandwidth is never shared with non-SAN applications. This has the lowest possible latency impact, and is practical to distances well in excess of 200km[107] with the Multiprotocol Router due to its ability to deliver high per-port buffer credits.

- **FC Over xWDM.** Native Fibre Channel connections are made to a dense or course wave division multiplexer. (DWDM or CDWM are collectively referred to as xWDM.) The traffic is carried on a dedicated wavelength, but the fiber it is carried on between sites may have other services running on different wavelengths. This is equally high performance to dark fiber as it does not add latency or constrain throughput, and is nearly as reliable. (It is only *slightly* less reliable because the WDM device itself might fail.) Distances supported may be in excess of those supported by dark fiber if intermediate WDMs are used as repeaters. Note that the FC switches or routers on each end may need to support a large number of buffer credits in some cases, unless the WDM itself does this.

- **FC Over SONET/SDH.** It is possible to carry Fibre Channel over Synchronous Optical Networks. (The analogous service is known as Synchronous Digital Hierarchy in Europe, Asia and other regions.) This may involve OC3, OC12, or even native FC services depending on the provider. Lower speeds such as E3/T3 may also be usable for connectivity at even lower cost points. SONET adds minimal latency, can often support up to

---

[106] This is how dark fibre got its name: there is no laser light coming out of the service provider's cable drop because – until the customer connects their equipment at the far end – there is nothing plugged into it that would generate light. Other services involve active equipment owned by the service provider and located at their facilities, which shine laser light down the pipe.

[107] This may require specialized SFPs and/or signal repeaters.

full FC bandwidth, is highly reliable, and can span arbitrarily long distances provided that the carrier has appropriate facilities.

- **FC Over ATM**. Mapping Fibre Channel over ATM was one of the first methods for providing long distance storage networks. (Brocade and CNT were pioneers in this space.) While ATM seems to be on the decline, it is still a "tried and true" approach. It can be configured to be highly deterministic, tends to perform better than FCIP from a delay standpoint, and is highly reliable. However, ATM routers and services tend to be fairly expensive.

- **FC Over IP**. Also known as FCIP, this technology is discussed extensively in Chapters 4, 8, 9, and 12. FCIP is characterized by its ability to connect to ubiquitously available IP MAN/WAN services at relatively low cost. It is also the least reliable and lowest performing option. This is because IP WANs typically involve many hops across different carriers equipment (so the environments are less controlled) and usually have high degrees of deliberately designed in over subscription. This causes high congestion (delay) and packet loss rates compared to localized SANs. Theoretically, FCIP can use either switched IP/Ethernet services or dedicated point-to-point Gigabit Ethernet connections, but as a practical matter the latter are not used. If point-to-point connections are available, it always is better to use native Fibre Channel.

Which MAN/WAN technology to use depends on a number of factors, such as:

- **Availability of Service**. Is there a provider that can deliver service at each site? For example, if dark fiber is not available between sites, then another technology will clearly need to be used no matter how well dark fiber otherwise would have met the network's requirements. FCIP tends to be the easiest fit in this category since IP services are almost universally available. It is somewhat harder to find IP services with appropriate bandwidth and service level agreements.

- **Application RAS Requirements**. For applications that require high reliability, availability, and serviceability, any of the technologies could be employed provided that appropriate SLAs are in place and only enterprise-class components are used. However, it is inherently easier to achieve RAS goals with native Fibre Channel solutions like dark fiber and xWDM since they involve fewer components from fewer vendors. The less equipment involved in a connection, the less that can go wrong with it. FCIP tends to be the worst performer in this category, with SONET/SDH and ATM in the middle.

- **Application Performance Requirements**. Many applications are extremely sensitive to delay and error rates on their storage devices, while others are less sensitive. For example, performance on hosts running synchronous mirrors over distance will be severely degraded unless WAN performance is best-in-class, whereas asynchronous applications can usually tolerate more delay and a higher error rate. Synchronous applications are better suited to SONET/SDH, ATM, xWDM, and dark fiber solutions; asynchronous applications could reasonably employ FCIP, but it is still critical to get an IP WAN with a top-notch service level agreement. Similarly, different applications will require more or less raw throughput. An IP SAN connection over an ISDN 128k link will not be useful for most customers. The best fit in the performance category is *always* native Fibre Channel either running across dark fiber or xWDMs for medium distances, and Fibre Channel over SONET/SDH or ATM for longer distances.

- **Distance Between Sites**. Some technologies are inherently limited to MAN and shorter WAN distances, such as dark fiber and xWDMs. Others, like FCIP or iSCSI, can support long distances, but not without incurring delay and loss that may impact applications. SONET/SDH and ATM tend to be the best fits for long distance.

- **Solution Cost**. How much does each service option and network infrastructure cost, both initially and on an ongoing basis? For example, if a customer has an application that would benefit from SONET/SDH, but only has half the budget necessary to deploy it, another solution will be needed or the project delayed. FCIP tends to cost less than the alternatives due to volumes and availability of IP networks.

In addition to choosing between protocols such as native FC, ATM, SONET/SDH, and IP, it is often necessary to select a lower-level protocol. Table 23 lists some MAN/WAN technologies and their speeds.

Table 23 – MAN/WAN Technologies and Speeds

Technology	Speed	Technology	Speed
ISDN BRI	128Mbits	OC12	622Mbps
FracT1	≤1.5Mbps	STM4	622Mbps
ADSL [108]	≤1.5Mbps	Native GE (1)	1Gbps
ISDN PRI	1.5Mbps	Native FC (1)	1Gbps
DS1/T1	1.5Mbps	Native FC (2)	2Gbps
E1	2Mbps	OC48	2.5Gbps
Ethernet	10Mbps	STM16	2.5Gbps
E3	34Mbps	Native FC (4)	4Gbps [109]
DS3/T3	45Mbps	OC192	10Gbps
Fast ENet	100Mbps	STM64	10Gbps
OC3	155Mbps	Native GE (10)	10Gbps [109]
STM1	155Mbps	Native FC (10)	10Gbps [109]

Only certain combinations of technologies are practical. For example, there may not be any method of mapping native FC over ISDN BRI, whereas mapping FCIP over ISDN could be supported. In addition, some of these technologies are only available at all in certain regions, such as T1 vs. E1.

---

[108] Some providers may offer multi-megabit ADSL, but this seems to be atypical.

[109] Denotes a protocol that is not widely available or cost effective at the time of this writing.

Note that speeds of less than 100Mbps may not be acceptable for *synchronous* SAN applications, and often multi-gigabit speeds are necessary for acceptable application performance to be maintained. OC3/STM1 are usually the baseline for this, and deployments using OC12/STM4 or beyond will probably have better results.[110]   *Asynchronous* applications will often be supportable with lower speeds.

FCIP vs. FC Performance

Just as with iSCSI, it is not possible to get close to performance parity with native Fibre Channel links when running FCIP. This is even true when comparing it to 1Gbit FC instead of 2Gbit. If high performance is a priority, use a technology like native Fibre Channel over dark fiber or xWDMs, or an ATM or SONET/SDH gateway.

For customers who need to use an IP SAN technology due to budgetary constraints, performance can be greatly enhanced by ensuring that the end-to-end connection between FCIP gateways has low error rates and low delays. If any piece of the network between the gateways does not have a top-of-the-line service level agreement, it is likely that the FCIP connection will have reliability problems. Be sure that the SLA specifies low error and loss rates[111] and low delays.[112]

In a realistically high-performance IP WAN network, each FCIP tunnel can be expected to sustain no more than about ½ of line rate in the best cases,[113] and this will reduce rapidly as reliability of the WAN degrades. If more performance is needed, other technologies are probably more

---

[110] It could take multiple FCIP portals on the gateway to fill these larger pipes.

[111] E.g. no greater than 0.01% [packet loss + error rate]

[112] E.g. no greater than one millisecond between FCIP ports

[113] This is caused by round trip delays. Some technologies purport to solve this by acknowledging writes on the near end before the far end receives them. This is a violation of SCSI standards and risks data corruption, especially in packet-loss-prone IP SAN solutions. The more responsible solution is to use a network that has less delay…

appropriate, but it is also possible to balance traffic across multiple parallel FCIP tunnels to improve throughput.

Distance Limits

There is no inherent distance limitation on the FCIP service. Rather, there are limits on loss and error rates that *tend* in the real world to be related to distance. In most cases it is impractical to support highly reliable (by SAN standards) IP connections for extremely long distances, such as coast-to-coast. Large IP networks like the Internet are possible because most IP applications handle IP's high latency and high packet loss gracefully. Storage applications are generally written assuming a reliable and fast infrastructure: sub-microsecond end-to-end delay and zero loss except in failure modes. As a result, the practical / supportable distance using the FCIP service is *usually* in the range of 200km to 400km.[114]

Some special purpose FCIP gateways are better at handling low-reliability networks. CNT in particular is recommended if either greater distances or "dirty" connections will be required.

If the IP WAN is going to carry both FCIP and data network traffic, it is critical to use QoS features to prioritize IP SAN traffic over other applications. Otherwise, data network traffic can act like a denial of service attack against the IP SAN, and even in the best of cases can further limit the practically supportable distance. Of course, prioritizing IP SAN traffic can have the same effect on data network applications, so it is recommended to physically separate data and storage network traffic if at all possible.

---

[114] Extremely long distance IP SAN solutions can be demonstrated to work under laboratory conditions, but this has little real world applicability. Since this section deals with practical limitations, describing a "science project" solution would not be productive. See the marketing literature distributed by other IP SAN vendors if proof-of-concept quality solutions are desired.

Fault Containment with FCR

It is always recommended to use the FC-FC Routing Service when building a long-distance SAN, whether using the integrated FCIP gateway or a third-party solution. This prevents WAN instabilities from affecting fabrics at the WAN endpoints to the greatest extent possible. Only devices in LSANs actively using the WAN will be impacted, which is unavoidable from the standpoint of the router.

Many of the figures throughout this book that show an FCR solution with a backbone fabric can be mapped to an equivalent FCIP+FCR solution. This is discussed in the detailed FCIP walkthrough (Figure 39 p96) and the combined usage examples (Figure 59 and Figure 60 p160, and Figure 62 p164). Simply use any valid Fibre Channel fabric distance extension solution in place of or in addition to the backbone fabric switches pictured.

Security Notes

Much about security for the router is the same as for any other network-attached mission-critical device. For example, one should follow existing policies regarding changing passwords and disabling or at least changing SNMP community strings. Many books have already been written about datacenter security, and most sites already have at least a basic security policy, so this subsection will not go into great detail on that subject.

In addition to general IT best-practices, there are some SAN-specific considerations. For example, fabric zoning is *always* recommended in SANs. This is true even if access control is being configured on storage devices as well. In this case it acts as a "belt and suspenders" security measure, and also helps fabric stability and scalability by limiting the propagation of RSCNs and limiting the impact of certain "bad citizen" behaviors in which nodes can engage. Zones should be configured with just one HBA per zone for greatest effect.

(This is because HBAs usually do not need to talk to each other, and can sometime create instabilities by doing so.)

Ideally, the router's management interfaces should be attached to an isolated (or at least firewall-protected) network management subnet rather than an exposed part of the greater corporate network.[115]

Similarly, all IP SAN interfaces (iSCSI and FCIP portals) should be on isolated or at least protected networks. It is rarely advisable to combine IP SAN and data network traffic.

Finally, always use authentication (e.g. CHAP or WWN) when building iSCSI and FCIP solutions.

Rollout and Change Control

Broadly, there are two categories of rollout for the router: "green field" deployments where the storage network is being built with the router from the ground up, and installed base upgrades, where existing FC fabrics are enhanced by adding a router.

Green Field Rollout

This is the easiest scenario to discuss, since there is no risk to production applications during the rollout phase. For most customers, the sequence for a green field rollout is as follows:

1. Create a high-level rollout plan, describing the phases below and giving schedule targets for each. Until the next steps are complete, this plan cannot be detailed.
2. Detail the business problem(s) that the storage network is intended to solve. For example, a customer may have many hundreds of enterprise-class storage arrays with inefficient utilization of their white space. The

---

[115] If the router is being used as an iSCSI gateway, then the iSNS servers must also have interfaces with access to this network. Also be sure that different gateways in the same fabric all have access to each other's management ports. That is, it should be possible to ping (or use any IP protocol) between the management ports of any iSCSI gateways that serve to the same fabric.

goal of the SAN might be to consolidate storage resources so that arrays with free space will be accessible
to the hosts that need them.

3. Design the storage network topology to solve the prob-
   lem(s). In the case of a router rollout, the design will
   specify FC HBAs, FC storage ports, FC switches, and
   routers. It should also include definition of storage-
   related software that will run over the SAN (like volume managers, value-added software on switches and
   routers, and multipathing drivers), applications that
   will use the SAN (like databases), and the anticipated
   IO patterns of these applications so that localization
   can be considered. Optionally, there will be iSCSI
   NICs, IP/Ethernet switches and/or routers, and
   CAN/MAN/WAN infrastructure as well.

4. Create a more detailed rollout plan, including a schedule for the remaining phases and a complete budget.
   Be sure to include professional services if a third party
   will be assisting with the deployment, and budget for
   support contracts on all hardware and software.

5. Source and acquire equipment and software. This may
   be done all at once, or in a phased manner.

6. Begin to deploy and test the SAN. Build out the core
   infrastructure first, so that the overall structure of the
   network does not need to keep changing during the
   rollout. This means deploying routers first, and connecting at least one switch per edge fabric that is
   intended to enter production in the first phase. Try using both localized and off-fabric connections to test the
   FC-FC router functions. If IP SAN technology is to be
   used, this is the time to test that as well.

7. Once the network is structurally complete and stable, it
   can enter production even if the entire rollout is not yet
   complete. For example, if the network design calls for
   sixty edge fabrics, and only thirty have been deployed,
   it would be safe to release the solution to production
   and add the remaining fabrics as needed.

Installed Base Upgrade Rollout

Adding a new category of network equipment to an existing mission-critical environment can be as simple as plugging it in and turning it on, or as complex as building a dedicated test environment and running months of stress-tests prior to entering production. It depends on site-specific change control procedures, the degree of confidence the network administrators have in the new equipment, and the impact to the company that would result from a failure during the rollout. It is advisable to do a risk assessment of mission-critical systems before installing any fundamentally new technology into a production environment.

For customers with extremely tightly controlled environments, release to production for the router may resemble a green field deployment. While the router should be non-disruptive to install, it is always possible that a complex device like a router might not function as intended, so these customers may take a conservative approach to the rollout. The routed solution could be built in an isolated environment and production applications migrated over to it gradually once it was verified to be stable.

Customers who have slightly less strictly controlled environments but still have robust change control procedures are likely to have A/B fabrics installed. If so, a reasonable precaution during rollout would be to install the routers on one of the redundant fabrics at a time, and perform a suite of tests prior to using them for production traffic. Only once all "A" fabrics are connected and verified to be stable would routers be connected to the "B" fabrics. Indeed, many administrators would let the router run in the "A" production fabrics for several weeks before rolling out the "B" routers. This process in combination with the redundant/resilient A/B Meta SAN approach (Figure 93 through Figure 98 on p210 through p214) can make rollouts into existing environments both easy and safe. For most customers, this is probably the right balance of cost, simplicity, and risk-mitigation.

Finally, some customers may have many fabrics, each with different levels of business relevance. If this is the case, the router can be used to connect to lowest-tier fabrics first, so that any unanticipated problems will impact only non-critical applications. By the time the router is connected to mission-critical fabrics, there should be a high degree of confidence that it will work as intended.

Meta SAN Change Control

Once a Meta SAN has entered production, it will fall under the existing change control procedures for the customer environment. Whatever procedures a customer employs, it is probable that they will have dependency analysis and notification components.

For example, if a change could affect two fabrics, all systems, application, storage, and SAN administrators associated with those fabrics would need to be notified, as well as the administrators for hosts using the FCR to access resources on those fabrics.

For FC-FC Routing Service deployments, this means looking for cross-fabric dependencies. For example, if an edge fabric needs to be taken offline, first check to see if any of its storage nodes are exported to other fabrics. If so, the owners of the remote hosts will need to be notified of the outage. Proper zone naming practices can facilitate this. (See Figure 108 p232 through Figure 110 and the surrounding text for an example.)

For IP SAN solutions, dependencies must be set up with the IP network. (This is another reason to physically separate IP SAN from data network traffic: it simplifies scheduling changes and outages.) It will be necessary for fabric, storage, systems, application, and IP network administrators to work in concert to make IP SAN changes safely.

Installation Procedures

This subsection gives guidance on how to sequence the installation of the Brocade Multiprotocol Router platform and each service. The manuals, release notes, and posted guides/whitepapers have more up-to-date syntax and procedures, so be sure to check the Brocade website before installing a router.

Each customer environment is unique, and these procedures will need to be adapted for each installation. They are intended to provide a starting point; not to be taken as strict installation checklists.

Multiprotocol Router Platform Installation

1. Unpack the router and check the contents of the box.
2. Insert all SFPs. If they were not shipped with the platform, check to see that they are supported and can run in the needed modes.
3. Install rail kit and mount if applicable.
4. Attach a PC or laptop to the serial RJ45 management port using the included adapter cable.
5. Configure the platform management IP settings.[116]
6. Attach the two RJ-45 copper Ethernet management ports to the LAN.[117]
7. Use either telnet (CLI) or WEB TOOLS (GUI) to set the remaining basic Fibre Channel parameters like backbone domain IP. This is just like configuring a standard Brocade FC switch.
8. If connecting to an existing production fabric, <u>disable</u> all ports that will be used as IFLs[118] or IP SAN portals

---

[116] IP address, gateway, netmask, hostname, etc.. Also, it is advisable to configure the two Ethernet management ports redundantly. This may require additional addresses.

[117] If configuring them redundantly, attach them to different LAN switches, preferably on different subnets.

[118] ISL ports may be left enabled. IFL ports should be disabled at this point to prevent accidentally merging fabrics.

in order to prevent accidental network misconfiguration. Use the *portDisable* command to do this. Note that this command *is* persistent across reboots.

9. Attach optical cables to the platform SFPs. If connecting ISLs, ensure that the fabric has formed properly using normal fabric commands, like *switchShow* and *fabricShow* on the router CLI.

10. Perform any additional site-specific configuration appropriate to Fibre Channel fabric switches, like setting SNMP community strings, time synchronization, or changing administrative passwords.

11. If using the platform exclusively as a Fibre Channel fabric switch, the installation is complete. If using it as a multiprotocol router, configure each desired service as described below.

12. Before proceeding, make sure that to have a detailed rollout plan. This should include documentation such as network topology diagrams, host names, IP addresses and gateways, domain IDs, a zoning plan (intra-fabric, IQN, and LSAN as applicable), fabric-wide parameters, and Fabric IDs if applicable. Remember to decide on the FID of the router itself. This is the backbone fabric FID. Also do not forget that FIDs – including those for backbone fabrics – need to be unique within a Meta SAN, but may be duplicated between different Meta SANs e.g. in a redundant / resilient A/B configuration.

FC-FC Routing Service Installation

1. Install the FC-FC Routing Service license using the *licenseAdd* command or equivalent GUI function.

2. Use *fcrConfigure* to set the FID of the router itself. This is the backbone fabric FID.

3. Use *portStop* < *port number* > on every port that will be configured as an EX_Port. This stops the ASIC rather than merely disabling the port in software via *portDisable*.

4. Use *portCfgEXport* to put the port into EX_Port mode, to set its FID, and to set fabric-wide parameters like TOVs and the PID format. This is also the time to set preferred xlate domain IDs and xlate PIDs if desired using *fcrXlateConfig* and *fcrProxyConfig -s*.

5. Verify that the port is in EX_Port mode and that the parameters are correct using *portShow*. Do not enable the port if it is still in U_Port mode, or you may accidentally merge the edge fabric with the backbone.

6. Use *portStart < port number >* to re-enable the port. It may be necessary to use *portEnable* as well.

7. Use zoning commands in two edge fabrics to configure LSAN zones. Use a meaningful scheme as discussed in Figure 110 (p232) and the surrounding text. Be sure that LSAN zones exist in both fabrics, and that each contains the <u>Port</u> WWNs (or aliases) of all nodes that are supposed to communicate in the LSAN, not just those from the local fabric. This will create xlate phantom domains and xlate PIDs as needed. Use *fabricShow* to verify that the xlate domains have been added to each edge fabric and *nsAllShow* to see if that domain has xlate PIDs. Running *lsanZoneShow* and *fcrProxyDevShow* on the router can also be helpful.

8. It should now be possible to access devices between fabrics. Use appropriate tools on the hosts to configure and test this.[119]

iSCSI Gateway Service Installation

If using iSCSI-FCR integration, configure FCR *first*. Then perform the following steps on each gateway:

1. At the time of this writing, the iSCSI Gateway Service does not require a license key. **Note**: In some versions of the gateway operating system, iSCSI requires manual activation using the command *serviceCfg -e iscsi*.

---

[119] E.g. set up the HBA drivers if applicable and then use the "Storage" tab in "Computer Management" under "Administration" in the control panel of Windows 2000.

If this is required, then the router is running a version of the operating system in which the iSCSI service is intended only for *demonstration* use, and *not* for *production* deployments.

2. Perform configuration and testing of the IP/Ethernet network between the iSCSI initiators and the portals.

3. Use *portStop* < *port number* > on every port that will be configured as an iSCSI portal. Note that this is *not* the same as *portDisable*.

4. Use *portType* < *port number* > *G* to put the port into Gigabit Ethernet mode.

5. Use *portCfgGigE* < *port number* > <*parameter list*> for settings such as IP address and gateway. This can also be used to set iSCSI parameters.

6. Use *portStart* < *port number* > to re-enable the port. It may be necessary to use *portEnable* as well.

7. Enable the FCS feature by running *iFCSenable* on one gateway. It will automatically be enabled in all other gateways in the fabric.

8. If configuring two gateways as an HA pair, use the *iscsiFailoverAdd* < *WWN* > command.

9. Configure parameters such as IP addresses, IQNs, and CHAP security in the iSCSI drivers for each host.

10. Configure a matching CHAP security policy on the gateways using *iscsiAuthConfig*.

11. Use *configureZoning* to ensure that NWWN zoning is enabled. This is the default in most fabrics.

12. Use zoning commands on the gateway platforms' CLI or WEB TOOLS interfaces to configure IQN-based zones. Running these commands on the gateway itself will allow the use of IQNs and will automatically create proxy WWNs for the iSCSI hosts.

13. It should now be possible to access FC disks from the iSCSI hosts. Use the iSCSI driver tools on the hosts to configure this, and OS tools test it.

FCIP Tunneling Service Installation

If using FCIP-FCR integration, configure FCR *first*. Also be sure to install and configure a Network Time Protocol (NTP) server if there is not already one in your environment. Then perform the following steps on each end of the tunnel:

1. Install the FCIP Tunneling Service license key using the *licenseAdd* command or equivalent GUI function.
2. Perform configuration and testing of the IP/Ethernet network between the FCIP portals.
3. Enable NTP on each gateway using *tsClockServer*.
4. Use *portStop < port number >* on every port that will be configured as an FCIP portal. Note that this is *not* the same as *portDisable*.
5. Use *portType < port number > G* to put the port into Gigabit Ethernet mode.
6. Use *portCfgGigE < port number > <parameter list>* for settings such as IP address and gateway.
7. Use *portCfgFCIP < port number > <parameter list>* for FCIP-specific settings like remote portal address and WWN, and the WAN_TOV timeout value.
8. Use *portStart < port number >* to re-enable the port. It may be necessary to use *portEnable* as well.

Once these steps have been completed on both gateways, the tunnel should form automatically. Use commands such as *fcipShow*, *fabricShow*, *portShow*, *switchShow*, and *topologyShow* to verify this. After the tunnel is verified to be up, continue with the following steps:

9. Configure fabric zoning (either LSAN or standard as appropriate) to allow connectivity between hosts and storage on opposite ends of the link.
10. It should now be possible to access disks from hosts at the opposite site. Use HBA driver tools on the hosts to configure this, and OS tools test it.

Meta SAN Documentation

Once a Meta SAN is designed and deployed, it must be documented.[120] It is difficult if not impossible to effectively manage and troubleshoot networks without this. Most IT departments will already have a standard format for documentation. It is perfectly acceptable to map Meta SAN documentation into different standard formats. However, to be complete, documentation for Meta SANs should include the following information:

- A summary diagram of the overall physical topology of the Meta SAN. This will generally use a roll-up technique that represents each fabric or subnet as a cloud. Each fabric should include its name and FID. Routers should include their names, management IP addresses, and addresses for IP SAN portals.

- An optional summary diagram of each fabric and subnet, showing the topology of switches and routers in some detail, but rolling up hosts and storage arrays by function. This might involve using a single icon to represent all servers running one application or all storage arrays of a specific type.

- A detailed diagram of each fabric and subnet, showing the physical topology of switches, routers, hosts, and storage, optionally including the specific ports to which each device is attached. Including WWNs, PIDs, domain IDs, IP addresses, and device names is beneficial.

- A block diagram showing the logical (phantom) topologies of each fabric, including the backbone. This should include the domain IDs and names of each device, and an indication of which remote fabric is represented by each xlate domain. It may also include WWNs of switches. It is not necessary to include hosts and storage devices in this diagram.

---

[120] Documentation usually will be created *while* the network is being designed and deployed. The finishing touches will be completed afterwards.

Also, text or spreadsheet files should be included and kept up to date with the following information:

- Output for *topologyShow*, *cfgShow*, *nsShow*,[121] and *fabricShow* for each fabric. Note that these are included in *supportShow*.

- A spreadsheet or table showing the xlate mappings for all devices that participate in LSANs. I.e. have a line for each mapped device stating that the physical device with WWN *xx* in FID=*yy* is used in an LSAN to FID=*zz*, and hangs off of xlate domain *qq* using xlate PID *qqrrss*.

- A spreadsheet or table showing firmware and driver versions of every SAN-related product in the Meta SAN. This includes switches, routers, HBAs, storage, drivers, volume managers, virtualizers, and so on.

In addition, once the Meta SAN is in a steady state of operation, each switch and router should have its *supportShow* data saved to a file off of the SAN. This should be re-done any time major changes are made. This way, if a problem occurs it will be possible for support personnel to compare before and after pictures of the network.

Also, it is recommended that before any changes, each switch and router should have its configuration saved to a non-SAN-attached host. Old versions should be kept to allow rollback if needed. See man pages for *configUpload* and *configDownload*.

Troubleshooting Tips

Like other networking technologies, from time to time it will be necessary to troubleshoot a routed SAN, and like any other network, this comes down to finding which piece of hardware, software, or configuration is malfunctioning between nodes.

---

[121] It may be desirable to run *nsShow* on each switch in each fabric. The intent is to capture what the entire fabric name server is supposed to look like when it is working.

Before going into the tools and techniques used specifically in routed SANs, it will be useful to review some basic questions to ask when troubleshooting any kind of network.

In the case of large-scale failures, it is usually easy to identify the impacted components. If an entire edge fabric is down, it is unlikely to be the fault of a multipathing driver on a single host. However, the *root cause* – that is the basic problem that is really causing the symptom of a down fabric – could be a malfunctioning HBA, a bad switch, a zoning misconfiguration, or a plethora of other issues. The goal of troubleshooting is always to find and correct the root cause.

Complex and large scale problems may require the intervention of support personnel, but for simpler issues affecting only a subset of nodes, self-help is usually straightforward and sufficient.

Assume for example that two nodes cannot communicate. There are standard troubleshooting techniques that have been developed for other IT technologies which can apply to SANs. Here are some sample questions derived from these techniques to ask before calling support, or using the SAN-specific methods discussed in the remainder of this subsection:

- Is everything powered on and plugged in?
- Are the end-point devices working at all? E.g. can you ping their LAN interfaces and access their management consoles.
- Can they communicate with any *other* nodes, or are they entirely "off the air?" If a host can access one storage port but not another, this is more than likely *not* a bad host. If it cannot access any storage ports at all, the issue is probably the host or the zoning configuration.
- Are the ports zoned together? Incorrect zoning configuration account for a massive portion of fabric communication issues. Check to see if WWNs and/or [domain,port] entries are correct, and if they or their aliases are used together in an *active* zone.

- Does one or the other have access controls? (Such as LUN masking on a RAID array.)

- Do their ports show up as online on the switches they are attached to? If a switch is showing a port as offline, check all cable(s) and media (SFPs and/or GBICs). Consider trying a different switch port.

- If they are FC nodes, are they in the fabric name server?

- Did connectivity between the devices ever work before?

- Are there any known problems with the fabric(s), even issues that might seem unrelated? If so, reconsider whether or not there *could be* a relationship.

- In an IP SAN, are there known problems with the IP/Ethernet network? (LAN, CAN, MAN, WAN.

- Are ports showing large or rapidly increasing numbers on their error counters?

- Has anything changed? At all? *Really?* (This item can be a big issue for troubleshooting, since people who make changes just prior to an outage are notoriously reluctant to mention it, and it is very hard to find certain kinds of problems without this knowledge.)

One of these questions may yield an answer that – if it does not solve the problem – at least may point out a direction of inquiry. For example, if there is a known network problem like a flapping WAN link, it will still be necessary to correct that problem before connectivity will work, but at least the SAN administrator will know what to concentrate on to return the network to a healthy state.

If a general-purpose network troubleshooting processes does not help, it will be necessary to move to router-specific methods as discussed in the next subsection.

Built-In Tools for Router Troubleshooting

The first (and often the last) step in troubleshooting any Brocade networking product is to use the built-in tools in the switch and router operating systems.[122]

Like most high-tech products, most problems with Brocade SANs turn out to be relatively simple configuration errors. All Brocade products have built-in tools for displaying configurations, and analyzing the output of these should be the first priority.

For example, when troubleshooting an LSAN problem, first make sure that the correct ports on the router are configured as EX_Ports and that their FIDs are set properly using *fcrConfigure*. Make sure that their fabric parameters (e.g. PID format and TOVs) match their edge fabrics' by looking at *configShow*[123] output on those switches. Check to see if the routers' EX_Ports are online using *fabricShow* on any switch in each edge fabric, or *switchShow* on the router. This should show the router front phantom domains and xlate phantoms for any remote fabrics to which LSANs are configured. Also run *switchShow* on the switches to which the EX_Ports are attached and on the routers themselves. Check to make sure that correct LSAN zones are present in each edge fabric by using *cfgShow*. From the router, use *lsanZoneShow*. Make sure that the devices to be exported are really online in their respective edge fabrics using *nsShow*, and that xlate entries are correctly built using the *fcrProxyDevShow*, *fcrPhyDevShow*, and *fcrXlateConfig* commands on the router itself.

If any of these commands comes up with a negative result, it usually means that:

---

[122] That is, it is the first step *after* making sure that everything is plugged in, powered on, and cabled properly. This footnote turns out to cover a counter-intuitively large number of support calls.

[123] Not to be confused with *cfgShow*.

- A port or device is shut down or misconfigured, as in an incorrect FID assignment, or an HBA driver set for the wrong fabric topology.

- An SFP or cable has failed or is of the wrong type, as in using an MMF cable to run a long distance link using ELWL SFPs, or using an unsupported SFP type.

- A cable is un- or misconnected, as in connecting an edge fabric to the wrong EX_Port or even the wrong router. Possibly an EX_Port is connected to the backbone, or two fabrics are merged that should be separate.

- A zoning configuration is incorrect, as in using the wrong WWN for a remote node, or not having all nodes in the LSAN present in the same LSAN zone in each edge fabric, or not starting the zone name with the "LSAN_" prefix.

Fixing problems in this category simply requires following common sense processes that are taken straight from existing Fibre Channel procedures.

In general, problems beyond simple misconfiguration exist at the fabric services level, and all fabric services activity is logged by the platform. Tools like *supportShow* and *portLog-Dump* can display these and other logs, and can solve the majority of Fibre Channel service problems, as well as node problems like HBA misbehaviors, or storage ports failing to log onto the fabric.

Finally, it is possible that a routing service itself may have a defect. This will of course require interacting with the correct support channel to determine and correct. Run the *supportShow* command on all switches in each fabric and on each router as soon after the incident as possible, as this will capture critical data to help support solve the problem.

FC Analyzers

Brocade products are mature after many years of mission-critical production service, so problems rarely occur that require Fibre Channel frame-level analysis. This was a relatively common event with first generation Brocade products, and still is today with other vendors new to Fibre Channel who have not finished debugging their products to that level. When an FC analyzer is needed outside of an engineering lab, it usually means that trained service personnel are on-site debugging a persistent problem and that all other debugging approaches have failed.

Analyzers *might* be used to troubleshoot defects in the router's xlate code (unlikely), to determine if nodes are responding improperly to PLOGIs or are sending with a >2048byte payload size, or are using PIDs in the payload (as in xcopy). Aside from standard fabric analysis techniques that service personnel will already be familiar with, the router has only a few caveats.

The main one is related to FC-NAT. Because the router changes the SID and DID of a frame, it will look differently to the analyzer depending on its location as it transits the Meta SAN. Figure 137 (p310) and the surrounding text discuss this in detail.

IP/Ethernet Analyzers

Unlike Fibre Channel networks where the use of protocol analyzers is now rare, for IP/Ethernet ports, it will from time to time be necessary to use an analyzer. IP/Ethernet networks are subject to problems that require analyzers frequently enough that almost all IT departments have already purchased and are familiar with such tools. In general, simply use whatever Ethernet analysis tools and practices are already in place. If no such tools exist, consider a free analysis tool like Ethereal. (http://www.ethereal.com/)

If IP SAN traffic is kept separated from data network traffic, it is less likely that an analyzer will be needed – and this is one reason that separate networks are recommended. If it *is* needed, make sure that it can decode the appropriate IP SAN protocol such as iSCSI or FCIP.

FC-FC Routing Service Troubleshooting

Here are some things to think about when troubleshooting FCR Meta SANs:

- Is the FCR service enabled on the router? (This requires a license key, so run *licenseShow.*)

- Are LSAN zones configured properly on each fabric? That is, are Port WWNs or their aliases zoned together in each fabric? (*nsShow* and *cfgShow*) If FID=1 and FID=2 are sharing nodes, and zoning is only done on one side, connectivity will not work. Similarly, if FID=1 has the LSAN zone, but it does not contain the FID=2 nodes, connectivity will not work.

- Are cables connected properly? Specifically, are EX_Ports connected to the correct edge fabrics? If an EX_Port for FID=1 is connected to the FID=2 fabric, it can potentially cause the router to segment off both fabrics. (Fabric ID Oversubscribe.)

- Are the ports that are supposed to be EX_Ports *really* configured that way? (*portShow*) Is the FCR configuration correct? (EX_Port FIDs, TOVs, PID formats, etc.)

- Do edge fabrics see the router? Look for front and xlate phantom domains in the fabric. (*fabricShow* and *topologyShow*) Look in the name server for xlate PIDs. (*nsAllShow*)

- Is one or another node using PID binding, and if so is it set correctly for the *xlate* PID of the other nodes? (Using the *real* PID will not be helpful.)

- If there is a backbone fabric, does it look "right?" (*fabricShow* and *topologyShow*) Look for a segmented fabric, missing domains, or down ports. Do all routers on the backbone have the same backbone FID set? (*fcrConfigure*)

- If everything looks like it should be working, but frames seem to be getting dropped by the router or the backbone, look for devices sending to the wrong PID or using a >2048 byte payload to inter-fabric destinations. This would indicate a defect in e.g. the HBA driver code. It would probably require an FC analyzer to solve this.

The following built-in CLI commands are helpful to run on the edge fabric switches:

Table 24 - FCR Fabric CLI Commands

portShow	nsAllShow
switchShow	nsCAMShow
fabricShow	configShow
topologyShow	cfgShow
nsShow	

The following built-in CLI commands are helpful to run on the router platform itself:

Table 25 - FCR Platform CLI Commands

portShow	fcrXlateConfig
switchShow	fcrFabricShow
fabricShow	fcrRouteShow
topologyShow	fcrResourceShow
lsanZoneShow	fcrProxyDevShow
fcrConfigure	fcrPhyDevShow

iSCSI Gateway Service Troubleshooting

Here are some things to think about when troubleshooting iSCSI Meta SANs:

- Are iSCSI hosts trying to access storage in the backbone fabric, or in edge fabrics (if FCR integration is used). The latter configuration is not supported at the time of this writing.

- Is iSCSI enabled on the gateway? (If not, it probably means that the gateway is running an OS version with iSCSI code only intended for demonstrations.)

- Are the ports that are supposed to be iSCSI portals *really* configured that way? (*portShow*) Is the iSCSI configuration correct? (IP addresses etc.)

- Are cables connected properly? Specifically, are iSCSI portals connected to the correct IP SAN subnets? Are FC E_Ports connected to the backbone?

- Does the backbone fabric look "right?" (*fabricShow* and *topologyShow*)   Look for a segmented fabric, missing domains, or down ports.

- Can iSCSI NICs ping their portals? (*ping* and *mPing*) If not, standard IP network troubleshooting will apply.

- Is there anything between the iSCSI hosts and the portals that might selectively block iSCSI? (E.g. a firewall, router, or switch with ACLs.)

- Are the iSCSI NICs running properly configured iSCSI drivers? Are they *supported* drivers running the right version of the iSCSI standard? (Since iSCSI is an emerging protocol, there are still about twenty different and incompatible versions of the "standard" that may show up in different drivers.)

- If there is an iSNS server, is it configured both on the iSCSI hosts and on the gateways? Is it a supported server running a compatible version of the standard?

- Do the FC storage ports show up on their switches and in the backbone fabric name server? (*switchShow* and *nsShow*)

- Do iSCSI hosts show up in the BB fabric name server? (*nsShow* should show the IQN in the SCSI inquiry field.)

- Are IQN- / Node WWN-based zones configured properly? (*nsShow* and *cfgShow*. *zoneShow −i* on the gateway itself will show IQNs instead of proxy WWNs.)

- Is the FCS service running on all routers? (*ifcsShow*)

- Do CHAP passwords match? (*iscsiAuthConfig*)

- Is node name zoning enabled on the backbone fabric? (*configureZoning*)

The following built-in CLI commands are helpful to run on the backbone fabric switches:

Table 26 - iSCSI Gateway Fabric CLI Commands

portShow	nsAllShow
switchShow	nsCAMShow
fabricShow	configShow
topologyShow	cfgShow
nsShow	

The following built-in CLI commands are helpful to run on the iSCSI gateway platform itself:

Table 27 - iSCSI Gateway Platform CLI Commands

portShow	nsCAMShow
switchShow	mPing
fabricShow	iscsiSessionShow
topologyShow	iscsiPortShow
nsShow	iscsiWWNAlloc
nsAllShow	ifcsShow

FCIP Tunneling Service Troubleshooting

Here are some things to think about when troubleshooting FCIP Meta SANs:

- Is FCIP enabled on the gateway? This requires a license.

- If the system is using FCIP/FCR integration, has the FCR configuration been completed and validated? (EX_Ports attached to the correct edge fabrics, and so on.)

- Have the edge fabrics on both ends of the WAN been set up and validated? Do the FC nodes show up on their switches and in their fabric name servers? (*switchShow* and *nsShow*)

- Are cables connected properly? Specifically, are FCIP portals connected to the correct IP SAN subnets?

- Are the ports that are supposed to be FCIP portals *really* configured that way? (*portShow*) Is the FCIP configuration correct? (*portCfgFCIP*) (IP addresses etc.)

- Does the backbone fabric look "right?" (*fabricShow* and *topologyShow*) Look for a segmented fabric, missing domains, or down ports. Note that FCIP VE_Ports are part of the backbone fabric.

- Can nodes on the IP network reach the FCIP portals? Can the portals ping each other? (*ping* and *mPing*) How about nodes from the remote site? If not, standard IP network troubleshooting will apply.

- Is there anything between the portals that might selectively block FCIP? For example, a firewall, a router, or a switch with ACLs.

- Are all portals running the same version of FCIP?

- If the portals were configured with WWN security, are the WWNs correct? (Try configuring both portals *without* WWN security to see if this is the issue.)

- Is WAN_TOV enabled on both ends or neither end? (Either is OK, but it should *not* be enabled on only *one* end.) If so, is the NTP configuration correct? (The clocks must be synchronized tightly for this to work.)

The following built-in CLI commands are helpful to run on the backbone and edge fabric switches:

Table 28 – FCIP Gateway Fabric CLI Commands

portShow	*nsAllShow*
switchShow	*nsCAMShow*
fabricShow	*configShow*
topologyShow	*cfgShow*
nsShow	

The following built-in CLI commands are helpful to run on the FCIP gateway platform itself:

Table 29 – FCIP Gateway Platform CLI Commands

portShow	*mPing*
switchShow	*tsClockServer*
fabricShow	*fcipShow*
topologyShow	*portCfgFCIP*

15: Deployment Guide FAQ

Design FAQ

Q: How many ISLs do I need within a fabric?

A: This is application dependant, but tends to be based on the ratio of initiators to targets. The industry average seems to be around six or seven to one. Environments with this h:s ratio and little locality would use 7:1 over-subscribed ISLs, so, for example, a 16-port switch would have 2 ISLs and 14 nodes.

Q: How many IFLs do I need between fabrics?

A: There tends to be more "built in" locality between fabrics than within them. Therefore inter-fabric over-subscription can be *much* higher than intra-fabric ratios. The rule of thumb is to configure at least two IFLs for redundancy, and add more as needed based on performance needs.

Q: How many routers do I need for my Meta SAN?

A: This depends on geographical, performance, redundancy, and scalability requirements. For example, if routers are being used for FCIP between two sites, at least two routers are needed. If this needs to be highly available, at least two routers per site are needed. If inter-site bandwidth needs to be high, it may be necessary to add more routers to support more VE_Ports. And if each site has many edge fabrics, it may be necessary to add routers to support more EX_Ports.

Q: Can the router's IP SAN options be used in conjunction with firewalls and/or VPNs?

A: Yes. It will be necessary to configure the firewall or VPN to allow unrestricted connectivity between the endpoint IP addresses. In addition, some firewalls / VPN gateways route frames very slowly by SAN standards, so be sure to check how much delay is added and how much throughput is constrained.

Q: It sounds like Fibre Channel and iSCSI solve the same SAN design problems, but FC has higher performance and a longer track record in the industry. Why would anybody deploy iSCSI?

A: In some situations, cost is more important than application performance and availability, and in some of those situations, iSCSI will cost less.

Q: Can the platform support multiple links between gateways for the FCIP Tunneling Service.

A: You can have more than one FCIP tunnel per switch pair. The algorithm for traffic distribution across TCP connections within the tunnel is the same as is used for E_Port distribution. That is, parallel tunnels will act the same way as parallel E_Ports without exchange-based trunking enabled.

Q: I don't want to manage LSAN zones on a daily basis. Can I just make all of my zones in all of my fabrics into LSAN zones?

A: This is possible, but not recommended. The router supports a limited number of LSAN zones, since it needs to do various processing tasks on a per-LSAN basis. Using the LSAN prefix on zones that do not traverse between fabrics might simplify management in certain cases, but it drastically increases the CPU load on the router since it bypasses quite a bit of optimized code. The best practice is to use the "LSAN_" prefix only on zones truly being used for LSANs.

Q: Can each FCIP gateway connect to more than one Ethernet switch, and if so, is it active/passive, or active/active?

A: Parallel VE_Ports operate the same way parallel ISLs do between FC switches whether they are connected to the same or different Ethernet switches. Traffic is actively shared across all available links using DLS, and failure of any link simply results in the reduction of aggregate bandwidth between domains.

Q: Does the AP7420 support compression for FCIP?

A: No. CNT has a better solution if compression is required, and this can still be used in conjunction with the FCR feature of the Multiprotocol Router. Note that compression does not improve performance with most data types.

Q: What is maximum performance for FCIP per port?

A: At the time of this writing, it is about 0.6Gbits/sec. per FCIP port, but this has been increasing as the service gets tuned more efficiently. (The first version of the code was an order of magnitude slower.) See the Brocade online documentation to check what the current version of the operating system supports. If more bandwidth is required than is supported per port, multiple FCIP ports can be used between sites. These can co-exist on shared MAN/WAN pipes, so multiple VE_Ports do not generally require multiple pipes.

Installation FAQ

Q: Is there a minimum firmware version I should be running on the Multiprotocol Router?

A: Yes. The latest firmware is always recommended. At the time of this writing, this is XPathOS 7.3.

Q: Will installing the router to my existing production environment be disruptive?

A: That depends on how you use it. For example: If you remove an existing switch and replace it with the router, it will be disruptive to any devices using the switch that you removed. Simply adding an EX_Port to a fabric is non-disruptive. It is just like adding a totally new, blank switch with no devices attached. Adding the platform as an iSCSI gateway is non-disruptive provided that the existing storage arrays do not have compatibility problems resulting from the introduction of iSCSI. (Any iSCSI usage cases should be tested in a pre-production environment first.)

Q: When creating Meta SAN documentation, is there anything special I should do beyond standard network / SAN documentation?

A: Make sure you document both the physical and logical topologies of each fabric, and the real-to-phantom mapping information for devices in LSANs. Make sure that your LSAN zoning configuration is saved. And be sure that your IP SAN documentation is in sync with your FC SAN methodology. Note that the *configUpload* / *configDownload* commands are very useful for saving entire switch or router configurations into a documentation repository.

Q: iSCSI doesn't seem to be coming up on my router. I can't get the configuration tools to work at all. What could that be? Is there a license key or something?

A: iSCSI should be enabled automatically with no license key for OS versions on which it is supported. With some OS versions, it is only supported for demonstration use, and needs to be enabled manually. Please engage with a Brocade SE if this is the case.

Q: I have iSCSI hosts that run at different speeds. Is there a rule of thumb about how to distribute these across the router?

A: Yes. Try to connect slower hosts to the same portals as other slower hosts, and faster hosts with other faster hosts. This can prevent a fast hosts from starving a slow one and causing it to time out.

Q: I have an Ethernet switch that I want to use for iSCSI fan-in. It only has RJ45 copper interfaces. The router has only optical interfaces. What do I do?

A: You need a converter or media interface adapter. See "Copper to Fiber Gigabit Ethernet Converter" p296.

Q: I'm installing a router and I can't make the serial port work. What could be the issue?

A: Are you using the cable and adapter supplied with the router? If so, are you using the correct serial port settings? (9600/8/none/1/no flow control) If not, did you make a correct custom cable? (See "RJ45 Serial Port " p287.)

Q: What is the CLI command to do _____?
A: Check out Table 24 through Table 29 (p267 - p270) for a start, and see the manuals for specific syntax.[124]

Troubleshooting FAQ

Q: Why won't my Brocade FCIP gateway work with the vendor *xxx* gateway?
A: FCIP is a relatively new standard. Like all IP SAN technologies, it will be some time before all vendors can interoperate perfectly. The good news is that FCIP is the industry protocol of choice for extending SANs over IP networks, and therefore this is the method vendors are working towards for interoperability. The bad news is that the standard was just ratified, so it may be some time before all interoperability work is complete.

Q: I have an FCIP gateway on one end, and an FC switch on the other end, and the link will not come up. What am I doing wrong?
A: FCIP is an encapsulation protocol. Each FC frame is "wrapped" in several layers of headers (TCP/IP/FCIP) on the transmitting end. In order to make sense to a Fibre Channel fabric again, each frame must be *de*-encapsulated at the far end. This means that FCIP gateways are required on both ends of a tunnel. Note that you can eliminate the gateways from *both* ends by using dark fiber or *x*WDM products.

Q: Is *pathInfo* supported across the router?
A: Not at this time, but it is planned for a future release. In the mean time, it can still be used within an edge fabric.

---

[124] It is not possible to keep a published book fully up to date as commands are enhanced, so the manuals are the best place for details about usage to reside.

Q: I see the router EX_Port online, but I cannot create LSAN zones in my fabric. What could be wrong?

A: LSAN zones are identical to regular zones. If you cannot create LSAN zones, it either means that you do not have a zoning license key installed, or that there is a problem with the management tools in that fabric. The router itself is not involved in the creation of LSAN zones, so standard fabric troubleshooting methods will apply.

Q: I created an LSAN zone, but the router seems to be ignoring it. What could be the problem?

A: The most common issues are (a) not using the "lsan_" prefix, (b) using port ID entries (domain comma port) instead of port WWNs, (c) using node WWNs instead of port WWNs, (d) not activating the zone set, (e) not creating matching LSAN zones on all relevant edge fabrics, and (f) not having the router EX_Ports properly configured.

Q: The iSCSI connections from my 100baseT hosts keep timing out, but my 1000baseT hosts are working. Is there a problem with 100baseT?

A: Not exactly. There can be a problem with combining streams from 100baseT hosts onto the same portal as 1000baseT hosts, because the faster hosts can starve the slower ones. Try distributing the iSCSI hosts differently, using only 100baseT *or* 1000baseT hosts on any given portal.

Q: I am using the iSCSI gateway feature, and my connections keep dropping. Is this normal?

A: Not exactly. However, with iSCSI, it isn't exactly abnormal either. Most IP networks have far lower performance and reliability characteristics than are required to make storage networks work even minimally. Try collapsing your iSCSI subnets down to a single Ethernet switch each as in Figure 21 (p56). In some cases, even this will not help if the Ethernet fan-out switches are too slow. In this case, it will be necessary to upgrade to faster (and more expensive) Ethernet infrastructure.

Q: I am using the iSCSI gateway for disk, and it is working, but when I try it for tape, my backups keep failing. Is there a problem with the gateway working with tape?

A: It isn't so much a problem with the gateway working with tape as it is a problem with tape devices working with slow and unreliable networks such as iSCSI invariably provides. If the network between the host and the tape becomes slow (either high latency or congestion) then you may get an under-run condition on the tape. This can cause massive performance issues and even backup failures. Since iSCSI is inherently *much* slower than Fibre Channel, these conditions are proportionally more likely to occur.

Q: It looks like my FCIP tunnel *should* be up, but IO is not making it across the link. Any ideas?

A: If you are using WAN_TOV, check to make sure that NAT is configured and synchronized between the sites. Even minor differences in system clock times can prevent this from working. Try turning off WAN_TOV on both ends to test this. If so, double-check to see if fabric services think the tunnel is up (e.g. using *fabricShow*). If so, it is likely a reliability issue with the IP network. Look for packet loss or excessive delays.

Q: I just plugged my router into an edge fabric, and I'm not seeing it come up. Thoughts...?

A: Is the router port plugged in and configured correctly? I.e. is it attached to the correct fabric, and configured as an EX_Port with the correct FID, TOV, PID format, etc.? This is usually the problem. It is also possible that the edge fabric does not have a full fabric license. For example, if the router is attached to a Value Line (VL) switch, that switch must have a license key upgrade first. (VL switches are priced at a substantial discount because the do not have this key.)

Q: I have a Meta SAN up and running. When I pull all of the IFLs to e.g. fabric #2, its phantom xlate domain remains in e.g. the fabric #1 *topologyShow*. Is this normal?

A: Yes. We do not pull the xlate phantom domain in order to minimize fabric disruption. (Domain loss causes a reconfiguration.) Instead, we pull all of the proxy PIDs out of the SNS. Try an *nsAllShow* before and after to see this effect.

Q: My Fibre Channel ports are all working, but my iSCSI or FCIP portals will not come online. I've checked the configuration and everything looks right. Is there anything specific to IP/Ethernet that could be the issue?

A: Yes. For example, you need tri-mode SFPs for Ethernet ports, but not for Fibre Channel interfaces. You should also check to make sure you do not have patch cables twisted such that transmit on the router is going to transmit (instead of receive) on the Ethernet fan-out switch.

Section Four

Reference Material

Section Topics

- Basic Reference
- Advanced Reference
- Glossary
- Index

Appendix A: Basic Reference

This chapter provides reference material for readers who may be less familiar with either Fibre Channel or IP/Ethernet technology. Topics covered include cabling and media options, and some of the external devices that might be connected to the router.

Cables and Media

Port Types

Figure 116 shows the locations of each port type for reference throughout this subsection.

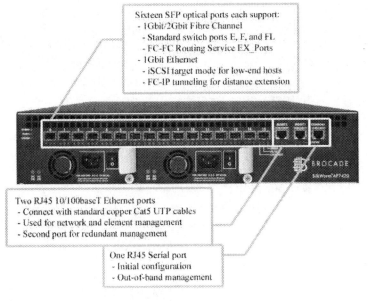

Figure 116 - Router Port Types

281

Optical Cables and Media

SFP Media

Small Form-Factor Pluggable (SFP) media are now the most popular removable transceiver modules for gigabit switches. Figure 117 shows a set of typical SFPs. Note that some SFPs (not pictured) have copper connectors. The router only supports optical SFPs at the time of this writing. Figure 119 shows an LC cable appropriate for attachment to an optical SFP.

Figure 117 - Examples of SFPs

The router provides sixteen SFP ports for data connections. They convert from the copper signals used on the motherboard of a switch, router, or HBA to the laser signals used in fiber optic cabling.

SFPs come in a number of varieties. The primary variations are the wavelength and the type of fiber optic cable the media is designed for. For a discussion of these variables, see LWL, SWL, MMF, and SMF below. For Gigabit Ethernet applications, 1000baseSX media are required, which uses shortwave lasers and generally runs over MMF cables. Note that many SFPs – including those that generally ship with the router – are capable of both Fibre Channel 1Gbit/2Gbit and Ethernet 1000baseSX operation. These are known as "tri-mode SFPs." If a customer is providing their own SFPs, this may not be the case. Be sure to check the SFP vendor's documentation on this matter before deployment.

GBIC Media

Older, 1Gbit Fibre Channel devices used Gigabit Interface Controller transceiver modules, as do some Gigabit

282

Ethernet devices. Figure 118 shows a set of typical GBICs. Note that the two GBICs pictured on the right use copper cables. Figure 120 shows an SC cable appropriate for attachment to an optical GBIC.

Figure 118 – Examples of GBICs

For newer 1Gbit/2Gbit Fibre Channel HBAs, switches, and routers, the SFP standard is ubiquitous[125]. However, it may sometimes be necessary to connect a 1Gbit Fibre Channel device to the router, and many Gigabit Ethernet devices still use GBICs as well. To do this, it is necessary to ensure that the wavelengths match (see LWL and SWL below) and that the optical cable type is the same (see SMF and MMF below).

SWL Media

Short Wavelength Laser media are by far the most common in use. They can be either SFPs or GBICs, are the least expensive of the laser optical media, and are used to connect either Gigabit Ethernet or Fibre Channel switches and nodes over short distances. They would typically be used within a datacenter, between different datacenters in the same campus, or over longer distances if using an intermediate extension device like a DWDM. SWL media are generally used with MMF cables. SFPs and GBICs are rarely labeled as SWL or LWL, but often have a number such as "850nm" on the label, which is the wavelength at which they operate.

---

[125] There are a few exceptions. 2Gbit FC**Error! Bookmark not defined.** GBICs do exist, but they are comparatively rare.

LWL and ELWL Media

Long and Extended Long Wavelength Laser media are used to run native point-to-point FC over dark fiber or xWDM for distance extension. Like SWL media, they can be either SFPs or GBICs, and can be used in either Fibre Channel or Gigabit Ethernet devices. As the name implies, they operate at longer wavelengths than SWL media, and can span longer distances as a result. They may be able to achieve distances in excess of 100km even without repeaters. In general, SMF cables are required for LWL and ELWL media. Look for indications like "1310nm" or "1550nm" on the label to differentiate these from SWL SFPs.

✓ Side Note

Long and Extended Long Wavelength Laser media can cause severe eye damage. Do not look directly into LWL or ELWL SFPs or GBICs, or into a cable-end carrying light from such media.

LC-LC Cables

LC connectors (Figure 119) are used to attach fiber optic cable to SFPs and patch panels. An LC-LC cable has this connector on each end. It could be used to connect two routers together, to connect a router to a 1Gbit or 2Gbit Fibre Channel device or switch, to a patch panel, or to many Gigabit Ethernet devices. These cables can be purchased in either MMF or SMF versions.

Figure 119 – LC Connecter

SC-LC Cables

SC connectors (Figure 120) are used to attach fiber optic cable to GBICs and patch panels. An SC-LC cable has this connector on one end and an LC connector on the other end. It could be used to connect a router to an older Fibre Channel node or switch, to a patch panel, or to many Gigabit Ethernet devices. Some 2Gbit FC devices use GBICs and therefore SC connectors as well, and the router would require this cable to connect to them. These cables can be purchased in either MMF or SMF versions.

Figure 120 – SC Connecter

MMF Cables and Media

Multi-Mode Fiber is used for short distances. It is less expensive than SMF, and is the most common cable type for use inside a datacenter or campus. These cables use a larger diameter (50/125µm or 62.5/125µm.) fiber core on the inside of the cladding. (Cladding is the sheath around the outside of the fiber.) Most often these cables are used with SWL GBICs and SFPs. Be sure to check that the transceiver is designed to work with the cable diameter (50 or 62.5) since there are two formats. Brocade switches all work equally well with either format, so it should work as long as the transceiver is supported by Brocade and matched to the cable. Usually, MMF cables are orange, but they can be ordered in non-standard colors so this is not a totally reliable way to distinguish them from SMF cables. Look for writing on the cable cladding as well.

SMF Cables and Media

Single-Mode Fiber can be used for short distances, but due to its greater cost it is almost exclusively used for much longer distance links in combination with LWL, ELWL or WDM solutions. Generally speaking, these solutions are designed for SMF cables, but it is appropriate to double-check since using SMF cables with media designed for MMF can cause problems. SMF cables use a much smaller diameter fiber core inside the cladding: 9/125μm. They are usually colored yellow, but like MMF cables they can be ordered in other colors.

Copper Cables and Media

Category 5, 5e, and 6 Unshielded Twisted Pair

Standard category 5 (Cat5) unshielded twisted pair (UTP) cables are used to connect hubs or switches to the RJ45 Ethernet management ports on the router. These standard cables are available widely from virtually any computer or network supplier at the time of this writing. Cat5 crossover cables are also available to connect the router directly to a host.

Category 5e (Cat5e) UTP cables were designed to run at higher rates than Cat5 could achieve. They can connect to the management interfaces, or provide Gigabit Ethernet connections to the router's sixteen data ports. Special optical to copper transceivers are required for the latter application. (See Figure 130 p296 and the surrounding text for details.)

Category 6 (Cat6) UTP is an even higher performance standard than Cat5. The router does not require Cat6 connections for any application, but since Cat6 is backwards compatible to Cat5 and Cat5e, it is possible to use Cat6 wiring if desired.

RJ45 Ethernet Ports

Both RJ45 Ethernet management ports are configured as MDI devices. This means that they use the same pin configuration as a host as opposed to a hub or switch. MDIX devices such as hubs and switches can be connected to the router with a standard cable; MDI devices like hosts require a crossover cable.

Note that RJ45 connections to the router's data ports are not supported. Some vendors supply 1000baseT SFP transceivers, so it might be tempting to use these to attach to the data ports when in Gigabit Ethernet mode. At the time of this writing, 1000baseT SFPs seems to be more expensive than using a media converter. Therefore these SFPs have not been tested with the router, and should not be used. As always, it is possible that support might be added, so discuss configurations with the appropriate support provider prior to implementation.

RJ45 Serial Port

The router has an RJ45 serial port for out-of-band management and initial configuration. This is strictly a serial port and *cannot* be connected to Ethernet. To connect a host with a DB9 serial port to the router, an adapter is required. One is supplied with the router. Figure 121 shows how one could be made.

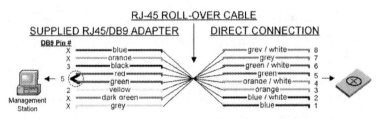

This diagram shows an RJ-45 ROLL-OVER cable terminated into the RJ-45 to serial adapter that is supplied with the router. Note that the adapter has both the red and green wires (4 & 5 from the RJ-45 side) connected to pin 5 on the DB-9 side. This cannot be used to connect the AP7420 to certain terminal servers if they do not have DB-9 connectors. Note that only three of the DB9 pins are used.

Figure 121 – RJ45 Serial to Host Connection

This diagram shows an RJ-45 rollover cable with the RJ-45 to serial adapter that is supplied with the router. (A rollover cable reverses pins between the two ends such that 1->8, 2->7, etc..) Note that the adapter has both the red and green wires (4 & 5 from the RJ-45 side) connected to pin 5 on the DB-9 side, and that only three of the DB9 pins are used. It would be possible to construct an adapter that used a straight-through cable by reversing the appropriate pins in the adapter itself.

Some users may wish to connect a router to a terminal server with an RJ45 serial port instead of a DB9. The pin-out used for the router is compatible with the RJ45 serial ports from many vendors (e.g. Cisco) in which case a simple rollover cable will work. In some cases it will need to be modified as in Figure 122.

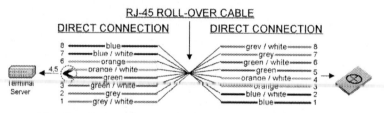

This diagram is an RJ-45 ROLL-OVER cable with the wires 4 & 5 connected together near one end. To connect the wires, strip back a few inches of the outer cable shielding and tie wires 4 & 5 together. Use a wire nut or twist together and protect with electrical tape.

Figure 122 – RJ45 Serial to Terminal Server Connection

This diagram shows an RJ-45 rollover cable with wires 4 & 5 connected together at one end. To connect the wires, strip back a few inches of outer cable shielding and tie them together. Use a wire nut or twist them together and protect with electrical tape.

To connect to a vendor with a radically different pin-out, a customized cable will be needed. Table 30 shows the pin configuration used by the port on the router, which would allow creation of such a cable by appropriately trained personnel.

Table 30 - RJ45 Serial Pin-Out

Pin #	Signal	In/Out
1	RTS	Out
2	DTR	Out
3	TXD	Out
4	GND	n/a
5	GND	n/a
6	RXD	In
7	DSR	In
8	CTS	In

Crossover Cables

An Ethernet crossover cable reverses the transmit and receive signals. It is designed to connect Ethernet nodes (MDI) to other nodes, or hubs/switches (MDIX) to other hubs/switches. When connecting the Ethernet management interfaces of a Multiprotocol Router to hubs or switches, crossover cables are *not* needed. When attaching directly to hosts, crossover cables are needed. Connecting to an IP router typically requires a crossover cable unless the router has both MDI and MDIX support.

HSSDC-2 Fibre Channel

It is possible to attach 2Gbit Fibre Channel devices using copper cables following the HSSDC-2 standard. At the time of this writing, HSSDC-2 connections directly to the router have not been tested or requested by end users. This means that copper Fibre Channel devices need to be connected to other Brocade switches within an edge fabric, such as a SilkWorm 3200 or SilkWorm 3800. Contact the appropriate support provider for details.

Ethernet and IP Network Equipment

This section does not provide a comprehensive tutorial on Ethernet or IP equipment. There are many books on that subject, and Internet searches can provide much information as well. Nor is it intended to supplement the manuals for those products. It is a high-level discussion of how such equipment relates to the Brocade Multiprotocol Router in particular.

Multiprotocol Router IP/Ethernet Modes

The router itself may be considered IP/Ethernet network equipment when used for iSCSI or FCIP.

For data links, the router has sixteen SFP ports that support optical Gigabit Ethernet 1000baseSX connections. These may be attached to a standard optical IP/Ethernet device such as a hub, switch, router, or host.

Different attachments require different cables. For example, an SC-LC cable is needed if the other device uses GBICs instead of SFPs. In any case, it is necessary to ensure that media on both ends of the cable have the same wavelength, and that both are designed for the mode of the fiber optic cable connecting them.

For management, the router has two RJ45 10/100baseT ports. These can be configured redundantly. They can connect to any standard 10/100baseT Ethernet device. The most common connection is to a hub or switch.

Ethernet L2 Edge Switches and Hubs

It is possible to use commodity 10/100baseT hubs to attach to the Ethernet management ports of the router. It is not recommended to use hubs for data links to iSCSI hosts or for FCIP connections.

When connecting the router to iSCSI hosts, it is *possible* to use accelerated Gigabit Ethernet NICs with optical transceivers to connect hosts directly to the router. However, this is not *recommended*: this approach has much higher cost and much lower performance than attaching the host to a Fibre Channel switch using a Fibre Channel HBA.

The value proposition of iSCSI vs. Fibre Channel only works if the low-end hosts are attached via already existing

NICs to a low cost Ethernet edge switch. Many iSCSI hosts then share the same router interface. (This may be called a fan-in, or port aggregation approach.)

There are many vendors who supply Ethernet edge switches. Figure 123 shows an example from Foundry Networks. (http://www.foundrynetworks.com) Figure 124 shows one way that this edge switch could be used to provide cost-effective iSCSI fan-in.

Figure 123 – Foundry EdgeIron 24 GigE Edge Switch

It is important when selecting an edge switch to be sure that it has appropriate physical media. The unit in Figure 123 has twenty four 10/100/1000baseT connections for iSCSI hosts with copper connections and four SFP optical connections for the router.

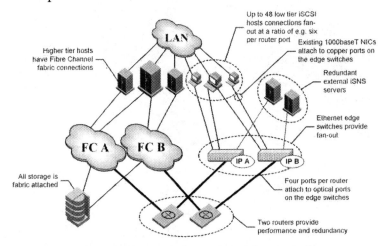

Figure 124 - Fanning Out iSCSI Using Edge Switches

IP WAN Routers

When connecting the Multiprotocol Router to a WAN in an FCIP solution, it is usually necessary to use one or more IP WAN routers. These devices generally have one or more Gigabit Ethernet LAN ports and one or more WAN interfaces, running protocols such as SONET/SDH, frame relay, or ATM. They almost always support one or more IP routing protocols like OSPF and RIP. Packet-by-packet path selection decisions are made at layer 3 (IP).

Figure 125 shows an IP WAN router from Tasman Networks. (http://www.tasmannetworks.com) There are many other vendors who supply IP WAN routers, such as Foundry Networks (Figure 126) and Cisco.

Figure 125 – Tasman Networks WAN Router

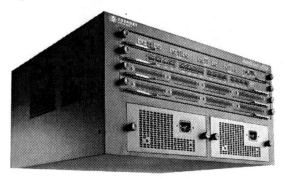

Figure 126 – Foundry Modular Router

Make sure that your WAN router and service are both appropriate for the application. Two considerations to keep in mind when selecting a WAN router for SAN extension are performance and reliability. Most WAN technologies were not intended for either the performance or reliability needs of SANs.

For example, a T1 line runs far less than 1% as fast as a Fibre Channel ISL. Some WAN routers solve this by trunking T1 connections together using link aggregation. Unless the scheme is balanced, it may not perform better than a single T1.

Similarly, some IP WAN carriers are notorious for packet loss and/or out of order delivery. These are not suitable for SAN extension. Make sure your vendor can ensure high end-to-end connection quality.

Finally, for redundant deployments it is strongly desirable for a WAN router to support a method such as the IEEE standard VRRP. Such methods can allow redundantly deployed routers to fail over to each other and load balance WAN links while both are online.

IP WAN routers might attach directly to the Multiprotocol Router, to the subnet that the router is connected to, or to an entirely different subnet reached through an IP/Ethernet layer 3 switch or LAN router. Figure 127 shows one way that an IP WAN router might be used in combination with the Multiprotocol Router. In this example, there are two sites connected across a WAN using FCIP. The Multiprotocol Routers each have two FCIP interfaces attached in a redundant manner to enterprise class Ethernet switches. These are connected redundantly to a pair of WAN routers, which are running VRRP. Those routers connect to the WAN using aggregated T1 interfaces for performance and further redundancy.

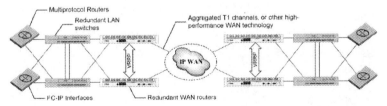

Figure 127 – WAN Router Usage Example

> ### ✅ Side Note
>
> *When using link aggregation, make sure the WAN router vendor supports* per packet inverse multiplexing. *Performance with* load sharing *schemes can be substantially inferior. Also, different routers have variations on redundant deployment protocols such as VRRP. Make sure your vendor can provide performance and reliability suitable to Fibre Channel across the board.*

IP/Ethernet L3 Switches

Layer 3 switches are hybrids of switching and routing technologies. They make packet-by-packet path selection decisions based on layer 3 information, which normally describes a router. Often they support IP routing protocols such as RIP and OSPF, and can act as gateways between IP subnets. However, they generally do this at wire speed, while routers are typically slower. Also, since layer 3 switches can make layer 2 decisions, it is possible to combine routing and switching functions into a single platform, improving performance and manageability. Figure 128 shows an enterprise-class layer 3 IP switch.

Figure 128 – Foundry BigIron L3 Modular Switch

When connecting the Multiprotocol Router to an IP management LAN, it may be connected to an IP/Ethernet

294

layer 3 switch. There are no caveats about this in general. From the point of view of the Multiprotocol Router it is just like connecting to a layer 2 Ethernet switch. It is necessary to ensure that VLAN tags are turned off at the ports to which the Multiprotocol Router is connected, since it does not support tags at the time of this writing.

One case where an IP layer 3 switch might be preferable to an L2 switch would be if a large number of iSCSI hosts are to be connected to a large number of Multiprotocol Routers. In this case, the ability of an IP layer 3 switch to contain broadcasts could be helpful. Figure 129 shows one way that an IP layer 3 switch could be used for iSCSI fan-in.

The primary caveat about this approach is that it is generally more expensive than using low cost Fibre Channel HBAs and Fibre Channel edge switches.

In this example, there may be hundreds iSCSI hosts. IP networks are notorious for broadcasts that cause unreliable behavior in large subnets, so these are divided into smaller VLANs. Each iSCSI gateway attaches to each VLAN with one or more different iSCSI portals.

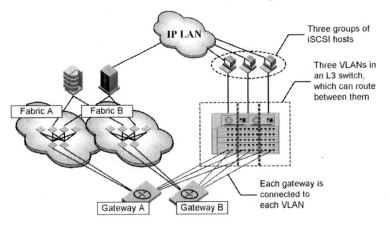

Figure 129 - iSCSI Fan-in Using L3 Switches

Copper to Fiber Gigabit Ethernet Converter

Some IT organizations supply Gigabit Ethernet connections using 1000baseT instead of 1000baseSX or LX. One solution is to use a Gigabit Ethernet switch with both copper and optical ports, attaching the router to the optical ports and the IT network to the copper ports. Alternately, a media converter (sometimes called a MIA) can be used.

There are a number of vendors who supply converters. Figure 130 shows one from TC Communications. (http://www.tccomm.com)

Figure 130 - Copper to Optical Converter

This MIA uses GBICs instead of SFPs for optical connections, and requires SC-LC cables. (See Figure 120 p285 and the surrounding text.) Converters are placed in-line with the connection to a router port. Figure 131 shows how a converter could be deployed.

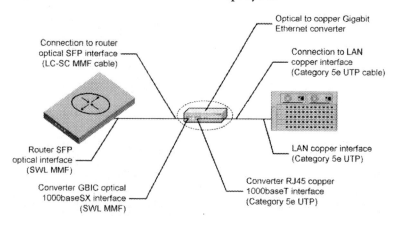

Optical to copper Gigabit Ethernet converter

Connection to router optical SFP interface (LC-SC MMF cable)

Connection to LAN copper interface (Category 5e UTP cable)

Router SFP optical interface (SWL MMF)

LAN copper interface (Category 5e UTP)

Converter GBIC optical 1000baseSX interface (SWL MMF)

Converter RJ45 copper 1000baseT interface (Category 5e UTP)

Figure 131 - Usage of Copper to Optical Converter

Appendix B: Advanced Ref.

This chapter provides "advanced topic" background and reference material.

Routing Protocols

This subsection is intended to clarify the uses for the different routing protocols associated with the multiprotocol router, and how each works at a high level. Broadly, there are three categories of routing protocol used: intrafabric routing, inter-fabric routing, and IP routing. The router uses different protocols for each of those functions.

To get from one end of a Meta SAN to another may require all three protocol groups acting in concert. For example, in a disaster tolerance solution, the router may connect to a production fabric with FSPF, use OSPF to connect to a WAN running other IP routing protocols, and run FCRP within the IP tunnel.

FSPF: Intra-Fabric Routing

Fabric Shortest Path First (FSPF) is a routing protocol designed to select paths between different switches within the same fabric. It was authored by Brocade and subsequently became the FC standard intra-fabric routing mechanism.[126][127]

---

[126] Much of the content in this subsection was adapted from "Fabric Shortest Path First (FSPF) v0.2" by Ezio Valdevit.

[127] This and other Fibre Channel standards can be found on the ANSI T11 website, http://www.t11.org.

FSPF Version 1 was released in March of 1997. In May of 1998 Version 2 was released, and has completely replaced Version 1 in the installed base. It is a link-state path selection protocol. FSPF represents an evolution of the principles used in IP and other link-state protocols (such as PNNI for ATM), providing much faster convergence times and optimizations specific to the stringent requirements of storage networks.

The protocol tracks link states on all switches in a fabric. It associates a cost with each link and computes paths from each port on each switch to all the other switches in the fabric. Path selection involves adding the cost of all links traversed and choosing lowest cost path. The collection of link states (including cost) of all the switches in a fabric constitutes the topology database.

FSPF has four major components:

- The FSPF hello protocol, used to identify and to establish connectivity with neighbor switches. This also exchanges parameters and capabilities.

- The distributed fabric topology database and the protocols and mechanisms to keep the databases synchronized between switches throughout a fabric

- The path computation algorithm

- The routing table update mechanisms

The first two items must be implemented in a specific manner for interoperability between switches. The last two are allowed to be vendor-unique.

The Brocade implementation of FSPF allows user-settable static routes in addition to automatic configuration. Other options include Dynamic Load Sharing (DLS) and In-Order Delivery (IOD). These affect the behavior of a switch during route recalculation, as, for example, during a fabric reconfiguration.

This feature works in concert with Brocade frame-by-frame trunking mechanisms. Each trunk group balances traffic evenly on a frame-by-frame basis, while FSPF balances routes between different equal-cost trunk groups.

The Brocade SilkWorm Multiprotocol Router further enhances FSPF by providing an optionally licensed exchange-based dynamic routing method that balances traffic between equal cost routes on an OX_ID basis. (OX_ID is the field within a Fibre Channel frame that uniquely defines the exchange between a source and destination node.) While this method does not provide as even a balance as frame-by frame trunking, it is more even than DLS.

FCRP: Inter-Fabric Routing

The Fibre Channel Router Protocol (FCRP) is used for routing between different fabrics. It was designed to select paths between different FC Routers on a backbone fabric, to coordinate the use of xlate domains and LSAN zoning information, and to ensure that exported devices are presented consistently by all routers with EX_Ports into a given edge fabric. Like FSPF, this protocol was authored by Brocade. At the time of this writing it is in the process of being offered to the appropriate standards bodies. (Fibre Channel expansion committee.)

Within FCRP, there are two sub-protocols: FCRP Edge and FCRP Backbone.

The FCRP Edge protocol operates on EX_Ports using ILS 0x45.[128] It first searches the edge fabric for other EX_Ports. If it finds one or more, it communicates with them to determine what other fabrics (FIDs) their routers have access to, and to determine the overall Meta SAN topology. It checks the Meta SAN topology, looking for duplicate FIDs and other invalid configurations. Assuming

---

[128] The full name is SW_ILS. ILS = Internal Link Service. This is discussed in detail in the FC-SW-3 specification in section 6.1, available from www.t11.org. In general, it is not necessary for users to know about this level of detail, but knowing the ILS number could come in handy if e.g. using a Fibre Channel analyzer.

that the topology is valid, the routers hold an election to determine ownership of xlate phantom domains for FIDs that they have in common.

For example, if several routers with EX_Ports into the FID 1 fabric each have access to FID 5, one and only one of them will "own" the definition of network address translation to FID 1 from FID 5. This router will request a domain ID from the fabric controller for the xlate domain intended to represent FID 5, and will assign PIDs under that domain for any devices in LSANs going from FID 5 to FID 1. All of the other routers with FID 5 to FID 1 paths will coordinate with the owner router and will present the xlate domain in exactly the same way. If the owner router goes down or loses its path to FID 5, another election will be held, but the new owner must continue to present the translation in the same way as the previous owner. (In fact, all routers save translation mappings to non-volatile memory and export the mappings if their configurations are saved to a host.)

Note that the owner of the FID 5 to FID 1 mapping does *not* need to be the same as the owner of e.g. the FID 4 to FID 1 mapping. Each xlate domain could potentially have a different owner.

It is important to stress that the Fibre Channel standard FSPF protocol works in conjunction with FCRP. Existing Fibre Channel switches are required by standards to use FSPF to coordinate with and determine paths to the phantom domains projected by the router. This only works correctly because FCRP makes the phantom domain presentation consistent.

On the backbone fabric, FCRP operates using ILS 0x44. It has a similar but subtly different set of tasks. It still discovers other FC Routers, but instead of operating between EX_Ports it operates between domain controllers over E_Ports. For each other FCR found, a router will discover all of its NR_Ports and the FIDs that they represent, each of which yields a path to a remote fabric. It will determine the FCRP cost of each path. Finally, it will transfer LSAN zoning and device state information to each other router.

When the initial inter-fabric route database creation is complete, routers will be consistently presenting EX_Ports with xlate domains into all edge fabrics, each with phantom devices for the appropriate LSAN members. Into the backbone fabrics, routers will present one NR_Port for each EX_Port. This is another situation in which FCRP and FSPF work together: FCRP allows the NR_Ports to be set up and their activities coordinated. Once traffic starts to flow across the backbone, it will flow between NR_Ports. FSPF controls the path selection on the standard switches that make up the backbone.

Side Note

Not only FSPF and FCRP are complementary. On an FCIP connection in a Meta SAN, all routing protocol types plus layer 2 protocols like trunking and STP can apply to a single connection. STP works outside the tunnel on LANs between FCIP gateways and WAN routers, IP protocols like OSPF work through the WAN outside the tunnel, FSPF operates at the standard FC level inside the tunneled backbone fabric, and FCRP operates above FSPF but still within the tunnel.

IP Routing Protocols

When a Brocade router runs iSCSI or FCIP, it uses standard IP routing to reach the far-end host (iSCSI) or router (FCIP). This subsection discusses how the router interacts with IP routing methods.

At the time of this writing, the IP SAN interfaces on the router look like nodes to the IP network. They support static routing. Each IP SAN interface is given a default gateway, and assumes that packets will make their way from that gateway to their destination. Along the way, it is likely that other IP routing mechanisms will come into play.

OSPF and RIP

When running FCIP across an IP WAN, it is likely that WAN routers will be running a protocol like Open Shortest Path First (OSPF) or the Router Information Protocol (RIP). In SAN applications, it is generally necessary to support faster convergence times than RIP can handle, so OSFP is likely to be more widely deployed. It is also possible to use a proprietary protocol like Cisco's EIGRP, but this is beyond the scope of this book.

OSPF is in some respects like a primitive version of FSPF: it is a link-state protocol that allows WAN routers within the OSPF network to perform optimal path selection with relatively[129] fast convergence. This allows redundant WAN paths to be shared in an active-active manner, and fail over to each other. A Brocade router uses static routing to send an IP packet to its default gateway, which may use OSPF to reach another gateway, which delivers the packet to the destination. Figure 132 illustrates an example of a simple FCIP configuration interacting with OSPF.

There are two sites in this configuration, each with two Multiprotocol Routers running FCIP and two IP WAN routers running OSPF. The lines connecting the routers indicate *paths*, not *ports*. For example, Routers A and B might each have one FCIP port. Similarly, Routers C and D might each have one LAN-side port. If these ports were connected to a Gigabit Ethernet switch then each FCIP port would have a path through that switch to each LAN-side port on the WAN routers. The two Site #1 FCIP ports also would be able to reach each other,

---

[129] "Relative" is an important caveat. FSPF tends to converge several orders of magnitude faster than "fast" IP routing protocols such as even highly tuned OSPF. FSPF can actually recalculate and assign routes in about half a second, whereas IP protocols tend to take many seconds if not minutes.

though there is no application for this currently. In some
failure cases it is important that the two WAN routers can
reach each other using the LAN.

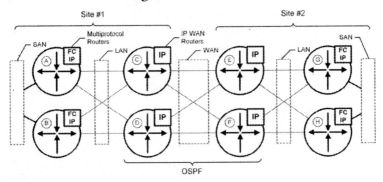

Figure 132 – OSPF Interaction with FCIP

Assume that Router A has one FCIP port that needs
to reach Router G at Site #2, and is configured to use the
LAN-side port of Router C as its default gateway. It will
use path AC to reach Router C, which can use either path
CE or path CF to reach Site #2. Routers C, D, E, and F
are running OSPF. If Router C decided to use path CE
to reach Site #2, and that path goes down (perhaps due to
a complete failure of Router E) then OSPF will allow it to
change relatively quickly to path CF.

If the WAN router should lose all of its WAN link(s),
OSPF will allow it to determine whether another router
on its LAN still has a path. In this case, if Router C lost
both CE and CF, it could use Router D to deliver packets
to Site #2. While this prevents certain WAN failures
from propagating to nodes, if a WAN router loses all of its
direct paths to the destination, packets using it may follow
a circuitous path. For example, if Router A sends a packet
to Router C in this failure mode, Router C will have to
send the packet to Router D, possibly even right back out
the same LAN interface it came in on in the first place.
Figure 133 shows how this would work.

First Router A sends a packet across the LAN to its
default gateway, Router C. That router has lost both

WAN paths to Site #2, but it knows via OSPF that Router D can still get there. It sends the packet back out its LAN interface, this time addressed to Router D, which then forwards it to Site #2. This takes two more hops than in normal operation.

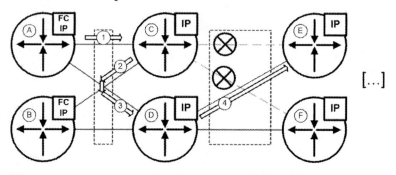

[...]

Figure 133 - OSPF WAN Failure

Note that this requires the gateway with the failed WAN path to take an action: it has to receive every packet and forward it to the alternate router. If the gateway itself should fail, this will not be helpful.

<u>VRRP, HSRP, and FSRP</u>

To solve this, WAN routers may run a protocol like HSRP, FSRP, or VRRP for redundancy between the routers themselves. If two routers at a site are configured with VRRP, one can take over the LAN-side interface of its partner should that router fail.

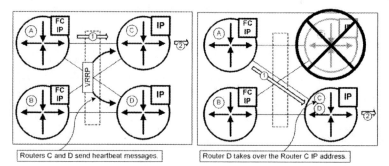

Figure 134 - VRRP Failover

Figure 134 shows a failure case in which VRRP allows continued WAN access between Sites #1 and #2.

STP and Ethernet Trunking

While it is not an IP routing protocol, it is worth discussing the Spanning Tree Protocol. (STP is defined in IEEE 802.1D.) STP operates at the Ethernet layer to provide path redundancy between bridges and L2 switches while preventing loops that could otherwise take down the network. Figure 135 shows how STP can be used to protect an FCIP solution against a link failure if the LAN between the FCIP ports and the WAN routers is slightly more complex.

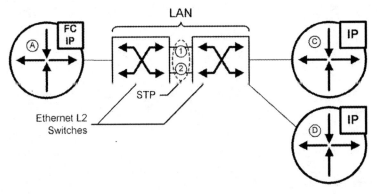

Figure 135 – STP Redundant LAN

In this figure, the lines between network devices represent physical ports, not paths. The FCIP router (A) is attached to an Ethernet switch, which has two ports (1 & 2) attached to another Ethernet switch, to which the WAN routers are attached. STP is running on the two Ethernet switches. If one link should fail, packets will be able to use the other link.

Unfortunately, standard STP takes a long time to reconverge around link failures: 30 seconds is considered "good." It is also generally an active/passive protocol. Some vendors now offer a rapid convergence version, which - though not up to Fibre Channel standards - is preferable for SANs compared to standard STP. However, not all vendors support this and it requires all switches to have the enhanced STP capability in order to work. This generally brings the cost of the solution up to native Fibre Channel levels and beyond, while still underperforming FC solutions considerably. For these reasons, it is generally more popular to use trunking (such as IEEE P802.3ad Link Aggregation) either instead of or in combination with STP as shown in Figure 136.

The two links between switches s1 and s3 form an Ethernet trunk, as do those between s1 and s4. Each trunk is physically two links, but treated as one virtual link by STP. These virtual links (1 & 2) must still be protected from loops, so STP operates on top of Ethernet trunking.

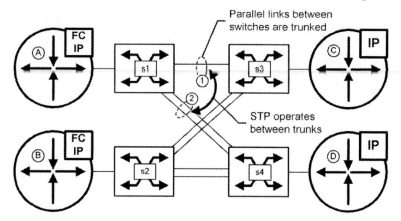

Figure 136 - Ethernet Trunking with STP

FC-FC Router Details

This subsection provides details on the Brocade router implementation. It is intended for use as a general reference, and for use in troubleshooting Meta SANs. There is also some information for those planning to build management tools for the router.

FCR Frame Header Formats

The FC-FC Routing Service defines two new frame headers: an encapsulation header and an Inter-Fabric Addressing (IFA) header. These are used to pass frames between NR_Ports of routers on a backbone fabric. These extra headers are inserted by the ingress EX_Port and interpreted and removed by the egress EX_Port.

The format for these headers going to be submitted for review in the T11 FC Expansion Study Group and is subject to change.[130] Since frame handling is performed by a programmable portion of the port ASIC on router platforms, header format changes can be accommodated without hardware changes.

Inter-Fabric Addressing Header

The Inter-Fabric Addressing Header (IFA) provides routers with information used for routing and address translation. Table 31 shows the header format. Only three fields are used at the time of this writing. The others are reserved for future use.

Table 31 – IFA Header Fields

0	R_CTL=0x51	·Ver	Type	L	M	DFID
1	L2.TTL	Pad	R	Prio		SFID

R_CTL – Set to 0x51, which means "Inter-Fabric Addressing Header"

DFID – The Destination Fabric ID. In the first implementation, only DFIDs from 1 to 128 are utilized, though more are possible. This is used to route the frame to the correct destination fabric.

SFID – The Source Fabric ID. In the first implementation, only SFIDs from 1 to 128 are utilized. The SFID field is used by the egress ASIC in conjunction with the SID field in the normal FC-FS frame header to derive the source proxy ID to use when sending the frame into the destination edge fabric.

Encapsulation Header

The encapsulation header is used to wrap the IFA header and data frame while it traverses a backbone fabric. Table 32 details the header format.

---

[130] The encapsulation and FC-SW headers already follow T11 standards, so it is unlikely that they will be change.

Table 32 - Encapsulation Header Fields

0	R_CTL	DID	
1	CS_CTL	SID	
2	TYPE	F_CTL	
3	SEQ_ID	DF_CTL	SEQ_CNT
4	OX_ID		RX_ID
5	Parameter		

R_CTL – 0x04 – Unsolicited Data
DID – PID of the destination NR_Port
CS_CTL – copied from the original FC header
SID – PID of the source NR_Port
TYPE – 0x59 – Proposed to T11 to mean "encapsulation tunnel"
F_CTL – Copied from the original FC header.
SEQ_ID/SEQ_CNT – The FC Expansion proposal outlines schemes for using the SEQ_ID and SEQ_CNT. For now, FCRS simply copies these fields from the original FC header.
OX_ID/RX_ID – Copied from the original FC header.
Parameter – Copied from the original FC header.

This header is formatted exactly like a normal FC-FS standard header, so an encapsulated frame is indistinguishable from a standard frame to switches on the backbone. This ensures that the router is compatible with existing switches, unlike proprietary tagging schemes proposed by other vendors.

Note that the SID and DID in the encapsulation header represent the source and destination NR_Ports. This is why standard switches can deliver the frame to the correct router without needing to know about FIDs, FCRP, or other Meta SAN extensions.

The standard FC-FS header format shown in Table 33. This is the header format used for FC frames in fabrics today, and is created by the originating device.

Table 33 - FC-FS Header Fields

0	R_CTL	DID	
1	CS_CTL	SID	
2	TYPE	F_CTL	
3	SEQ_ID	DF_CTL	SEQ_CNT
4	OX_ID		RX_ID
5	Parameter		

As you can see, the FC-FS header format is identical to the encapsulation header format. The contents of this header change as the frame traverses between fabrics. It is rewritten by the routers to reflect the FC-NAT translated values for SID and DID. When the frame arrives at the ingress EX_Port (the one attached to the source fabric), the fields reflect the *source* device's view of the Meta SAN:

DID – PID of the proxy device that represents a destination device in another fabric. I.e. this is the source fabric's xlate PID for the destination device.
SID – the real PID of the source device.

When the frame is sent between NR_Ports on a backbone fabric, the normal FC-FS header that was generated by the source device is encapsulated along with the IFA header within the encapsulation header. The DID field of the header is also modified, so the SID and DID both represent the two devices' *real* PIDs:

DID – Modified by the ingress EX_Port to the PID for the destination device in its own fabric.
SID – Unchanged. It still represents the PID of the source device in its own fabric.
OX_ID – Utilized along with DID/SID to load balance across multiple destination NR_Ports.

When the frame exits the egress EX_Port (attached to the destination device's fabric), the fields reflect the *destination* device's view of the Meta SAN:

DID – Unchanged since the previous stage. This field contains the real PID of the destination device.
SID – Modified by the egress EX_Port to the PID of the proxy source device that represents the real source device on another fabric. I.e. this is the destination fabric's xlate PID for the source device.

Note that the encapsulation and IFA headers add length to the frame while it is on the backbone. To accommodate this, proxy devices throttle the negotiated frame payload size as 2048 for nodes that try to negotiate the FC maximum frame length. This keeps frame sizes on the backbone fabric at or below 2112 bytes as required by FC standards. This has not been observed to have any performance impact, since most HBAs negotiate 2048 byte payloads, and the power of two payload size aligns better with typical filesystem block sizes anyway.

Advanced Reference

Putting it all together, the frame headers can be represented as in Figure 137.

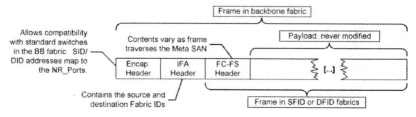

Figure 137 – FCR Frame Header Detail

FCR Manageability Extensions

The router supports extended commands for LSAN and router-specific operations in both the GUI and CLI management interfaces. Some areas in which additional management commands or extensions to existing commands are provided are:

LSAN Devices – These are devices that have been included in LSAN zones. Information that an administrator may need about an LSAN device includes its WWN, the FID where it is attached, its real PID in that fabric, and its xlate PID in any given remote fabric.

LSAN Zones – Each router can display all of its own LSAN zones and any received from other routers on the same backbone fabric.

NR_Ports – Each router can display all NR_Ports in the backbone fabric as well as which edge fabric is represented by each NR_Port.

Phantom Domain Management – Users can set a preferred ID for phantom domains. Xlate domains are specified by the edge fabric (FID) in which the domain exists and the remote fabric it represents. If the principal switch assigns a different domain ID, the new value is accepted. Information about the xlate domain can be displayed, such as its WWN and the actual domain ID assigned.

Backbone Fabric Management – An administrator may want to set the FID of the BB fabric, or display the routers in the backbone. It is also possible to display information about these routers, like their attached edge fabrics' FIDs and principal switch identities.

In addition, each EX_Port has a number of per-port configured parameters, such as:

EX_Port Admin - Enables/disables an EX_Port.

EX_Port Fabric ID - Sets the FID for the EX_Port.

EX_Port R_A_TOV - Sets the R_A_TOV value that the EX_Port uses for port initialization.

EX_Port E_D_TOV - Sets the E_D_TOV value that the EX_Port uses for port initialization.

EX_Port Front Phantom Domain ID - The persistently stored domain ID of the front phantom domain. If this value is configured by a user, then this value is used by the front domain to request its preferred domain ID. If the domain ID provided by the principal switch of the edge fabric is different, then the new value is stored.

EX_Port PID Format - PID format for edge fabric.

EX_Port Interoperability Mode - The Interoperability Mode for the EX_Port. Determines which vendor's E_Port implementation the EX_Port will use.

To support element management in these and other areas, the router CLI has extensions for:

- switchShow
- portShow
- licenseAdd and licenseShow
- supportShow

In addition to enhancements to existing commands, new commands are provided for functions with no prior analogue. The FCR manuals have descriptions of and in-

Advanced Reference

structions for these commands, as well as FCR extensions to existing commands.

- fcrFabricShow
- fcrRouteShow
- fcrConfigure
- fcrPhyDevShow
- fcrProxyConfig
- fcrProxyDevShow
- fcrResourceShow
- fcrXlateConfig
- lsanZoneShow
- portCfgEXport

The GUI element management interfaces (e.g. Web Tools) provide equivalent functionality in most cases.

FCR PID Format Support

There are certain parameters that must be set identically on all switches within a given fabric. One such parameter is the fabric's PID format.

Port Identifiers (PIDs) are one of the two addressing mechanisms used in Fibre Channel. Specifying a PID of a device is analogous to specifying the physical switch and port a device is attached to in data networks. PIDs are *not* analogous to IP addresses. PIDs are assigned by a Fibre Channel switch when a device logs into the fabric. An example PID might look like this: 011F00.

The method Brocade switches use for assigning PIDs has changed over time as the requirements for Fibre Channel fabrics have matured. One older PID format (native PID mode) was XX1YZZ, where "Y" was a hexadecimal number specifying a particular port on a switch and "1" was a constant. XX was used for the domain ID and ZZ for the AL_PA. Since all Brocade switches had sixteen or fewer ports at the time that method was established, one hexadecimal digit was entirely adequate to specify the port.

One new format (core PID mode) is XXYYZZ, where "YY" represents a port. This was necessary to support switches with more than sixteen ports. Using the entire middle byte for the port allows addressing up to 256 ports per switch.

A variation on the core PID format is called "extended edge format." This was designed to ease integration of large switches into installed base fabrics. The entire middle byte is still used for specifying the port, so up to 256 ports per domain are possible. However, the port address is offset by sixteen. This means that port 0x10 (16 decimal) refers to port zero, port 2F is port 31 instead of port 47, and port 0x0F wraps around and refers to port 255.

When a switch with one PID format is introduced into a fabric with a different format, the format needs to be synchronized between all switches to prevent segmentation. There are procedures for doing this without application downtime in many environments, but these do not cover all cases, and in any event these procedures may require considerable planning and effort.

The router addresses this issue. It supports using different PID formats on different fabrics and still routing frames between them. EX_Ports support native, core, and extended edge PID modes. (PID formats 0, 1, and 2 respectively.) "VC encoded" format (SilkWorm 1000 series only) is not supported. This is a user-configurable parameter on a per-EX_Port basis, though as a practical matter all EX_Ports on a given FID must be synchronized.

> ### ✔ Side Note
>
> *The PID format of a switch is not the only parameter that needs to be consistent between all switches in a fabric. Parameters like TOVs, zoning configurations and domain addresses must be in sync to merge fabrics, but do not need to be in sync to form a Meta SAN.*

FCR Fabric Services Support

Two different sets of fabric services exist on each router. There is one kind for the backbone fabric, which is just like a normal AP7420. There is another kind for EX_Ports. This section discusses EX_Port fabric services behavior.

An EX_Port is a light-weight version of an E_Port. It is never used as a "real" switch port, and is guaranteed to be on the edge of a fabric, so it does not need to support fabric services in the complete way that a regular switch would. Indeed, there are enormous scalability advantages to *not* supporting fabric services in exactly the same way as other switches. The overall EX_Port strategy is to ensure that edge switches do not need to know the difference between "lite" support and "full" support, while still preventing the router platform from needing to do CPU and other resource intensive operations that would be required for traditional switches.

Zoning – Zoning commands are supported in order to satisfy other switches within the fabric that want to share the zoning database. In addition, the router searches the zoning database to extract WWNs for LSANs and to determine the zoning policy for the imported/exported devices.

RCS – Supported for zoning only.

Fabric Build – Enough is supported to convince an edge fabric of the presence of phantom switches. EX_Ports provide fabric parameters (such as E_D_TOV,

314

R_A_TOV and PID format) at port initialization. Users are allowed to configure these parameters to allow EX_Ports to merge with edge fabrics.

FSPF – Enough is supported to convince the fabric of the phantom topology presented by the router. Routes to xlate domains are advertised as maximum cost links to prevent the fabric from establishing *intra*-fabric routes using these links. Should the loss of a path cause the fabric to want to utilize these links for intra-fabric routing anyway, the router will disable the EX_Ports.

SNS – A small subset of SNS is supported in order for the router to satisfy other switches within the fabric that want share SNS databases. In addition, a router needs to determine the presence and state of devices to be exported. SNS queries from end devices are not supported.

Secure Fabric OS – Not supported at the time of this writing, but planned for a subsequent release. Check with the appropriate support personnel for up-to-date information on availability of this feature.

Frame Trunking - Not supported on the AP7420 since the platform hardware doesn't have the capability. Exchange-based load balancing of IFLs and ISLs is supported.

Management Server (MS) – A small subset is supported so that MS support does not need to be disabled within an edge fabric. In addition, a small subset of the topology commands are supported so that the Brocade API can create its object hierarchy.

FCR Conflicts and Resolutions

There are a number of failure or misconfiguration scenarios that the router needs to support. These are driven by real-world events like "an EX_Port SFP fails" or "an administrator reboots a router" or "a user plugs a router port into the wrong edge fabric." Each failure mode results in changes in connectivity that the routers must handle gracefully, and must communicate to – and *only* to

– relevant devices and switches. This section discusses a few of the more common failure modes.

ELP conflicts - If an edge fabric has fabric-wide parameters like a TOV or PID format that do not match the EX_Port, it will segment. An administrator can configure the EX_Port to match values to correct the problem. This does not require changing parameters on EX_Ports attached to other fabrics.

Fabric ID Conflict - If an EX_Port uses a FID to connect to an edge fabric and that FID is already used by a different edge fabric that the router has visibility into, the EX_Port is disabled and an error message is printed. The existing edge fabric continues to operate normally. An administrator needs to correctly set the FID of the EX_Port for the new edge fabric and re-enable the EX_Port.

Fabric ID Oversubscribe - If an EX_Port uses a FID to connect to an edge fabric that already has an EX_Port with a different FID, the EX_Port is disabled and an error message is printed. This happens when an edge fabric tries to connect to a router using an EX_Port which is configured with a FID that is different than the FID of the EX _Port(s) already connected to it. The existing EX_Ports continue to operate normally. An administrator needs to correctly set the FID and re-enable the EX_Port.

Edge Fabric Merge - If two or more edge fabrics merge, this creates a FID conflict. However, unlike the oversubscribe case where existing FID can take precedence, the router cannot make an assumption about which FID to assign to the newly created edge fabric. All EX_Ports connected to the new edge fabric are disabled and an error message is printed. An administrator needs to correctly set the FID for all EX_Ports and re-enable the relevant ports, or segment the edge fabric back to its original state.

Edge Fabric Split - If an edge fabric segments, this is an example of the FID oversubscribe case. However, unlike the case where existing EX_Ports take precedence, the router cannot make an assumption as to which edge fabric segment retains ownership of the original FID. Therefore, all EX_Ports connected to the resulting set of edge fabrics are disabled and an error message is printed. An administrator needs to correctly set FID for all EX_Ports and enable the ports, or merge the fabric back to its original state.

FCR Timeout Values and Hop Counts

The router supports using different Timeout Values (TOVs) on each fabric. It is theoretically possible for edge devices to misbehave if end-to-end hop count is not matched to the TOVs.   Such misbehavior is *highly* unlikely, and most customers simply do not need to be concerned with TOV calculations.   Some customers, however, may have complex topologies that would – at least in theory – react badly to differing TOVs.

The safest approach is to use the default R_A_TOV and E_D_TOV settings for all fabrics and to restrict the end-to-end hop count to seven hops. The remainder of this subsection provides information and guidance for customers that are not able to operate within these constraints.

TOV and Hop Count Background Information

Fibre Channel specifies a number of TOVs in order to facilitate error detection and recovery. Two major timers are E_D_TOV and R_A_TOV.

E_D_TOV (Error Detect Time-Out Value) is a medium length timer with a default value of two seconds. It is used to detect frame and sequence level errors.

R_A_TOV (Resource Allocation Time-out Value) is a long duration timer that is used to determine how long

317

resources allocated for a particular operation need to be re-served.

These timers are fabric-wide parameters, but may dif-fer from fabric to fabric in order to accommodate various fabric topology complexities and/or high-latency links such as WAN extenders. Existing SilkWorm switches use R_A_TOV, E_D_TOV, and maximum hop count (a static value of seven) to calculate a very conservative HOLD_TIME per switch within a fabric. This is the time a switch can hold a frame before dropping it. In order to calculate HOLD_TIME at each switch, the following for-mula is used:

```
HT = ( (R_A_TOV-E_D_TOV)/(max_hops+1) ) / 2
```

Based on default value of 10,000ms for R_A_TOV, 2,000ms for E_D_TOV, and a maximum hop count of 7, the calculation becomes ((10000 − 2000) / (7 + 1)) / 2 = 500ms for HOLD_TIME.

This is a conservative value since the hold time of 500ms is applied to all switches regardless of actual hop count between devices, and − more importantly − regard-less of the amount of time any other switches actually *did* hold the frame. For example, say that there are actually seven hops between endpoints. Perhaps six are traversed in <1ms each, but if one switch holds the frame for 501ms, that switch will drop the frame. The calculation essentially assumes that there are always seven hops, and that all of them are highly delayed.

Conservative HOLD_TIME enforcement is imple-mented to prevent situations where end devices free resources for an I/O upon R_A_TOV expiration while the frames for the I/O are still active in the fabric. Poorly designed end devices may exhibit "bad" behavior in the-ory up to and including data corruption. Of course, switches rarely hold frames for significant durations: the typical port-to-port latency within a Brocade switch is less than 2.1μs, and may be as little as 0.7μs. In addition, end devices typically do not reuse resources quickly enough to cause a problem.

FCR TOV and Hop Count Discussion

Each EX_Port will respond to the attached E_Port with R_A_TOV and E_D_TOV as configured on a per-EX_Port basis, to allow link bring-up. These values are no longer used once links are established and are *separate* from the R_A_TOV and E_D_TOV that router actually uses to establish a backbone fabric with other routers.

Again, the safest approach is to use the default R_A_TOV and E_D_TOV for all fabrics, including the routers themselves. If that isn't possible, then the internal R_A_TOV and E_D_TOV of each router should be configured to the lowest of R_A_TOVs and to highest of E_D_TOVs from any edge or backbone fabric.

Each edge fabric's E_D_TOV should be set to the highest E_D_TOV from the edge fabrics with which the local edge fabric communicates. Each edge fabric's R_A_TOV should be set to the lowest R_A_TOV from the edge fabrics with which the local fabric communicates. It is possible to configure LSAN connectivity even if this isn't the case, but if maximum hop count occurred simultaneously with maximum congestion/latency *and* edge device drivers also behaved very badly, then data corruption could theoretically occur. Therefore if it is necessary to configure a mismatch in TOVs – e.g. to support a high latency WAN connection in one fabric – then for conservative deployments the end-to-end hop count should be reduced from seven by an amount proportional to the difference in the TOVs. For example, if one fabric has a 2x delta vs. the default R_A_TOV, then an end-to-end hop count of three or four hops would be conservative.

In any case, careful consideration should be given to keep the HOLD_TIME of all switches in the global fabric above 250 ms.

Advanced Reference

319

FC Protocols and Standards

The router generally adheres to Fibre Channel standards in the same way as other Brocade switches, which is why it is backwards compatible. Extensions such as FCRP operate at higher layers, and to the extent that standard services are enhanced, it is transparent to other switches. This is analogous to the difference between IP routing protocols and Ethernet: adding a new routing protocol on top of IP that sits on top of Ethernet does not violate Ethernet or IP standards. It is irrelevant to them since they apply to different layers in the protocol stack.

For example, an EX_Port implements a subset of the name server standard because it doesn't need any of the pieces that relate to direct attachment of nodes. The router *platform* implements the complete SNS for backbone fabric connections, but it is not possible to plug a node into an EX_Port, so implementing a name server-to-node protocol on an EX_Port would be superfluous.

Some standards that apply to the router include:

- FC-SW-*x*
- FC-FLA
- FC-AL-*x*
- FC-GS-4
- FC-MI-2
- FC-DA
- FCP-*x*
- FC-FS
- FC-PI-*x*

For more information on these and other Fibre Channel standards, visit the ANSI T11 website, www.t11.org.

Side Note

Following standards is necessary but not sufficient to ensure interoperability between networking devices. Standards documents often leave much to the imagination of vendors' engineering teams. It is necessary to check with support providers in addition to looking at standards before assuming multi-vendor interoperability. This is particularly true with emerging IP SAN standards like iSCSI and FCIP. For example, at the time of this writing, no vendors have demonstrated interoperability between different FCIP gateways, and there have been twenty incompatible drafts of the iSCSI standard so far. Existing IP standards do not guarantee real-world compatibility for IP SAN devices.

IP/Ethernet Protocols and Standards

Ethernet

When in Gigabit Ethernet mode, the router's data ports comply to all applicable Ethernet standards for SFP optical Gigabit Ethernet connections such as IEEE 802.3z. They also comply with all applicable IP standards. This means that the ports can be directly connected to standard off-the-shelf Gigabit Ethernet switches with optical interfaces, or to 1000baseT ports using optical to copper media converters. (See Figure 130 for an example of a converter.)

IPv4 and IPv6

The router complies with the IPv4 standard. This is the familiar four byte decimal delimited standard used by the vast majority of IP equipment in production today. IPv6 was developed for Internet backbone equipment. It is not implemented by the Multiprotocol Router at this time and is not expected to be required in the future.

321

✓

≡ **Side Note**

Did you know... The IEEE 802.3z Gigabit Ethernet standard was created by merging IEEE 802 Ethernet and ANSI T11 Fibre Channel? They took the FC-0 and FC-1 layers and tacked on 802.2 LLC and 802.3 CSMA/CD. Fibre Channel actually predates *Gigabit Ethernet!*

802.1q/p VLANs

The IEEE 802.1q standard is a method for inserting VLAN information into Ethernet frames. VLANs provide another method (besides routers) to break up large networks. The intent is to act as a container to prevent broadcast and multicast traffic from causing performance and reliability problems. VLANs also provide a primitive security mechanism. For almost all real-world IT applications, a router, firewall, or L3 switch is also required in order to provide connectivity between VLANs. IEEE 802.1p provides a L2 VLAN priority mechanism.

In a Fibre Channel fabric, the analogous mechanism to VLANs is provided by zoning. Zones limit the propagation of RSCNs, which could otherwise have the same effect as Ethernet broadcast storms. Zones also provide greater and more flexible security than VLANs, and even provide a method for getting between zones. Within a fabric, no router is required to configure connectivity between zones, since it is possible to configure zones that overlap in arbitrarily complex ways.

When attaching the router to an IP network to run iSCSI or FCIP, it is perfectly acceptable for that network to use 802.1q/p VLANs. The only caveat is that the network interface the router is plugged into must have the VLAN tags turned off since the router itself does not support VLAN tagging. This is likely to be supported in a future release as a "checkbox" item, though it has not actually been requested from customers at the time of this writing.

IP Routing Protocols

The router does not either explicitly support or disallow IP routing protocols such as RIP and OSPF at the time of this writing, though support may be added in the future. These can be present anywhere in the IP network without impacting the router: it simply does not interact with them.

Each Multiprotocol Router interface supports the configuration of a single default route. If redundancy is required, it is possible to configure different interfaces or even entirely different Multiprotocol Routers to use different gateways. It is also possible to use HSRP or a similar protocol to create redundancy for the gateway address itself.

iSCSI Protocols and Standards

While IP and Ethernet standard are very well defined, IP SAN standards are still moving targets. One advantage of the Brocade iSCSI implementation is that it uses a programmable portion of the platform's port ASICs. This means that the platform can be software updated as iSCSI standards change or are extended without forklift hardware upgrades. With a technology like iSCSI, this is of overriding importance since standards and preferred implementations tend to change radically often for several years even after a "standard" is finally ratified.

At the time of this writing, the service is based on the IETF IP Storage Working Group iSCSI draft #20, available on their website, at www.ietf.org. As the emerging iSCSI standards continue to change, the gateway will continue to be updated.

The gateway acts as a bridge between the iSCSI and Fibre Channel protocols and services. It understands both

Fibre Channel and iSCSI names. It generates a unique Fibre Channel name for each iSCSI name and registers this with the appropriate Fibre Channel services. The intent is to apply existing Fibre Channel access control (i.e. zoning) to iSCSI initiators. Figure 138 shows how the gateway service relates to the IP and Fibre Channel protocols, and how those relate to hosts, storage, and external services.

The gateway presently acts only in iSCSI target mode. This means that iSCSI initiator nodes can use the gateway to access Fibre Channel targets, but Fibre Channel initiators cannot access iSCSI storage. The usage cases that drove the creation of the gateway did not require the latter communication method, though of course this may change in the future. Therefore only the standards relevant to iSCSI target mode are applicable at this time.

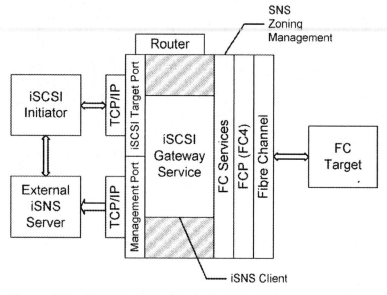

Figure 138 – iSCSI Protocol Relationships

Similarly, customer feedback has indicated that an iSNS server on the gateway is not a top priority. Instead, the gateway implements an iSCSI client that can interface with an external iSNS server.

FCIP Protocols and Standards

FCIP standards, like other IP SAN standards, are not entirely settled down at the time of this writing, so no vendor truly has a "standards compliant" FCIP product. Brocade, like other vendors, is aggressively working towards a standard. The service uses a programmable portion of the router's port ASICs, and Brocade is committed to delivering updates as standards solidify.

In the mean time, the service is based on draft twelve of "Fibre Channel Over TCP/IP (FCIP)" specification from the IETF IP Storage Working Group. The encapsulation method was based on draft eight of "Fibre Channel Frame Encapsulation," which has since been superceded by RFC 3643. At the time of this writing, the update to this new specification has not been completed. The current implementation of the service also has performance enhancements that deviate slightly from the drafts.

Figure 139 shows how the tunneling service relates to the IP and Fibre Channel protocols, and how those relate to hosts and storage. Two routers are depicted with one tunneled ISL between them. From the point of view of the Fibre Channel fabric, this is an FC standard E_Port-to-E_Port connection. The IP tunnel is invisible to the interior protocol.

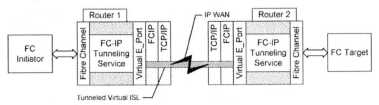

Figure 139 – FCIP Protocol Relationships

325

Glossary

AL_PA Arbitrated Loop Physical Address is used to identify a device in an arbitrated loop.

AS Alias Server standard that maintains identifier mappings to support multicast group management

Alias Server See AS

American National Standards Institute See ANSI

ANSI American National Standards Institute is the governing body for standards in the United States. The ANSI T11 committee sets standards for FC.

AP Application Platforms enable fabric-based storage applications such as mirroring, data migration, snapshots, virtual tape, etc..

API Application Programming Interfaces provide a layer of abstraction between complex lower-level processes and upper level applications development. They facilitate building complex applications by providing building blocks for programmers to work with.

Application Platform See AP

Application Programming Interface See API

Application-Specific Integrated Circuit See ASIC

Arbitrated Loop Shared Fibre Channel transport supporting a theoretical maximum of 126 devices

ASIC Application-Specific Integrated Circuits are fixed-gate microchips designed to perform specific functions very well

Asynchronous Transfer Mode See ATM

ATM Asynchronous Transfer Mode is a cell-switching transport used for transmitting data over CANs, MANs, and WANs. ATM transmits short fixed-length units of data. Characterized by relatively high performance and reliability vs. switched IP solutions.

Availability Strictly speaking, whenever a component is able to perform its intended function, it is "available." Unless otherwise specified, this refers to *higher-level* functions, such as application-level availability. For example, if a power supply on a switch fails, and the switch has a redundant power supply, this would generally be a *reliability* event, but not an *availability* event, since the switch would still be online and able to provide disk access to the host running the application.

Backbone Fabric See BB Fabric

Bandwidth Transmission capacity of a link or system.

BB_Credit Buffer-to-buffer credits are a flow control mechanism used to determine how many frames can be sent to a recipient from any given port

BB Fabric The FCR allows an optional Backbone Fabric to interconnect routers for more scalable and flexible Meta SANs. Routers connect to the BB Fabric via E_Ports.

Broadcast Transmitting to all nodes on a fabric.

Bridge Connects segments of a single network

Brocade Founded in 1995, Brocade rapidly became the leading provider of Fibre Channel switches. At the time of this writing, the company carries switches, directors, and multiprotocol routers.

Buffer-to-Buffer Credits See BB_Credit

CAN Campus Area Networks tend to be under a kilometer or so in size. They are distinguished from LANs in that those tend to be in the ~100 meter range, but more importantly CANs cross between buildings. This characteristic tends to imply thinner cabling, potentially higher speeds running over that cabling, and higher locality.

Carrier Sense Multiple Access with Collision Detection See CSMA/CD

CHAP Challenge Handshake Authentication Protocol is a method of securely verifying over a network that nodes are authorized to connect to one another.

Class Of Service See COS

CLI Command Line Interfaces are text-oriented methods of managing devices. The FCR uses a CLI based on the Brocade Fabric OS CLI to make administrator training easier.

Coarse Wave Division Multiplexer See CWDM

Command Line Interface See CLI

COS Class Of Service represents connection quality: a profile for attributes such as latency and data-rate.

CRC Cyclic Redundancy Check is a self-test for error detection and correction. All Brocade ASICs perform CRC checks on all frames to ensure data integrity

Credit Numeric value that represents the maximum number of receive buffers provided by an F/FL_Port to its attached N/NL_Port such that the N/NL_Port may transmit frames without overrunning the F/FL_Port.

CSMA/CD Carrier Sense Multiple Access with Collision Detection defines how Ethernet NICs behave when two or more attempt to use a shared segment at the same time

CWDM Coarse Wave Division Multiplexer. See also WDM and CWDM.

Cyclic Redundancy Check See CRC

Dark Fiber A leased fiber optic cable running between sites characterized by *not* having a service provided on the wire by the leasing company. All services are provided by the customer.

DAS Direct Attached Storage is the method of connecting a single storage device directly to one and only one host. In the enterprise datacenter, DAS is obsolete and has been replaced by storage networking. DAS is still used in desktops and laptops, and in lowest-tier hosts, although low-cost Fibre Channel HBAs seem likely to eliminate that last application.

DB9 This is the standard interface for serial ports. This is a "D" shaped connector with nine pins inside it. Since the Multiprotocol Router uses an RJ45 serial interface, connecting it to a DB9 port on e.g. a laptop requires an adaptor. (Included.)

DB25 This is much like a DB9 interface, but larger and with 25 pins. DB25 is commonly used for serial and parallel printer interfaces.

Dense Wave Digital Multiplexer See DWDM

Destination Fabric ID See DFID

Destination Identifier See DID

DFID Destination Fabric ID in a global header is the FID of the destination fabric for a frame. See also FID.

DID Destination Identifiers are three-byte Fibre Channel addresses that used to specify the physical location - switch domain, port on the switch, and position if applicable on the loop - of the receiver of a frame. A DID represented as 010100 would designate domain 1, port 1, no loop. Typically written in hex.

Direct Attached Storage See DAS

DLS Dynamic Load Sharing allows for recomputing of routes when ports go up or down

Domain ID Unique number between 1 and 239 that identifies an FC switch, router port, or translation address to a fabric

DWDM Dense Wave Digital Multiplexer.   See also WDM and CWDM.   Allows more wavelengths than a CWDM.

Dynamic Load Sharing See DLS

E_D_TOV Error-Detect Time Out Value is the maximum round trip time an operation is allowed before declaring an error condition

E_Port Expansion port connecting two switches to form a fabric. Connected E_Ports form ISLs. E_Ports may also now connect to EX_Ports to form IFLs.

Edge Fabric Fibre Channel fabric connected to an FCR via an EX_Port. This is largely the same as any standard Fibre Channel fabric. This is where the hosts and storage are attached in a Meta SAN

ELWL Extended Long Wavelength Laser transceivers may be based on 1550nm lasers. They are used to run native Fibre Channel connections over even greater distances than LWL media can support. Generally these media types use SMF cables.

Entropy See Operational Entropy

Error-Detect Time Out Value See ED_TOV

Ethernet The basis for the widely implemented IEEE 802.3 standard. Ethernet is a LAN protocol that supports data transfer rates of 10Mbps. It uses the CSMA/CD to handle simultaneous access to shared media. Fast Ethernet supports data transfer rates of 100 Mbps, and Gigabit Ethernet supports 1 Gbps and there is also an emerging 10Gbps standard.

EUI Extended Unique Identifiers are used by some iSCSI devices in much the same way that Fibre Channel devices use WWNs. However, unlike Fibre Channel, the emerging iSCSI standard actually has three competing name formats: EUI, NAA, and IQN, with the latter being most prominent.

EX_Port Enhanced E_Port used to connect a router to an edge fabric. From the point of view of a switch in an edge fabric, an EX_Port is virtually indistinguishable from an E_Port. It follows applicable Fibre Channel standards other Brocade E_Ports. However, the router terminates EX_Ports rather than allowing different fabrics to merge as would happen on a switch with regular E_Ports. Each EX_Port presents a set of translation phantom domains representing remote fabrics, each with "attached" proxy devices representing devices on those fabrics.

Exchange The highest-level FC mechanism used for communication between N_Ports. Exchanges are composed of one or more related sequences.

EX-IFL Inter-Fabric Link between an EX_Port and an E_Port. This is shortened to "IFL" if context is clear.

EX^2-IFL Inter-Fabric Link between two EX_Ports. Not supported at the time of this writing.

Expansion Port See E_Port

Exported Device Nodes in one fabric can be exported to other fabrics through an FC Router by using LSAN zoning. A node exported from one fabric must be imported into another, as in, "The host was exported from Fabric 1 and imported into Fabric 2."

Extended Long Wavelength Laser See ELWL

F_Port Fabric port on a switch to which an N_Port attaches

Fabric (1) The Fibre Channel topology that occurs when N_Ports are connected to F_Ports on a switch. (2) One or more Fibre Channel switches in an ISL networked topology. (3) A collection of ISL connected Fibre Channel switches and their devices such as hosts and storage. (4)

The software known as Fabric Services, which consists of the Storage Name Server, Management Server, FSPF routing, etc., etc..

Fabric Identifier See FID

Fabric Loop Port See FL_Port

Fabric Operating System See FOS

Fabric Port See F_Port

Fabric Shortest Path First See FSPF

FC Fibre Channel is the protocol of choice for building SANs. Unlike IP and Ethernet, FC was designed from the ground up to support storage devices of all types.

FC-0 Physical layer in Fibre Channel

FC-1 Fibre Channel 8b/10b encoding layer

FC-2 Handles framing, protocol, sequence/exchange management, and ordered sets for Fibre Channel

FC-3 Common services for Fibre Channel

FC-4 Mapping of ULPs such as SCSI or IP onto FC

FC-FC Routing Service A.k.a. FCR service. Brings hierarchical networking capabilities to Fibre Channel fabrics, allowing creation of LSANs so that devices located on separate fabrics can communicate without merging the fabrics. See also FCR.

FCIP Tunneling Service FCIP is a TCP/IP-based tunneling protocol that allows a transparent interconnection of geographically distributed fabrics through an IP-based network. This allows SANs to span longer distances than could be supported with native FC links. The service allows mapping an E_Port through an FCIP transparent tunnel to another FCIP gateway and switch on the other end. The port itself is both an E_Port and an FCIP port at the same time.

FC-NAT Fibre Channel Network Address Translation allows devices in fabrics to communicate even if the name spaces of those fabrics should overlap. This is similar to "hide behind" NAT in data networks.

FCP Fibre Channel Protocol is the mapping of SCSI over Fibre Channel. Probably the most popular ULP used in storage networks at the time of this writing.

FCR Fibre Channel Routers are platforms running the FC-FC Routing Service. Note that an FCR may also be running other software, so one platform could theoretically be an FCR at the same time as an FCIP tunnel or iSCSI gateway.

FCRP Fibre Channel Router Protocol is a Brocade-authored router-to-router protocol that allows FCRs to perform routing between different edge fabrics, optionally across a backbone fabric.

FFFFFC Well-known address for the name server

FFFFFD Well-known address for the fabric controller

FFFFFE Well-known address for the fabric F_Port

FFFFFF Well-known address for broadcast

Fibre Channel See FC

Fibre Channel Router See FCR

Fibre Channel Router Protocol See FCRP

FID Fabric IDs uniquely identify a fabric in a Meta SAN. See also Global Header, SFID, and DFID.

Field Programmable Gate Array See FPGA

Field Replaceable Unit See FRU

FL_Port Fabric loop port to which a loop or loop device attaches. It is the gateway to the fabric for NL_Ports on a loop.

FOS Brocade's Fabric Operating System is the software architecture that runs on most Brocade platforms. At the time of this writing, the most current Fabric OS version is 4.x. See also XPath.

FPGA Field Programmable Gate Arrays are similar to ASICs, except that their hardware logic is not fixed. It is possible to reprogram an FPGA in the field. Generally more expensive and possibly slower than an ASIC, but more flexible.

Frame Data unit containing a Start-of-Frame (SoF) delimiter, header, payload, CRC and an End-of-Frame (EoF) delimiter. The payload can be from 0 to 2112 bytes, and the CRC is 4 bytes. When operating across EX_Ports, the maximum payload is 2048 bytes.

Front Domain See Front Phantom Domain

Front Phantom Domain Tier of domains between xlate domains and the edge fabrics. Allows FSPF multi-pathing to work properly. The router uses one front domain per EX_Port. No FC-NAT devices are attached to front domains.

FRU Field Replaceable Units are components that can be swapped out by users or service personnel

FSPF Fabric Shortest Path First was created by Brocade, and has since been adopted as the industry standard for routing between Fibre Channel switches within a fabric

Full Duplex Concurrent transmission and reception of data on a single link

G_Port Generic port that auto negotiates to support E_, F_, or FL_Port functionality

GBIC Gigabit Interface Controller (or Converter) is a removable optical-to-copper transceiver module that has been largely superceded by SFP media.

Generic Port See G_Port

Gigabit Interface Controller See GBIC

Global Header Information on a BB fabric that identifies devices in full Meta SAN context. It consists of the inter-fabric addressing header (IFA header) and a normal FC-FS frame header containing an SID and DID that correspond to the actual PIDs of the source and destination devices. This is transparent to switches in the BB fabric.

Global Port Identifier See GPID

GPID Global Port IDs uniquely identify nodes in Meta SANs. Includes the PID and the FID of the device.

HBA Host Bus Adapter is an interface between a server or workstation bus and the Fibre Channel SAN

HCL/A Hot Code Load and Activation is the process of loading a new firmware image onto permanent storage such as compact flash on a switch or router, and then making that the active operating system without causing an interruption to the flow of data. It is possible for there to be a brief *management* interruption when the new code is activated, usually measured in seconds. For this and many other reasons, it is never recommended to make changes to a fabric (such as zoning updates) while simultaneously loading new firmware on switches.

Host Bus Adapter See HBA

Hot Code Load and Activation See HCL/A

Hot Swappable Component that can be replaced while the system is under power

IEEE Institute of Electrical and Electronics Engineers defines standards used in the computer industry

IETF Internet Engineering Task Force is the group that develops protocols for the Internet

iFCP Internet Fibre Channel Protocol was a standard proposed to compete with FCIP for extending Fibre Channel over IP WANs. At the time of this writing, only one vendor has implemented it, while many have implemented FCIP. Since the sole iFCP vendor has an FCIP roadmap as well, the future of iFCP is doubtful.

IFL Inter-Fabric Links are connections between routers and edge fabrics. Similar to ISLs. Architecturally, these can be EX_Port to E_Port or EX_Port to EX_Port, though only the former is implemented at the time of this writing. See also EX-IFL and EX^2-IFL.

In Order Delivery See IOD

In-Band Transmission of management or service protocol over the Fibre Channel transport. FSPF and FCRP are both in-band.

Initiator Server or workstation on a Fibre Channel network that initiates transactions to tapes or disks. See HBA.

Institute of Electrical & Electronics Engineers See IEEE

Inter-Fabric Link See IFL

Internet Engineering Task Force See IETF

Internet Fibre Channel Protocol See iFCP

Internet Protocol See IP

Internet Storage Name Server See iSNS

Inter-Switch Link See ISL

IOD In Order Delivery is a parameter than when set guarantees that all frames will be delivered in order or not at all. If they cannot be delivered in order, they will be dropped by the fabric.

IP Internet Protocol is the addressing part of TCP/IP

IPsec Internet Protocol Security is a set of protocols that provide network layer security. This is often used to create VPNs. It may be used to authenticate nodes, encrypt data, or both.

IQN iSCSI Qualified Names uniquely identify iSCSI nodes such as hosts and storage

iSCSI Gateway Service iSCSI is a mapping of the SCSI protocol to the IP transport. The gateway service projects iSCSI hosts onto the backbone fabric of a gateway switch.

iSCSI Qualified Name See IQN

ISID An iSCSI session identifier has an initiator and a target portion. The ISID is the initiator side.

ISL Inter-Switch Link is a connection between two switches using E_Ports

iSNS Internet Storage Name Server is the iSCSI equivalent of the Fibre Channel SNS.

JBOD Just a Bunch Of Disks; disks typically configured as an Arbitrated Loop within a chassis

Just a Bunch Of Disks See JBOD

L_Port Node Loop port supporting the FC_AL protocol

LAN Local Area Network; a network where transmissions are typically under 5km.

Latency The period of time that a frame is held by a network device before it is forwarded, ant the time that it sits on a cable between devices. (The latter is usually only significant on long distance links.)

LED Light Emitting Diodes. Used as status indicators.

Light Emitting Diode See LED

Logical Storage Area Network See LSAN

LSAN Logical Storage Area Networks span between fabrics. The path between devices in an LSAN may be local to a fabric, or may cross one or more FC Routers and up to one BB fabric. Administered using zones.

LSAN Zone The mechanism by which LSANs are administered. An FC Router attached to two fabrics will "listen" for the creation of matching LSAN zones on both fabrics. If this occurs, it will create phantom domains and FC-NAT entries as appropriate, and insert entries for them into the name servers on the fabrics. LSAN zones are compatible with standard zoning mechanisms. Their only distinguishing features are that they can only contain WWNs or WWN aliases, and that they must start with "LSAN_".

Local Area Network See LAN

Long Wavelength Laser See LWL

LUN Logical Unit Numbers are used to identify different SCSI devices or volumes that all have the same SCSI ID. In Fibre Channel, LUNs differentiate devices or volumes that share a WWN/PID address.

LWL Long Wavelength Laser transceivers may be based on 1310nm lasers. They are used for long distance native FC links. Generally these media types use SMF cables.

MAC Media Access Control is one of the sublayers in the OSI Data Link layer. It is responsible for moving packets between NICs using a shared media.

MAN Metropolitan Area Networks typically cover longer distances than LANs, but shorter distances than WANs. MANs may connect different campuses within a city, or between cities in a closely linked group. The size tends to be that of a metropolitan region: they can be tens of miles in radius, but cannot generally be more than a hundred miles or so. They tend to be provided by a single carrier from end-to-end, whereas WANs may involve different carriers.

Mean Time Between Failures See MTBF

Mean Time To Repair See MTTR

Media Access Control See MAC

Meta SAN The collection of all devices, switches, edge and BB fabrics, LSANs, and FC routers that makes up a physically connected but router-partitioned storage network. LSANs span between edge fabrics in a Meta SAN using FCRs, which provide both isolation and connectivity between the edges. In a data network, this might be called an "internetwork," or sometimes just "the network."

Metropolitan Area Network See MAN

MMF Multimode Fiber is a fiber-optic cabling specification that allows up to 500-meter distances between devices. MMF cables can have either 50 or 62.5 micron optical cores. Generally used with SWL media.

MTBF Mean Time Between Failures is the average time between the failure of any component in a system. This equates to how often service needs to be performed, and does not necessarily imply an *availability* impact.

MTTR Mean Time To Repair is the average amount of time it takes to repair a failed component.

Multicast Transmitting to a set of nodes on a fabric. More than one (which would be unicast) and less than all (which would be broadcast). This is often used in video applications.

Multimode Fiber See MMF.

Multiprotocol A device capable of using more than one protocol. For example, a router that has both Ethernet and Fibre Channel interfaces would be a multiprotocol router.

N_Port Fibre Channel host or storage port in a fabric or point-to-point connection. Stands for "Node Port."

NAA IETF Network Address Authority assigns worldwide unique names, such as Fibre Channel WWNs.

Name Server/Service See SNS

NAS Network Attached Storage is a common name for network filesystem (usually CIFS and/or NFS) servers that are specially optimized for that task. Often the only difference between a NAS filer and e.g. a UNIX NFS server is packaging.

Network Attached Storage See NAS

Network Interface Card See NIC

NIC Network Interface Cards connect a host's bus to a network. Similar to an HBA.

NL_Port Node Loop port supporting FC_AL protocol

Node Loop Port See L_Port and NL_Port

NR_Port An NR_Port appears to the BB fabric as being an N_Port "hanging off of" the BB domain of the FC router. It is a "router" port to which global capable devices (such as other routers) send frames with Global Header information.

Open Shortest Path First See OSPF

Open System Interconnection See OSI

Operational Entropy In this book, operational entropy refers to the tendency for IO patterns to become disordered as business needs change over time. There are other kinds of operational entropy as well: any ad hoc change from the network plan could be considered entropic.

OSI Open System Interconnection is a standard for implementing network protocols. The OSI reference model has seven layers. The OSI model is not widely implemented, but is the reference standard for other protocols.

OSPF Open Shortest Path First is a link–state router-to-router protocol for IP networks. By IP routing protocol standards, it is fairly robust.

PID Port IDs are three-byte addresses that describe the physical location of a Fibre Channel node within a fabric. PIDs are divided into a three-level hierarchy: Domain_ID, Area_ID, and Port_ID, which Brocade uses to represent switch domain, switch port, and FC-AL AL_PA respectively. A typical PID might look like this: 010f00.

Point-to-Point Dedicated Fibre Channel connection between two devices, usually a host and storage port

Port Identifier See PID

Proxy Device Also known as an "xlate device," this is how a device looks to a fabric to which it has been exported. The PID of a proxy device will start with the xlate phantom domain that represents its fabric.

QoS Quality of Service is a somewhat generic term that can refer to a mechanism that can guarantee priority, bandwidth, latency, error rate, and similar characteristics for the network path between nodes.

Quality of Service See QoS

R_A_TOV Resource Allocation Time Out Value; maximum time a frame can be delayed in a fabric and still be delivered

RAID Redundant Array of Independent (or Inexpensive) Disks. A set of disks that looks like a single volume. There are several RAID levels used to solve different storage performance, scalability, and availability problems. Most are fault-tolerant and/or high performance.

RAS Reliability Availability and Serviceability collectively refers to the overall quality of a component, device, or network. Factors that influence RAS include things like the MTBF and MTTR of components, software architecture, and redundant deployment strategies.

Redundancy Having multiple occurrences of a component to maintain high availability

Redundant Array of Independent Disks See RAID

Registered State Change Notification See RSCN

Reliability, Availability, and Serviceability See RAS

Reliability This is a measure of how often a component requires service. For example, if one CP in a redundantly configured SilkWorm 24000 chassis fails, there should be no application or network impact, so this is not an *availability* event. However, service personnel would need to replace the CP blade, so this is a *reliability* event .

Resource Allocation Time Out Value See RA_TOV

RETMA Radio Electronics Television Manufacturers Association in the context of storage networks is a standard specification for datacenter racks. A typical rack-mountable network device is designed to fit into a standard 19 inch RETMA rack, and its height is usually referred to in terms of RETMA "rack units." (Each unit is about 1.75 inches for obscure historical reasons.)

Route (1) The path between two switches in a fabric in the context of FSPF. (2) The path between different fabrics in a Meta SAN in the context of FCRP.

Router Device for interconnecting at least two different networks into an internetwork.

RSCN Registered State Change Notifications allow notification to nodes if a change occurs within a fabric

SAN Storage Area Networks link computing devices to disk or tape arrays. Almost all SANs at the time of this writing are Fibre Channel fabrics.

SAN Island When a SAN has no connectivity to other SANs in an organization, it is called an island to indicate its isolation. Islands can be merged into large fabrics or interconnected via FC-FC routers.

SCR State Change Registrations are used by devices to register to receive RSCNs

SCSI Small Computer Systems Interface as originally defined was a family of protocols for transmitting large blocks up to of 15-25 meters. SCSI-2 and SCSI-3 are updated versions of this. As the direct attachment of storage moved to a network model, SCSI has been mapped to protocols such as FC and IP.

SCSI Inquiry SCSI command that generally causes a target to respond with a string telling the requester information such as its make, model, and firmware version. Used by the SNS to further identify Fibre Channel devices. The iSCSI Gateway Service inserts IP and IQN strings using this SNS field.

SDH See SONET/SDH

Sequence Group of related frames transmitted from one N_Port to another

Serial The transmission of data bits in sequential order over a single line

SFID In a global header, the Source Fabric ID byte represents the FID of the source fabric of a frame

SFP Small Form-Factor Pluggable media have supplanted the GBIC as the removable optical-to-copper transceiver module of choice for Fibre Channel and Gigabit Ethernet equipment, though some Gigabit Ethernet devices still use GBICs.

SID Source Identifiers are three-byte Fibre Channel addresses that are used to specify the physical location - switch domain, port on the switch, and position if applicable on the loop - of the sender of a frame. A SID represented as 010100 would designate domain 1, port 1, no loop. Typically written in hex.

SilkWorm Registered trademark brand name for the Brocade family of switches, directors, and routers

Simple Name Server See SNS

Single Mode Fiber See SMF

SMF Single Mode Fiber is a cabling specification that allows 10km or even greater distances. SMF cables have nine micron optical cores. Generally used with either LWL or ELWL media.

Small Computer Systems Interface See SCSI

SNS Simple (or Storage) Name Server (or Service); the service provided by a switch that stores names, addresses and attributes related to Fibre Channel objects. Also known as the directory service.

SONET/SDH Synchronous Optical Networks are used in MANs and WANs. FC can be mapped to SONET/SDH. Characterized by high performance and reliability. The analogous service is called SDH in other countries.

Source Fabric Identifier See SFID

Source Identifier See SID

State Change Registration See SCR

Storage Device used to store data like disk or tape

Storage Area Network See SAN

Storage Subsystem See Subsystem

Storage Virtualization See Virtualization

Subsystem Synonym for storage device. Often external. On a SAN, may be shared between many compute nodes.

SWL Short Wavelength Laser transceivers based on 850nm lasers are designed to transmit short distances. This is the most common type of media.

Synchronous Digital Hierarchy See SDH

Synchronous Optical Networks See SONET/SDH

T11 ANSI committee chartered with creating standards for data movement to/from central computers

Target Disk array or a tape port on a SAN

Target Portal Group Tag See TPGT

TCP/IP Transmission Control Protocol over Internet Protocol is the standard communication method for the Internet

TCP Transmission Control Protocol is a connection-oriented protocol responsible dividing a message into packets, passing them to IP, and reassembling them into the original message at the other end. Detect errors / lost data and triggers retransmission if needed.

TCP Offload Engine See TOE

TCP Port Sub-addresses beneath IP that allow remote nodes to access a *specific service* for a given address. There are many well-known ports that allow standard upper-layer protocols like HTTP to work: web servers know to listen on the same port, and web clients know to attach to that port.

TOE TCP Offload Engines are used on iSCSI NICs to accelerate performance an prevent the host's CPU from being overloaded. Even the fastest TOE NICs can achieve at best half of Fibre Channel HBA speeds, and tend to cost as much as or more than HBAs.

TPGT An iSCSI session identifier has an initiator and a target portion. The Target Portal Group Tag (TPGT) is the target side.

Topology The physical, logical, or phantom arrangement of devices in a networked configuration

Transceiver Device that converts one form of signaling to another for transmission and reception. Fiber-optic transceivers convert from optical to electrical.

Translation Phantom Domain Also known as an "xlate domain," this is the FC-NAT mechanism to "attach" exported devices to their destination fabrics. If an FC router is attached via an EX_Port to an edge fabric, it will create xlate domains in that fabric corresponding to the remote edge fabrics that export devices into it.

Transmission Control Protocol See TCP

Tunneling Technique for making different networks interact where the source and destination nodes are on the same type of network, but there is a different network in between

U_Port Universal Ports can operate as G/E/F/FL_Ports. All Silkworm 2xxx and higher switches use Universal Ports to allow any device to connect to any port. Selection of actual port type is automatic.

ULP Upper Level Protocols run on top of Fibre Channel through the FC-4 layer. Examples include SCSI, IP, and VI.

Unicast Sending a frame between just two endpoints. Distinguished from broadcast and multicast where one transmitter has multiple receivers.

Universal Port See U_Port

Upper Level Protocol See ULP

Virtual Local Area Network See VLAN

Virtual Private Network See VPN

Virtual Router Redundancy Protocol See VRRP

Virtual Storage Area Network See VSAN

Virtualization The manipulation and abstraction of storage devices such as disks and tapes. Generally performs functions above and beyond those performed by traditional RAID applications. Examples include LUNs that span multiple subsystems, LUN over-provisioning where the size of a presented LUN is larger than the underlying storage capacity, and application-invisible data replication and migration.

VLAN Virtual Local Area Networks allow physical network devices to be carved into smaller logical segments. This is done in IP/Ethernet networks to prevent broadcast storms from creating instability. The analogous feature in Fibre Channel has been provided for years by zoning.

VPN Virtual Private Networks use high-speed encryption to create tunnels through public networks, so devices on

Glossary

347

one either end appear to be located on a physically isolated network.

VRRP Virtual Router Redundancy Protocol allows one router to take over the duties of another in the event of a failure. It can be thought of as a router clustering method. This prevents IP network nodes (like ports on the Multiprotocol Router in iSCSI or FCIP mode) from needing to support routing protocols like OSPF or RIP.

VSAN Virtual SANs are a vendor-unique implementation of a feature similar to zoning, though more limited. This should not be confused with LSANs. VSANs partition a network that previously allowed connectivity, whereas LSANs selectively allow connectivity where it was previously absent.

WAN Wide Area Networks span between cities, states, countries, and even continents. They tend to have higher delays due to their longer distances. WANs are often used by storage networks in disaster tolerance or recovery solutions.

Wavelength Division Multiplexer See WDM

WDM Wavelength Division Multiplexers allow multiple wavelengths to be combined on a single optical cable

Wide Area Network See WAN

World-Wide Name See WWN

WWN World-Wide Names are registered 64-bit unique identifier for nodes and ports in a fabric. A typical WWN might look like this: 10:00:00:60:69:51:0e:8b.

XPath Similar to Fabric OS, XPath is an OS architecture that runs on Brocade platforms. At the time of this writing, it is used on the SilkWorm AP7420.

xWDM See DWDM and CWDM

Zoning Allows fabric access control by port (PID) or WWN address. FC-FC routers require WWN zoning.

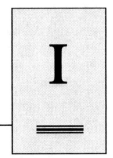

Index

Index